Confrontation and Liberation
in Southern Africa

About the Book and Editors

The 1984 "Nkomati Accord"—a bilateral security agreement between South Africa and Mozambique to eliminate guerrilla threats on both sides of a common border—was a milestone in regional confrontation and cooperation. Yet, the real challenge to the white South African regime is not external; it is internal opposition to apartheid.

This volume, written by leading African scholars, begins by exploring the origins of racism and nationalism in Southern Africa. The contributors discuss the spread of nationalist movements throughout the region, arguing that South Africa has attempted to resist, divert, or undermine the domino effect by capitalizing on the Nkomati Accord. The authors focus on the legal aspects of the Accord, its impact on the foreign and defense policies of the Front Line States, prospects for regional development and economic integration, and potential outcomes of the national liberation struggles in Southern Africa.

Ibrahim S. R. Msabaha is director of studies and programs at the Centre for Foreign Relations in Tanzania and lecturer in political science at the University of Dar es Salaam. **Timothy M. Shaw** is professor of political science and director of the Centre for African Studies at Dalhousie University. He is the coauthor of *Nigeria* (Westview, forthcoming).

Confrontation and Liberation in Southern Africa

Regional Directions After the Nkomati Accord

**edited by
Ibrahim S. R. Msabaha
and Timothy M. Shaw**

Westview Press • Boulder, Colorado
Gower • London, England

DT
747
86
C65
1987

LC

Westview Special Studies on Africa

Map of Southern Africa reprinted with permission. Copyright © by Joseph Hanlon, *Apartheid's Second Front: South Africa's War Against It's Neighbors* (Penguin Books Ltd, 1986), p. 14.
Chapter 10, by Douglas G. Anglin, is a revised version of an article that appeared in *African Affairs* 84(335), April 1985, 163–181. Reprinted by permission.
Conclusion by Robert Davies and Dan O'Meara reprinted with permission from *Journal of Southern African Studies* 11(2), April 1985, 183–211, © Oxford University Press, Oxford.

All rights reserved. No part of this publication may be reproduced or transmitted in any form or by any means, electronic or mechanical, including photocopy, recording, or any information storage and retrieval system, without permission in writing from the publisher.

Copyright © 1987 by Westview Press, Inc.

Published in 1987 in the United States of America by Westview Press, Inc.; Frederick A. Praeger, Publisher; 5500 Central Avenue, Boulder, Colorado 80301

Published in 1987 in Great Britain by Gower Publishing Company Limited, Gower House, Croft Road, Aldershot, Hampshire GU11 3HR

Library of Congress Cataloging-in-Publication Data
Confrontation and liberation in southern Africa.
  (Westview special studies on Africa)
  Bibliography: p.
  1. Africa, Southern—Foreign relations—South Africa.
2. South Africa—Foreign relations—Africa, Southern.
3. Africa, Southern—Foreign economic relations—South
Africa.   4. South Africa—Foreign economic relations—
Africa, Southern.   5. National liberation movements—
Africa, Southern.   6. Mozambique. Treaties. etc.
South Africa, 1984 Mar. 16.   I. Msabaha, Ibrahim S. R.
II. Shaw, Timothy M.   III. Series.
DT747.S6C65   1987   327.68   86-9059
ISBN 0-8133-7219-4

British Library Cataloguing in Publication Data
Confrontation and liberation in Southern
  Africa: regional directions after the
  Nkomati Accord.—(Special Studies on
  Africa)
  1. South Africa—Foreign Relations—Africa,
  Southern   2. Africa, Southern—Foreign
  relations—South Africa.
  I. Msabaha, Ibrahim S.R.   II. Shaw,
  Timothy M.   III. Series
  327'.0968   DT771.A356
  ISBN 0-566-05458-2

Composition for this book was provided by the editors.
This book was produced without formal editing by the publishers.

Printed and bound in the United States of America

The paper used in this publication meets the requirements of the American National Standard for Permanence of Paper for Printed Library Materials Z39.48-1984.

6   5   4   3   2   1

7-9-87

Contents

Tables

About the Contributors

Douglas G. Anglin is Professor of Political Science at Carleton University in Ottawa, Canada. Dr. Anglin was the first Vice-Chancellor of the University of Zambia and is author of essays on Southern Africa in <u>African Affairs</u>, <u>International Journal</u> and <u>International Organization</u>.

Reg H. F. Austin lectures in law at the University of Zimbabwe in Harare.

Horace Campbell holds a Ph.D. from the University of Sussex in England and is lecturer in political science and public administration at the University of Dar es Salaam. His articles on Eastern and Southern Africa have appeared in <u>African Review</u>, <u>Review of African Political Economy</u> and <u>Third World Quarterly</u>.

Robert Davies holds a Ph.D. from the University of Sussex and works at the Universidade Eduardo Mondlane. He is author of <u>South African Strategy towards Mozambique in the 'Post-Nkomati' Period</u> and <u>Capital, State and White Labor in South Africa, 1900-1960</u>, and is co-editor of <u>The Struggle for South Africa</u>.

Jeannette Hartmann holds a Ph.D. from the University of Hull in Britain and lectures in the social sciences at the University of Dar es Salaam. She has published in <u>African Review</u>.

Colin Legum is editor of <u>African Contemporary Record</u> and a prolific writer on African, especially Southern African, affairs. He was Associate Editor of <u>The Observer</u> and coauthor of <u>Africa in the 1980s: a continent in crisis</u>.

Nguyuru H. I. Lipumba lectures in economics at the University of Dar es Salaam.

E. N. Maganya is a Fellow of the Institute of Development Studies at the University of Dar es Salaam.

D.A.K. Mbogoro lectured in economics at the University of Dar es Salaam until his appointment as Minister of State for Finance and Economic Planning in the Government of Tanzania.

A. K. Mhina lectures in political science at the University of Dar es Salaam.

Ibrahim S. R. Msabaha is Director of Studies and Programs at the Center for Foreign Relations in Tanzania as well as lecturer in international relations and diplomacy at the University of Dar es Salaam. Dr. Msabaha holds a Ph.D. from Dalhousie University in Canada and has published on Tanzania's foreign policy in Holsti (ed) Why Nations Realign and Mushi & Matthews (eds) Foreign Policy of Tanzania.

Dan O'Meara is a researcher at CIDMAA in Montreal, Canada, a research and information centre on Southern Africa, author of Volkskapitalisme: class, capital and ideology in the development of Afrikaner nationalism and co-editor of The Struggle for South Africa.

C. M. Peter lectures in the Faculty of Law at the University of Dar es Salaam.

Timothy M. Shaw is Professor of Political Science and Director of the Center for African Studies at Dalhousie University in Nova Scotia. Dr. Shaw is co-editor of Conflict and Change in Southern Africa and of Southern Africa in the 1980s.

Hawa Sinare lectures in law at the University of Dar es Salaam in Tanzania.

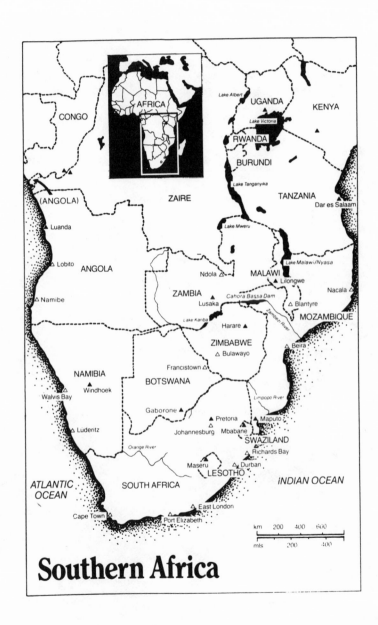

Southern Africa

Introduction: Southern Africa Before and After Nkomati

Timothy M. Shaw
Ibrahim S. R. Msabaha

... there have been set-backs in the struggle. The
Nkomati Accord was forced on the government of
Mozambique by the overwhelming pressure of innumerable
murderous attacks from South African forces and the
South African surrogates, combined with 'mediation' and
'assurances' from American and British diplomats and
conditional promises from the South Africans. So the
ceremony took place, the Mozambicans breathed a sigh of
relief in the expectation of an end to the attacks on
them, and P.W. Botha went off on a tour of Europe as 'a
reasonable man'.

- Julius K. Nyerere "Forward" to Phyllis Johnson &
  David Martin (eds) Destructive Engagement:
  Southern Africa at war[1]

Based on Nkomati and its newfound political
acceptability, South Africa declared itself a 'regional
power'. Pik Botha explained that this meant that 'no
problems in Southern Africa can be resolved unless the
legitimate interests of this regional power, South
Africa, are taken into account' ...

Within a few months (however), white South Africa's
newfound euphoria and arrogance had collapsed like a
pricked balloon. Its claims to be a 'regional power'
proved to be all hot air. It could not control its own
townships. Its economy was in crisis, with the rand
collapsing and foreign banks and transnational
corporations disinvesting. The cracks between business
and government widened into a yawning chasm. And far
from being the region's peacemaker, Pretoria was shown
to be violating its peace agreements with Mozambique and
Angola.

- Joseph Hanlon, Beggar Your Neighbours: apartheid
  power in Southern Africa[2]

South Africa's intimidation of its neighbours has rested
upon a persistent campaign of destabilization and
economic disruption ... Several states have entered into
'non-aggression pacts' or security arrangements with
South Africa in an attempt to stave off further attacks;
the Lusaka Accord of February 1984 with Angola and the
Nkomati Accord of March 1984 with Mozambique are the
best known of these. South Africa violated both these
Accords from the very outset, giving the region further
proof that it could not be trusted to honor even solemn
treaty obligations.

- Mission to South Africa: the Commonwealth Report[3]

The experience of the past twelve months has
concentrated the collective mind wonderfully on the
interdependence of economics and politics in South
Africa; unfortunately it has not taught us how to
extricate ourselves from the present impasse and realize
the potential for renewed growth. The potential is
great: we have a large number of people who are
unemployed or under-employed, considerable underutilised
manufacturing capacity, and a sizeable current account
surplus.

- Anglo American Corporation Chairman's Statement
  1986[4]

Southern Africa as regional studies and as regional
system will never be the same again.[5] If the Portuguese coup
of 1974 constituted one turning point in the regional affairs
then the mid-1980s - from Nkomati-type Accords and States of
Emergency to triple attacks and sanctions debates - surely
constitute another. Although fundamental change may yet
remain elusive, the intensity and visibility of ongoing
contradictions can no longer be ignored. Both South and
Southern Africa have long exercised a fascination over
scholars and statepersons alike; now they are once again
"high politics" on the global agenda, as they were fleetingly
in the early-1960s and mid-1970s. The spell cast by the
beauty and agony of the sub-continent will continue to grip
both media and mandarins as the interrelated mixtures of
conflict and cooperation, change and continuity evolve. This
introduction seeks to place intellectual and political
concerns in context: the evolution and projection of

Southern African studies and systems in the mid-1980s.[6]

SOUTHERN AFRICAN STUDIES IN THE MID-1980s

Analysis tends to lag behind the train of events. Thus J.A. Hobson's original social analysis of the Boer War did not appear until 1900.[7] While early studies of Southern African post-war and post-independence integration did not appear until the late-1960s and early-1970s with the seminal article on "The Subordinate State System of Southern Africa" by Larry Bowman[8] and Kenneth Grundy's comprehensive book on Confrontation and Accommodation in Southern Africa.[9] As the pace of change accelerated with post-liberation independence and struggles in Angola, Mozambique and then Zimbabwe, scholarship could hardly keep pace until, in the mid-1980s, there was a veritable outpouring.

Characteristic of the evolution of the field, the authors of the latest regional overviews have already produced major country case studies. So Phyllis Johnson & David Martin wrote the definitive investigation of The Struggle for Zimbabwe: The Chimurenga war in 1981[10] before editing Destructive Engagement: Southern Africa at War while Joseph Hanlon produced Mozambique: the revolution under fire in 1984[11] a couple of years before his pair of books on Southern Africa: the overview Penguin Special on Apartheid's Second Front: South Africa's war against its neighbours and the encyclopedic Beggar Your Neighbours: apartheid power in Southern Africa.[12] In the late-1960s Bowman could write the definitive piece on the region using the then-fashionable "subordinate state system" perspective without concern for duplication. But almost two decades later, the multiplicity of texts displays some replication as well as competition. Hopefully, this welcome over-attention will advance understanding and generate debate rather than produce overkill. In particular, it is to be hoped that the Johnson & Martin collection symbolizes something of a turning point: Southern African studies by Southern (not only South) Africans rather than by apartheid defenders (cf Gann & Duignan Why South Africa will survive or Richard E. Bissell & Chester A. Crocker (eds) South Africa into the 1980s[13]) or Africanist authors, however well-intentioned. The present volume on the region is primarily by Southern Africans just as an earlier co-edited collection with which one of us was associated was by West Africans, mainly Nigerians.[14]

Because of the current escalation in regional relations – both conflict and cooperation have increased markedly since the mid-1970s and the successful liberation wars let alone

4

from the mid-1960s of BLS non-violent independence - the
latest wave of writing is likely to be relevant for some time
to come. Indeed, the landmark Johnson & Martin and Hanlon
volumes were published in early-1986 as the Commonwealth
Eminent Persons Group was pursuing its active diplomacy in
Southern Africa only to be blasted-out of its idealism by
South Africa's triple attacks in mid-May. Thus Mission to
South Africa is available alongside Apartheid's Second Front
and Destructive Engagement: contextual backdrop to current
stalemates. In general, these volumes reinforce each other-
the background, historical and regional, to apartheid,
dependence and destabilization - and together they
demonstrate the realities of South African power and the
limits of external diplomacy.

Nevertheless, although this genre is radical and
relevant it lacks a certain depth and so its analysis is
ultimately superficial, even unsatisfactory. The
deficiencies of contemporary Southern African studies (with a
few exceptions to which we will turn) lie in their
unwillingness, first, to examine sub- rather than superstructure and, second, to offer comparative inter-regional
insights.[15]

First, then, despite a fine tradition of materialist
analysis in South Africa in particular and in a few
neighboring states as well,[16] regional studies have rarely
examined modes and relations of production; rather, they have
concentrated on exchange, infrastructure and communication.
Thus they overlook patterns of regional social contradiction
and coalition: why do trade and migration continue despite
repeated destabilization and sanction? And second, partially
because they treat state and race rather than capital and
class, these studies tend to assume that Southern Africa is
sui generis rather than a comparable case of regional
dominance in terms of both economics and strategic
resources.[17]

Whilst there clearly are unique elements and
combinations in Southern Africa there are also comparable
relationships: the South African "military-industrial
complex" is distinctive but not unique.[18] Likewise,
antagonism between Southern African capital and labor are
different but still comparable. In short, Southern African
studies to date are deficient because they pay insufficient
attention to the workings of transnational capitalism and too
much attention to interstate diplomacy, disagreements and
deceptions.

Yet the remedy for this oversight is already at hand in
the tradition of sophisticated analyses of and debates about
South Africa's political economy, as well as its political

structure and culture. And some other national case studies notably those on Zimbabwe,[19] also display a degree of rigor and nuance. Southern African studies need to transcend the inherited, inherent biases of their sub-field and go beyond (ie. to the international or global division of labor) and below (ie. to national modes and relations of production) the regional level and thereby put change and continuity, conflict and cooperation into historical, holistic perspective.

One of the immodest claims we may make for this collection is that it treats capitalism as well as conflicts and class as well as race. It also seeks to put Southern Africa into comparative perspective - regional institutions and relations elsewhere - and examine the legal implications of Nkomati. And, in addition to representing critical African scholarship on the region, it begins to relate foreign policy and political economy to each other and to regional developments. Moreover, the May 1985 Arusha conference from which these original papers derive was significant in at least two other ways: it brought diverse interests in Tanzania together - academe, media, bureaucracy, party, military and non-governmental organizations - and it brought several international analysts together, from the rest of Southern Africa, Europe and Canada. And finally, the subsequent selection, revision, editing and reproduction of the papers was also a trans-Atlantic endeavour, leading to their publication just 18 months after their initial presentation: an essentially indigenous contribution to an ongoing and intensifying debate and struggle.

FROM CONTINUITY TO CHANGE

The edifice of apartheid has clearly begun to crumble because of internal contradictions and external conditions. But this post-liberation prospect was not always so apparent: for the first three post-war decades, South Africa's regional dominance seemed assured. Indeed, it is only over the last ten or twelve years that racism in the region has seemed to be at all vulnerable. To be sure, the "winds of change" did blow into Southern Africa in the 1960s as African decolonization progressed southward. But the crucial "dominoes" of Angola, Mozambique and Zimbabwe did not fall until the second half of the 1970s: and even their liberation was limited by regional reactions, notably South Africa's support for opposing armies.

So the formal independence of BLS, Malawi and even Zambia did not undermine the essential fabric of regional relationships. Indeed, to an extent, the demise of British and then Portuguese colonialism served to advance South African control: <u>divide et imperium</u> was facilitated. Apartheid's ascendancy was apparent in the successive diplomatic forays labelled "dialogue" and "detente". After 1948, the Nationalist Party was able to implement apartheid at home and regionalism abroad because of the combination of orthodox decolonization and economic expansion. But if the post-war era was characterized by continuity - protection of white prosperity through the advancement of white power - the post-liberation period was marked by change.[20] From the perspective of the 1980s, the 1974 Portuguese coup <u>did</u> constitute the beginning of the end of regionalism defined by racism. But the end is not yet nigh and the legacies of South African hegemony will not be easy to transcend.

The last decade has been marked, then, by change rather than continuity and by conflict rather than cooperation, with the start of the 1980s being the most significant - the independence of Zimbabwe and the launching of SADCC - at least until the mid-1980s' conjuncture of State of Emergency inside South Africa and states of insecurity in the region. This transformation has notable historic roots, particularly the long 75 year history of the ANC, and was advanced by several "shocks" in the global economy: the high price of oil (then gold) followed by stagflation and recession. But perhaps the most fundamental cause of the conjuncture was reflected in the inability of the apartheid regime to reassert control over its own population in 1985-6 unlike its ability to do so after Sharpeville (1960) and Soweto (1976). For the real driving force for change in Southern Africa is neither regional diplomacy nor global debate but opposition inside South Africa itself: the relentless, courageous and sophisticated demands of labor, church, peasants and womens' group.[21] The initiative in South Africa now more than ever lies with the ANC and UDF rather than with the State Security Council (SSC) or Defense Forces (SADF), <u>Inkatha</u> or vigilantes.[22] To be sure, the ability of ANC-UDF to organize effectively is limited by repression, harassment and insolvency. And yet despite myriad obstacles and tensions the ANC-UDF association has built-up a head of steam that previously effective regime responses can no longer contain.[23] SADCC and FLS provide legitimacy and publicity for this continuing struggle; but neighbors do not make revolution,[24] neither do more distant supporters and sanctions.

Nevertheless, despite ANC-UDF seizing the initiative, the resistance of the apartheid regime remains formidable, including its ability to undertake seemingly endless acts of regional destabilization. The emergence of black unions,[25] as well as media and churchmen, is one indication of contradictions and changes within South African capitalism, the internal correlates of the new international division of labor and South Africa's role within it. For South Africa cannot become a Newly Industrializing Country (NIC) like its fellow "pariah", Taiwan, because it lacks the internal market and indigenous technology, which even regional exchange cannot replace.[26] Moreover, its ambition to become a regional "military-industrial complex" (MIC) is frustrated by its inability to secure sufficient external strategic materiel (cf NICs like Brazil or South Korea)[27] while its access to foreign capital is increasingly circumscribed.[28] South Africa is no longer – because, not despite, apartheid-able to generate and remit the super-profits which international business demanded in exchange for supporting apartheid. Rather, the stage is now set for the final battle of the long-standing Boer War: national capital is buying-up transnational because of the opportunities or threats involved in dis- and di-vestment. But it is unlikely that the British-Boer understanding of the late-nineteenth century can be repeated at the end of the twentieth: the further impoverishment of the Black population can no longer be arranged between the white tribes.[29]

In her comprehensive and controversial magnum opus on Capitalism and Apartheid, Merle Lipton rightly points out to the set of social actors and alliances which have constituted South Africa's political economy with an emphasis on politics as well as economics:

> Apartheid cannot simply be explained as the outcome of capitalism or racism. Its origins lie in a complex interaction between class interests (of white labor as well as sections of capital) and racism/ethnicity, reinforced by ideological and security factors.[30]

Yet even her focus on "the ambiguous process of authoritarian reform ... and black radicalization" fails to treat or situate the current trend towards militarization and neo-facism.[32] If South Africa has failed to become a NIC through international finance and exchange it may yet reinforce its claims to being a regional MIC through the final, ultimately self-defeating, fling of the dice: "total strategy" against alleged "total onslaught".

TOWARDS A REDEFINITION OF REGIONALISM

Despite appearances to the contrary until _circa_ 1975, South Africa has failed to defend apartheid or advance capital through orthodox forms of regionalism – economic cooperation, infrastructural integration and diplomatic communication (and _cordon sanitaire_ with Portugal and Rhodesia). Instead, over the last decade it has moved towards a more high-risk and -cost strategy which mixes regional cooperation with regional destabilization: regional power without being a NIC. This apparently contradictory stance is, of course, a reflection of internal contradictions, notably between big business and the military establishment,[33] but it also constitutes a forlorn attempt to "internationalize" domestic difficulties; ie. to realize myths of nationalist-communist "conspiracies". In fact, the policy is ultimately self-destructive as well as unacceptable: the internalization of contradictions as ANC loses its rear-bases in the region and FLS adopt ambivalent stances. Regional destabilization and sanctions constitute the _denouement_ of South African ambitions, not their zenith. As Reginald Green and Carol Thompson argue,

> South Africa does have regional interests which have been defined in fairly stable terms for almost 200 years, since the early nineteenth century. Regional strategy since 1970 has been intensely ideological and remarkably consistent in objectives – the preservation of _apartheid_ at home and the acquisition of _lebensraum_, especially economic and security, throughout the region. However, the balance among strategic elements and tactics has shifted sharply over time with temporary selective reversals of course overlying a secular trend toward rising levels of violence.[34]

However, the established pattern of regional cooperation of dialogue and detente, albeit amongst unequals, was replaced with South African adventurism in Angola and subsequent series of interventions in almost all FLS/SADCC members. Thus together "total strategy" and "constellation" – internal cohesion, regional power and Bantustan-neighbors integration – constitute a unilateral redefinition of regionalism:[35] away from cooperation and towards coercion. As Green and Thompson assert, these operational strategies do form a framework, albeit a contradictory one:

> ... there are at least five strategic elements, and these are not totally consistent in the abstract:

economic incentives, economic threats and penalties, a
dual outward-looking approach involving a forward or
'strike kommando' policy coupled with one of
'constellation' or political-economic domination, and an
inward-looking 'laager' approach.[36]

Total strategy thus had regional as well as internal
implications; it sought to export South African
contradictions and corporatism. Yet it is inherently short-
term and self-destructive given the history of national and
regional political economies.

Authoritarian reform is ultimately a contradiction in
terms: white establishments - bureaucratic, economic,
military, political and religious - cannot be coerced or
cajoled into new relations with black labor, political and
religious leaderships, even if the latter were willing,
without fundamental not superficial reform. Hence the
essential foolhardiness of "total strategy (which) required
four critical and interrelated changes ...: streamlining
apartheid, strengthening the military, supporting business
and bringing it into partnership, and creating a new regional
policy."[37] Such an ambitious and intricate prospectus would
be problematic even in a context of political support and
economic growth. As neither of these conditions have been
present in South(ern) Africa since the mid-1970s, total
strategy cannot be sustained. Thus the white regime's
unilateral redefinition of regionalism - security through
coercion rather than either cooperation or cooptation - is
doomed,[38] even if attempts continue to assemble supportive
internal coalitions and external compradors.

TOWARDS A REDEFINITION OF SOUTHERN AFRICA

In the final analysis, the only way in which peace and
security, along with basic needs and rights, can be achieved
and assured for all the peoples and states of Southern Africa
is through a transformation in the regional political
economy: from racism and capitalism to non-racial
cooperative relations of production and distribution. But
despite the idealism of liberals and radicals alike in South
and Southern Africa (as reflected in several chapters in the
present volume) such a dream is as yet both ill-defined and
elusive, awaiting the harsh light of praxis to shape it. And
destabilization and sanctions as integral elements in total
strategy make it ever more so. Aside from engendering
mistrust and alienation, in the longer term, the short-term
costs of destabilization for impoverished economies are

staggering. As Hanlon asserts:

> So far the war is a costly draw ... The dreams of 1980,
> of steady regional progress towards economic growth and
> independence, have been shattered. Destabilization now
> costs the SADCC states more then $4,500 million per
> year.   Development efforts are undermined.   The
> political fabric is weakened.   Whatever the internal
> political faults and economic errors of the region's
> various governments, their effects have been dwarfed by
> destruction from outside.[39]

And the real costs of containing rebellion inside the
citadel of apartheid are also immense: physical destruction
and lost production as well as thousands dead in the short-
term and the trend towards exponential militarization,
extremism and distrust in the longer-term.[40]   Moreover,
depending on the length and degree of violence, capitalism
and racism in South and Southern Africa will not disappear at
the midnight of majority rule. As Robin Cohen cautions, with
implications for Southern as well as South Africa:

> The achievement of state power does not, however,
> dislodge imbedded social structures, or alter the
> economic 'facts of life'.   In tropical Africa,
> decolonization signalled the formal end of empire; it
> did not prefigure substantive independence.   Likewise,
> in South Africa, the achievement of black majority rule
> will not signify the end of apartheid, but its legal and
> formal abolition.   The Freedom Charter boldly states
> 'All apartheid laws and practices shall be set aside'-
> the first is easy to achieve by proclamation, but the
> heritage of apartheid practices will not be so easy to
> root out and destroy.[41]

Any transition towards democratic government in South Africa
will be difficult and protracted: the movement from white
minority affluence to black affirmative action will be
complex.   But South Africa's political economy has already
produced an impressive range of human resources, such as
Nelson Mandela, Bishop Desmond Tutu, Reverend Allan Boesak,
Chief Lutuli, Percy Qoboza, Oliver Tambo, Donald Wood, Cyril
Ramaphosa, and Dr. Frederick Van Zyl Slabbert.   Yet these
talents cannot be mobilized until the edifice of apartheid is
formally ended.   And the institutionalization of Bantustans
and legitimization of Chief Gatsha Buthelezi and Inkatha
complicate such movement.
There are clearly major issues of political economy yet

to be settled but, curiously, South Africa has been, since 1948, a state capitalist system with significant state intervention. It has become a relatively industrialized country so that, like Zimbabwe after UDI, it could, even after a limited period of escalating sanctions, provide a sound basis for further development under a new dispensation. As the Commonwealth Eminent Persons Group warns, however, slowness in dismantling apartheid affects the whole region:

> The cost of South Africa's 'total strategy', in terms of human life, is incalculable, although some estimate the loss of life at 100,000 and those made homeless at one million ... The total cost to those nine countries is estimated at over US $10 billion in the period 1980–1984. That huge sum far exceeds the total foreign assistance received by SADCC, and is equivalent to about one third of all Member States' exports earnings during that period. Some argue that this growing burden may well be of the order of US $4 or 5 billion a year for the SADCC region as a whole.

> Nobody who cares for the future of a free and non-racial South Africa, rich in resources and productive in its trade and commerce, would wish to see the destruction of its economic and industrial base. Yet that will be the consequence if the continuing failure to dismantle apartheid and peacefully negotiate a political settlement is allowed to run in parallel with an external policy of conflict and destruction, involving the whole sub-continent.

> Apartheid South Africa poses a wide threat well beyond its borders.[42]

One major South African institution which has always been in the vanguard of liberal white bourgeois opinion and which has considerable Southern African as well as South-South links,[43] the Anglo American Corporation,[44] has continued to call on the intransigent and indecisive Afrikaner regime for change. The 1986 Chairman's Statement by Gavin Relly is in the Harry Oppenheimer mold; he warned against further repression and advocated accelerated liberalization – an end to states of emergency and a call for freedom of all political leaders and parties:

> ... there is no course open to South Africa which does not involve risk. The least dangerous, I am convinced, is to confront the issue of politically motivated

violence by opening up the opportunities for direct
political action. There is encouraging evidence that if
this were done, the majority of South Africans would
wish to take part in the political process on a
democratic basis and would favor negotiation rather than
violence. A failure of nerve at this juncture will lead
to a calamitous situation of political drift, with the
economy sliding toward a state of seige as the
initiative passes to the men of violence and the
international pressures to change us or isolate us
steadily increase.[45]

Symptomatic of the potential for renewal and redirection
in South Africa is its indigenous version of "liberation
theology". The powerful "Kairos Document", with its critique
of state and church theologies and its call for Christian
relevance, is an optimistic and progressive "comment":
"Christians, if they are not doing so already, must quite
simply participate in the struggle for liberation and for a
just society."[46] Stripped of its theological aura, the
promise and position of Kairos are revealing of the depth and
feeling and promise in South Africa once apartheid is
abandoned:

The time has come. The moment of truth has arrived.
South Africa has been plunged into a crisis that is
shaking the foundations and there is every indication
that the crisis has only just begun and that it will
deepen and become even more threatening in the months to
come. It is the Kairos or moment of truth not only for
apartheid but also for the church.[47]

And not only for the church but for all involved institutions
in the national, regional and global political economies.
We hope that this collection will advance both analysis
and practice of change in and around Southern Africa. In
focusing on the impact of Nkomati on the region we are
concerned to focus on the dialectic between process and
resistance. The future of South and Southern Africa is of
profound concern not only to their citizens but also to the
rest of Africa and the world. The international conference
from which these edited papers derive was itself an indicator
of regional, continental and global attention. It was
arranged through the initiative of Ibrahim Msabaha who
brought together local and international scholar,
statespersons, decision makers, commentators, soldiers and
activists. It was facilitated by the support of the
University of Dar es Salaam, particularly the Department of

Political Science, and the Centre for Foreign Relations in
Tanzania. And it was produced through the editorial skills
and devotion of Susan Slipp in the Centre for African Studies
at Dalhousie University. A luta continua.

NOTES

1. Julius K. Nyerere "Forward to Phyllis Johnson &
David Martin (eds), Destructive Engagement: Southern Africa
at war, (Harare: Zimbabwe Publishing House, for Southern
African Research and Documentation Centre, 1986), p. x.
2. Joseph Hanlon, Beggar Your Neighbours: apartheid
power in Southern Africa, (London: James Currey and
Bloomington: Indiana University Press, for CIIR, 1986), pp.
41, 45.
3. Mission to South Africa: the Commonwealth Report.
The Findings of the Commonwealth Eminent Persons Group on
South Africa, (Harmondsworth: Penguin, June 1986, for
Commonwealth Secretariat), pp. 126-127.
4. Anglo American Corporation of South Africa Limited,
Chairman's Statement, 1986, (Johannesburg: AAC, July 1986),
p. 5.
5. cf Christian P. Potholm and Richard Dale (eds),
Southern Africa in the 1980s, (London: George Allen & Unwin,
1985).
6. The War in South Africa: its causes and effects,
(New York: Howard Fertig, 1969. Reprint of 1900 edition).
7. International Studies Quarterly 12(3), September
1968, pp. 231-261.
8. Subtitle The limits of independence, (Berkeley:
University of California Press, 1973) cf note 15 below.
9. (Harare: Zimbabwe Publishing House, 1981).
10. (London: Zed, 1984).
11. (Harmondsworth: Penguin, 1986) and note 2 above,
respectively.
12. (London: Croom Helm, 1981) and (Boulder: Westview,
1979) respectively.
13. Olajide Aluko & Timothy M. Shaw (eds), Southern
Africa in the 1980s, (London: George Allen & Unwin, 1985).
14. For treatment of both these issues see Kenneth W.
Grundy's follow-up to Bowman's conceptual overview
"Intermediary power and global dependency: the case of South
Africa," International Studies Quarterly 20(4), December
1976, pp. 553-580. See also notes 25 to 29 below and Timothy
M. Shaw Africa's International Affairs: an analysis and
bibliography, (Halifax: Centre for Foreign Policy Studies,
1983).
15. See, inter alia, John S. Saul & Stephen Gelb, The

Crisis in South Africa, (New York: Monthly Review, 1981), Dan O'Meara and Robert Davies, "Total Strategy in Southern Africa: an analysis of South African regional policy since 1978," Journal of Southern African Studies 11(2), April 1985, pp. 183-211, (reprinted as Conclusion to this collection);and John Saul, The State and Revolution in Eastern Africa, (New York: Monthly Review, 1979).

16. H.J. & R.E. Simons, Class and Colour in South Africa, 1850-1950, (Harmondsworth: Penguin, 1969), and F.A. Johnstone, Class, Race and Gold, (London: Routledge & Kegan Paul, 1976) as well as the series of essays by, inter alia, M. Legassick, H. Wolfe, S. Trapito, D. Kaplan, J. Slovo, R. Davies and D. O'Meara.

17. cf Arnold H. Isaacs, "South Africa and BLS: a Galtung approach to dependence relations" in Jerker Carlsson & Timothy M. Shaw (eds), The Political Economy of South-South Relations: case studies of Newly Industrializing Countries, (London: Macmillan, 1987).

18. See Timothy M. Shaw & Lee Dowdy, "South Africa" in Edward A. Kolodziej & Robert Harkavy (eds), Security Policies of Developing Countries, (Lexington: Heath, 1982), pp. 305-327, and Timothy M. Shaw & Edward Leppan, "South Africa white power and the regional military-industrial complex" in Aluko & Shaw (eds), Southern Africa in the 1980s, pp. 251-277. See also Abdul S. Minty, "South Africa's military build-up: the region at war" and "South Africa's nuclear capability: the apartheid bomb" in Phyllis Johnson & David Martin (eds), Destructive Engagement: South Africa at war, (Harare: ZPH, 1986), pp. 171-220.

19. See especially Colin Stoneman (ed), Zimbabwe's Inheritance, (London: Macmillan, 1981) and Andre Astrow, Zimbabwe: a revolution that lost its way, (London: Zed, 1983).

20. For an informed if uncritical overview of South African foreign policy which point to its organizational and operational weaknesses see Deon Geldenhuys, The Diplomacy of Isolation: South African foreign policy making, (London: Macmillan, 1984). For a more critical introduction to a somewhat earlier period see Sam C. Nolutshungu, South Africa in Africa: a study in ideology and foreign policy, (Manchester: Manchester University Press, 1975) and on one regional "theatre" see Robert S. Jaster, South Africa in Namibia: the Botha Strategy, (Washington: University Press of America for CFIA, 1985).

21. See South Africa in the 1980s: state of emergency, (London: CIIR, 1986. Third edition), South Africa Review, (Johannesburg: Raven Press, annually), Don Ncube, The Influence of Apartheid and Capitalism on the Development of

Black Trade Unions in South Africa, (Johannesburg, Skotaville, 1985).

22. On the rise of regime-supported or tolerated right-wing vigilantes, both black and white – "fathers" or "fascists" versus "comrades" – see Nicholas Haysom, Apartheid's Private Army: the rise of right-wing vigilantes in South Africa, (London: CIIR, 1986).

23. See South Africa in the 1980s and South African Review.

24. Although they do suffer for being seen to support it; see Joseph Hanlon Apartheid's Second Front: South Africa's war against its neighbours, (Harmondsworth: Penguin, 1986).

25. See Ncube, Black Trade Unions, Robin Cohen Endgame in South Africa? The changing structures and ideology of apartheid, (London: James Currey, and Paris: UNESCO, 1986), pp. 38-59, and Roger Southall, "Special issue on South Africa," Labour, Capital and Society 18(2), November 1982.

26. On inter-pariah or "Fourth bloc" linkages which "reinforce South Africa's movement towards the position of national security state" see South Africa in the 1980s, p. 21.

27. See Carlsson & Shaw (eds), The Political Economy of South-South Relations.

28. See Julius Nyang'oro & Timothy M. Shaw (eds), Corporatism in Africa: state-society relations in a continent in crisis, (Boulder: Lynne Rienner, 1987).

29. On the history of white capital, particularly fractions concerned with agriculture, mining and manufacturing, see Merle Lipton, Capitalism and Apartheid: South Africa, 1910-1986, (Aldershot: Wildwood, 1986).

30. Ibid., p. 365.

31. Ibid., p. 377.

32. See Nicholas Haysom, Apartheid's Private Army, South Africa in the 1980s and Roger Omond, The Apartheid Handbook, (Harmondsworth: Penguin, 1985).

33. See Lipton, Capitalism and Apartheid, 277-398 and Reginald H. Green & Carol B. Thompson, "Political Economies in Conflict: SADCC, South Africa and Sanctions" in Johnson & Martin (eds), Destructive Engagement, pp. 259-260. The latter argue that "middle" rather than "high" capitalism is most concerned about regional access, with the latter being preoccupied by preserving capitalism at home rather than markets abroad: "The standard presentation is business versus the military. That is an oversimplification. There are three distinguishable capitalist sub-classes in South Africa, which broadly correlate with the main white political groupings" (p. 259).

16

34. Green & Thompson, "Political Economies in Conflict," p. 257.
35. See Hanlon, Beggar Your Neighbours, passim, especially pp. 51-65.
36. Green & Thompson, "Political Economies in Conflict," p. 248.
37. Hanlon, Beggar Your Neighbours, p. 13.
38. See Roger Southall, "Regional trends and Africa's future" in Timothy M. Shaw & Olajide Aluko (eds) Africa Projected: from recession to renaissance by the year 2000?, (London: Macmillan, 1985), pp. 81-111.
39. Hanlon, Beggar Your Neighbours, p. 259. Green & Thompson estimate that the 6-year cost of South African aggression against SADCC to be $16-17 billion not SADCC's own estimate of $12-13 billion; Green & Thompson "Political Economies in Conflict", pp. 271-272.
40. See South Africa in the 1980s.
41. Cohen, Endgame in South Africa? cf Martin Legassick, "South Africa in crisis: what route to democracy?" African Affairs 84(337), October 1985, pp. 587-603.
42. Mission to South Africa, p. 129. On the political and economic costs to Mozambique, for example, see John S. Saul, "Nkomati and after" in A Difficult Road: the transition to socialism in Mozambique, (New York: Monthly Review, 1985), pp. 391-418, and "Briefing – Socialist Transition and External Intervention: Mozambique and South Africa's War," Labour. Capital and Society 18(1), April 1985, pp. 153-170.
43. See David Fig, "South African Penetration of Brazil," in Carlsson & Shaw (eds), The Political Economy of South-South Relations.
44. See Duncan Innes, Anglo American and the Rise of Modern South Africa, (London: Heinemann, 1984).
45. Chairman's Statement. 1986, p. 5.
46. The Kairos Document. The Challenge to the Church: a theological comment on the political crisis in South Africa, (London: CIIR and BCC for Kairos Theologians, 1985), p. 25.
47. Ibid., p. 4. See also Breaking Down the walls: World Council of Churches' statements and actions on racism, (Geneva: WCC Programme to Combat Racism, 1956).

PART ONE

Present Struggles
in South Africa and Namibia

1. Liberation Struggles in Southern Africa After Zimbabwe

A. K. Mhina

Since the liberation of Zimbabwe in 1980, liberation struggles in Southern Africa have declined, contrary to the rather optimistic expectations of many observers. This chapter will attempt to examine the present position of liberation struggles in Southern Africa, their setbacks, and the currently favorable position of the regime in South Africa. Also, I will attempt to establish why many liberation struggles have suffered such setbacks since the independence of Zimbabwe, and will conclude with prospects for the liberation of Southern Africa.

The present setback in the liberation process followed a period of great optimism, not only in Africa, but also in many parts of the world. In the early 1970s, many nations achieved independence or succeeded in their liberation struggles. For example, in early 1975, liberation of the Vietnamese from United States imperialism led to unprecedented optimism over the possibility that a small, Third World nation could liberate itself from a super power.

Armed struggles in Portuguese colonies in Africa-Angola and Mozambique – eventually led to the defeat of the Portuguese army. In 1975, after a costly liberation struggle between Portuguese soldiers and African guerrillas, a military coup in Portugal led to a transfer of power and the liberation of the African colonies. Although Seiler argues that officers benevolently handed power to the former colonies, in actuality the armed struggles necessitated changes in Portugal, which in turn necessitated the success of liberation struggles.[1]

Negotiations with Portuguese coup leaders were based on the strength of the liberation movements, otherwise they would never have succeeded. When Spinola attempted to peddle a neo-colonial variant in the form of independence within the orbit of Portugal it was flatly rejected. When Spinola stalled he was kicked out by younger officers. Likewise, during discussions with FRELIMO the Portuguese proposed that there should be a referendum in Mozambique on whether or not Mozambicans wanted independence. FRELIMO refused on the basis that it was an insult and continued with the armed struggle.

Apart from the liberation of the Portuguese colonies, another blow befell the minority white regimes in Southern Africa: the liberation of Zimbabwe, after intensification of armed struggle following the independence of Mozambique. The Lancaster agreement which laid the basis for independence followed the realization of both the Rhodesian and South African armies that they could not win the war.

The independence of Zimbabwe had serious implications for the situation in Namibia and South Africa. There was a strong belief in the "domino theory", substantiated because of assistance from Mozambique to Zimbabwe with the guerrilla group ZANLA of ZANU-PF. Although South Africa had started a series of attacks against Angola to prevent SWAPO attacks in Namibia by 1980, it was believed that South Africa was in deep trouble due to increasing hostile borders.

It was felt that independence of Namibia was therefore imminent. The OAU Liberation Committee laid a strategy which gave priority to Namibia so as to hasten its path to independence, which would then allow all efforts to be concentrated on the liberation of South Africa. By 1980 supporters of the liberation of South Africa were very optimistic about the possibility of liberation of Namibia and South Africa. Optimism for others bordered on euphoria.

However, in the opposite camp, the fascist regime and supporters of South Africa were in a panic: the regime felt it was being cornered. A number of plays on peace were revived.

According to Utete, the collapse of Portuguese rule disrupted South Africa's carefully conceived regional strategy which had been based on two contradictory premises:

a)   White minority regimes would survive into the indefinite future in Mozambique, Angola and Zimbabwe, with South African assistance to bolster them economically and militarily; and

b)   The black ruled regimes of Southern Africa, although opposed to racism and white minority rule, might nonetheless be brought into the Southern African orbit through offers of aid coupled with threats of military retaliation for participation in anti-South African military activities.[2]

The failure of this strategy of <u>cordon sanitaire</u> which had originally sought to draw a line from Angola to Mozambique delineating South African following a period of dialogue proved to be a great disappointment to South Africa. "Dialogue" with Ghana, Ivory Coast, Senegal and Liberia was brief, and never really flowered. After this, a period of "detente" followed, providing military and economic support to Ian Smith and the Rhodesian government, later failing. The South African government did not give up its struggle for survival, however, and intensified its efforts to remain dominant despite setbacks.

According to Ingram, the debate within the Afrikaner establishment has been whether the regime should adopt the historic <u>laager</u> concept, which means pulling back within its borders and securing its position against all adversaries, or whether it should take an offensive posture and push its area of influence northwards and exercising its economic power in the dozen or so countries which have become economically dependent.[3]

The South African regime unleashed attacks on all South African neighbors. Attacks on Angola increased and, according to President Santos, the aim of such attacks was to destabilize Angola by attacking economic installations and uprooting the people in Southern Angola. The South African regime claimed it was making pre-emptive attacks on SWAPO bases. In reality the majority of casualties were civilians and refugees. One such raid in June 1980, "Operation Smokeshell", killed approximately 400 people. Another raid in August 1981 killed 700 people, and left 130,000 refugees. The raid was carried out by 15,000 South African soldiers, who travelled 200 miles into Angola. It was estimated by President Santos that by the end of 1980 raids led by the South African regime had cost Angola roughly U.S. $7 billion.[4]

The South Africans occupied part of Southern Angola where they stayed until the recent announcement of their withdrawal. Apart from direct South African army incursions South Africa has supported UNITA led by their puppet, Jonas Savimbi, whose main area of activity is in Cuando-Cubango Province. Apart from supporting UNITA by giving the group arms, there are South African soldiers from the so-called Buffalo Regiment fighting alongside the UNITA regiment.[5] Attacks have been against railways and other heavy economic installations, along with capturing foreign expatriates.

South Africa has also attacked Mozambique, with its initial raid in January 1981. Twelve South African refugees were killed in one commando raid of Matola suburb. In May 1983, the South African airforce attacked Maputo killing six _ivilians, and carried out another raid in October.[6]

[The most effective South African destabilization strategy in Mozambique has been the support of MNR guerrillas, creating chaos by attacking economic and infrastructure targets consistently. Direct aggression by South Africa cost Mozambique U.S. $333 million in 1982-83. MNR destroyed 900 rural shops, affecting 1.5 million people, 500 primary schools were destroyed and so were 86 secondary schools. In 1982 alone 130 communal villages were destroyed.[7]]

Apart from the raids of Mozambique and Angola many other countries have either been raided or are threatened with attack, including Zimbabwe and Zambia. According to Ingram, [South African intentions were to keep neighboring countries in some form of turmoil with the object of showing the world that black rule does not work.[8]]

Thus, the South African regime reacted to the independence of Zimbabwe with a very strong will to survive. The attacks were so effective that Mozambique signed the Nkomati Accord which heavily favors the position of South Africa. [Mozambique has protested against South African failure to implement its side of the Accord, but seems incapable of withdrawal from the agreement. It has been reported, for instance, that in a recent meeting between South Africa and Mozambique at Maputo, Foreign Minister Botha of South Africa arrogantly taunted Mozambican Interior Minister Viera with the words, "If you say Nkomati is dead, then what will you do."[9] To make things worse, it is said the Front Line States could not promise help to Samora if he scraped Nkomati.[10]]

Apart from the Nkomati Accord, Angola has also discussed peace with South Africa in Lusaka under the auspices of Chester Crocker. Crocker calls the move "constructive disengagement." The agreement is supposed to involve the withdrawal of Cuban soldiers in exchange for South African withdrawal from Angola. Not much has happened although the South African regime is claiming to have withdrawn from southern Angola.

Such has been the setback to the liberation process in Southern Africa. The question is how to explain the situation from the point of view of the liberation struggle. For the purposes of this chapter, this will be described from two different perspectives: the strategy of the liberation movements, and the capacity of the Front Line States to provide an effective rear base.

After the liberation of Zimbabwe, there was a great deal of optimism that Namibia would soon be liberated. The main focus has been 1978 United Nations Resolution 435, which

outlines the strategy for South African withdrawal from
Namibia in the following stages:

a)   7,500 U.N. troops replace South African army;

b)   South Africa decrease troops to 1,500 over three
     month period;

c)   four month election campaign; and

d)   last South African troops withdraw within one week
     of certification of election results.[11]

The plan seemed to be a genuine solution to the Namibian
question, and there appeared to be a coincidence of interest
between the Western Contact Group, South Africa, SWAPO and
the Front Line States.   The Contact Group, comprising the
United States, Canada, Britain, West Germany and France, was
supposed to "deliver" South Africa, while the Front Line
States were supposed to "deliver" SWAPO.
All participants claimed to support the U.N. plan
including South Africa.   However, in reality South Africa
appeared to be determined to maintain a puppet regime in
Namibia – something for which SWAPO is obviously ill-suited
and vehemently opposed.
Thus, while the Front Line States and SWAPO were
striving for a settlement, South Africa increased attacks on
Angola.   The invasions of 1981 were carried with all signs
that South Africa believed it had the moral support of at
least the United States.[12]   The Contact Group watched as
South Africa battered Angola, intending to beat SWAPO into
submission.   The Americans supported this action, and Reagan
has been accused of being the reason for the inactivity of
the contact group which led to the French statement regarding
its withdrawal from the group.
The United Nations Conference on Namibia, held in Geneva
in January 1981, was intended to cement the U.N. Plan for
Namibia.   However, discussions broke down during the initial
stage.   It was obvious that while SWAPO was ready to
negotiate, the South African government was not.
When the U.N. Security Council proposed sanctions
against South Africa in retaliation for Pretoria's
intransigence over Namibia, the Western powers vetoed the
move.   It was only at this stage that the Front Line States
began to doubt the sincerity of the Western powers on the
Namibian question.
To some observers, the reason for the support of South
Africa by the Western Contact Group is clear: South Africa

and Namibia are rich in minerals, including diamonds, copper, lead, zinc, cadmium and the strategically important mineral, uranium. Capitalist multinational corporations have heavy investments in South Africa and Namibia. With the exception of Scandinavian countries, the West will only support change as a means to stall a complete defeat of the South African regime. The line dividing them from South Africa is thin. Hugo Young, on the position of the United States government, and particularly that of Reagan, writes,

> Congress is not the whole of Washington. There is also the President hooked on a policy of 'constructive engagement' which being decoded means that the best way of making South Africa better for blacks is to make it safe for Western capitalism. Reagan can veto any anti-investment bill and his benignly conciliatory reaction at Langa suggests he will do so.[13]

The position of Britain under Thatcher is similar. The British government is prepared to take no risk and pay no price in practical support of its moralizing.[14]

On Namibia, the South African regime is ignoring everybody and going on with plans for 'internal settlement', in the form of interim administration. The basis of interim administration will be the Multiparty Conference (MPC) which in 1983 replaced the pro-South African Turnhalle Democratic Alliance (DTA).[15]

The South African regime apparently feels it can ignore SWAPO and establish an administration composed of numerous small parties, gaining credibility. However, while South Africa will not achieve the required aim, the main issue is the fact that South Africa seems to believe it has already done enough damage to SWAPO to be able to ignore it.

One explanation for the setback to the liberation struggle in Namibia is the complacency of SWAPO on the possibility of victory through negotiations. Expectations were based on the peaceful path to independence and quick results were expected. One author argues that the South African army has had some success in reducing the level of guerrilla activity in Namibia. However, this was based on the observation that during a period when SWAPO usually launched an intensified struggle, such activity did not seem to materialize at all.[16]

Needless to say, it has been recognized that Angola has been heavily attacked by South Africa. It is also recognized that the terrain in Namibia is very difficult for guerilla warfare activity. However, SWAPO ought to be fully aware of the serious constraints. After the liberation of Zimbabwe,

it appears that the limitations of dealing with the powerful
South African regime were underestimated.

As well, it is difficult to understand SWAPO's recent
optimism.   The President of SWAPO speculated that within one
year Namibia would be free.   The Zambian News Agency
observed,

> The SWAPO President's optimism stems from the moral and
> material support the liberation movement was receiving
> from the international community.[17]

Internationally, the pressure is for the implementation of
the U.N. Plan. However, South Africa has blatantly ignored
the proposal and is attempting to undermine all peaceful
resolutions by creating a puppet regime.   Certainly, one
cannot expect the 'fortunes' of SWAPO to change in a few
months, especially when expectations are based on
'international pressure'. This possibility becomes even more
remote, in consideration of what Crocker terms 'Constructive
Disengagement' - the removal of Cuban soldiers from Angola.
Bitter and protracted struggles will have to be waged to
successfully liberate Angola.

As for South Africa, the liberation struggles have been
stepped up.   The African National Congress (ANC) has been
very active, whereas the Pan African Congress (PAC) has for a
long time been inactive. PAC inactivity has been attributed
to a leadership crisis which seems to have been resolved.
The liberation process has, regardless, been affected to some
extent by the prescription of ANC activities in the countries
bordering on South Africa. To understand this problem it is
imperative that one examine what has been happening in the
rear base.

Obviously, several neighboring countries have been
subjected to attack by South Africa. Such attacks led to the
Nkomati Accord, and there are attempts at reaching a solid
agreement between Angola and South Africa under the auspices
of the U.S. government.

Many have described the agreements as a setback but many
have also pointed out that they understand the circumstances
which forced Mozambique and Angola into negotiating with
South Africa.   The question is why has the South African
strategy been so effective at least in the short run? Part
of its success should be attributed to the political and
economic strategies of the rear bases.

Mozambique had suffered severe problems before signing
the Nkomati Accord.   During the struggle for Zimbabwean
independence, Mozambique endured a great deal of hardship and
destruction.   According to Guy Arnold, damage resulting from

the neighboring war totalled approximately U.S. $120 million, while another U.S. $500 million was in lost reserves.[18] Further damages were caused by South African direct and indirect infiltration. Coupled with drought, these attacks precipitated a serious food crisis which led to starvation for many Mozambicans.

Some blame for these problems has to be placed on the Mozambican government, especially concerning reconstruction after independence. The economic strategy was not well planned and was implemented haphazardly. In agriculture this strategy was catastrophic. The emphasis was placed on highly capital intensive state farms in a situation where the technological culture to run and maintain the mechanized farms was absent. This was a blunder and it is only after the damage was done that the correct strategy of concentration on small-holders was announced.

In the manufacturing sector, a management crisis was evident partly because of a lack of skilled labor. It is only very recently that there has been a realization that these organizations have to be run as public business enterprises not on the civil service line.

In the political arena, despite good intentions on the part of Samora Machel, power has been personalized in Mozambique with no representative institutions. Political penetration in the rural areas is yet to be fully achieved. The frequent reshuffles of the Cabinet have not brought any serious changes and the Politburo has not changed its composition since independence.

The vulnerability of Mozambique to South African incursions has thus been blamed by many upon poor economic and political strategies. Campbell, for example, has argued that,

> the representative tendencies which are expressed in the forms of state operations hinder the full mobilization of the people and represent anti-democratic politics and practices which are to be found all over the underdeveloped world.[19]

In the fourth congress of FRELIMO of April 1983 it was acknowledged by the leadership that the major reasons for the spread of the MNR in provinces were:

a)   the slow responses of the party to the threat of South African destabilization;

b)   the tactics of the army in engaging MNR;

c)   the excesses of the army vis-a-vis rural peasants; and

d)   the absence of the party in the rural areas.[20]]

One can also observe at this stage that while the forces working against Mozambique were of a great magnitude and the traditional Mozambican economy were very weak and dependent on the South African economy, the state in Mozambique could not cope because of a poor economic strategy which failed to deal realistically with the nation's problems. [The uncritical adoption of Eastern European models in a situation far from peaceful was a blunder.]

Poor political mobilization, especially in the countryside, led to the alienation of FRELIMO from the people. It should be recognized that Mozambique sacrificed a lot for liberation, and that not all countries in Africa, particularly the Southern African region, were prepared to help these liberation struggles. Uwechue of Africa commented following the Nkomati Accord, that it exposed a fatal flaw in Africa's approach to the liberation struggle in Southern Africa: many African governments pay lip service to it but few tried to rescue Mozambique.

In contrast with the Mozambican approach has been that of Zimbabwe. After independence, Mugabe's major priority was to rebuild his own country. He quickly held out an olive branch to Pretoria, stating from the outset that although his government would always oppose apartheid, it did not intend to provide the guerrillas of ANC with bases in Zimbabwe.[21] This decision was made easy by the fact that the ANC had been an ally of ZAPU and not ZANU-PF during the liberation struggle in Zimbabwe.

In the economic arena, Mugabe had gone for only modest change. Having seen the chaos caused elsewhere in Africa through economic reforms, Mugabe sought to avoid such a crisis of shortages. In the process, however, burning problems which had precipitated the war of liberation had yet to be tackled. Howard Barrell, quoting a South African political scientist, wrote that if rhetoric determined reality, Zimbabwe could be a Marxist-Leninist society. He states, however, that in reality few people have recognized that yet another African revolution has thus far merely served to unleash individual entrepreneurship.[22]

Thus the whites who were worried when Mugabe took power are now concerned that he may lose power, and upwardly mobile blacks also fear that he may turn rhetoric into reality. As Thornycroft observes,

Few wars ended the way the Rhodesian conflict was concluded. The enemy was forgiven his sins, his property was left intact, his privileged lifestyle remained unaltered.[23]

For the Africans who fought the war, the land question remained a central issue. According to Roger Riddell, there are three related dimensions that add to the significance and complexity of the land question:

a) access to agricultural land is extremely unequal and remains along racial lines despite elimination of the legislation that created existing problems;

b) problems of land scarcity and landlessness persist alongside areas of unused and under-utilized land; and

c) the largely white commercial farming subsection contributes in a major way both directly and indirectly to the economic prosperity of the modern sector of the economy.[24]

There have been improvements, however, particularly when considered within the parameters of the Lancaster House Agreements. At the time of writing, approximately 150,000 landless peasants had been resettled on white farms and the overall contribution of peasants and small farmers increased. Before 1980, they contributed less than 10% of maize production, a strong contrast to the 40-50% of present output. Regardless, some critics still feel resettlement has been slow.

In Matabeleland dissidents have attacked European farmers. Over 40 white farmers have been killed in Matabeleland since 1980, and despite Mugabe's decision to rearm the farmers, many have been forced to quit in some areas. The Kezi area in Matabeleland is a case in point.[25]

Unlike Mozambique, Zimbabwe has tried to avoid confrontation with South Africa. The fear has been that South Africa could add fuel to the conflict in Matabeleland, also a stronghold of Mugabe's opponent Nkomo. Economically, not much has changed. Mugabe has repeatedly stated that he foresees the displacement of capitalism in a process of 'transformation' rather than precipitate 'revolution' which he believes would endanger the country's productive base.

The liberation movements in South Africa should

therefore not expect much in terms of an access route through Mozambique and Zimbabwe at this stage. What, then, are the prospects for the liberation of Southern Africa? Of the contradictions within the Southern African subsystem, the most profound exist within South Africa and Namibia, as well as terrorizing neighboring countries. The peoples of South Africa and Namibia, where the majority group comprise the African people, have been robbed of their land and subjected for many years to the ruthless exploitation of the South African government and international capitalists. The system of apartheid which has subjugated the African people to the myth of white supremacy is so revolting that people of all races throughout the world have condemned it.

The contradictions of South Africa have led to a situation where peace will be unattainable until the majority African people have achieved power and established a democratic state. The situation is likewise in Namibia. Circumstances are against the fascist regime of South Africa. Thus, despite the effectiveness of the attacks on neighboring countries, the struggles have intensified in South Africa.

A new phase of struggle in South Africa began with the Soweto uprising of 1976. Along with the two earlier liberation organizations, the ANC and PAC, the Black Consciousness Movement which began in 1971 led to coordination of activities among various student organizations. Two other major movements have emerged – the United Democratic Front (UDF) and the Azanian Peoples Organization (AZAPO), the latter of which is more radical. The Black Consciousness Movement together with the ANC has kept the struggles in South Africa at a high level.

Despite the savagery of the regime in dealing with peaceful demonstrations, the struggles have continued. The anger of Africans is increasing and methods of counteracting oppression by the regime are becoming increasingly sophisticated. The recent bomb attacks on the offices of the Anglo American Corporation and another mining multinational after the expulsion of black workers because of trade union activities show the ability of the ANC and other organizations to launch attacks within South Africa.

CONCLUSION

This chapter has attempted to show that the setbacks of the liberation struggles after the independence of Zimbabwe have been the result of a variety of factors.

In the first place, there has been an underestimation of the capabilities of the South African regime. Many African es have been aware of the military machine of South Africa and the backing it receives from capitalist countries. However, dealings with South Africa reveal a certain naivete. An example is the expectation that South Africa can let the rear base recover to be able to attack it. The failure of Nkomati should be placed in this context.

Second, and related to the first factor, are the high expectations placed on peaceful settlement following the success of the Lancaster House talks. This is especially relevant to the case of Namibia. While a peaceful settlement is a possibility, it usually follows a realization on the part of the oppressor that the war is lost. The Portuguese negotiated with the liberation movements after the campaign by Portugal to wipe out movements failed. In Mozambique such an attempt was carried out by Arriagha in the Gordian Knot campaign.

In Zimbabwe, the Lancaster negotiations were held after it was clear that Muzorewa's Zimbabwe-Rhodesia could not stop the war. It is not intended here to argue that SWAPO's achievements have been small, but to note that before the enemy is defeated there should be no reason for the struggle to relax. Intensive attacks by South Africa within Angola have been a setback to SWAPO. What is important, however, is to understand the struggles will be protracted and SWAPO should not put all its eggs in the international pressure basket.

Third, the problems of reconstruction have affected the strongest rear base of the struggles in South Africa. Mozambique has made tremendous sacrifices to achieve liberation. As well, Mozambique has been vulnerable due to weaknesses in its political and economic strategy. Politically, FRELIMO inherited the Portuguese colonial state with its trappings including personnel such as policemen. Leaders feared a vacuum, but by keeping such institutions they alienated a variety of people including those in the rural areas. Economically, and particularly in agriculture, capital-intensive state farms have been a failure.

Despite these setbacks, however, the struggle continues. South Africa is still cornered. Principle contradictions lie within South Africa itself, and not from outside sources as the regime would presume. So long as the contradictions exist, the struggle will intensify.

NOTES

1. John Seiler, ed. Southern Africa since the Portuguese Coup, (Boulder: Westview Press, 1980). See Introduction.

2.   C. Munhamu Utete, "Zimbabwe and Southern African 'Detente'", Ibid., p. 63.
3.   Derek Ingram, "Southern Africa after Zimbabwe", Africa Guide 1982, p. 16.
4.   Roy Laishley, "Angola", Ibid.
5.   Ibid.
6.   The Economist Intelligence Unit No. 4, 1983, p. 22.
7.   Colin Legum, "Mozambique–South Africa: Is it a Deal?", New Africa, March 1984.
8.   Ingram, p. 17.
9.   "Mozambique: Cold Comfort at Lusaka", Africa Event, May 1985, p. 48.
10. Ibid., p. 49.
11. D. Ingram, "South Africa Goes Down the Muzurewa Road in Namibia", Daily News, (Dar es Salaam), 14 May 1985.
12. Ingram, "Southern Africa after Zimbabwe," p. 18.
13. Hugo Young, "The Limits of Political Rhetoric", Africa Events, May 1985, p. 50.
14. Ibid.
15. Ingram, "South Africa Goes Down the Muzurewa Road in Namibia".
16. Ibid.
17. Daily News, 10 May 1985.
18. Guy Arnold, "Mozambique", Africa Guide 1982,
19. Horace Campbell, "War, Reconstruction and Dependence in Mozambique", Third World Quarterly, 6(4), October 1984, p. 842.
20. Ibid., p. 847.
21. Ingram, "Southern Africa After Zimbabwe," p. 17.
22. Howard Barrel, "Which Way Mugabe", New Africa, January 1984, p. 12.
23. P. Thornycroft, "Mugabe: marking time or backing down?", Africa Events, May 1985, p. 51.
24. Roger Riddel quoted in B.H.Kinsey, "Forever Gained: resettlement and land policy in the context of national development in Zimbabwe", Africa: Journal of the International African Institute, 52(3), 1982, p. 93.
25. New Africa, March 1984.

2. The Decolonization Process in Namibia

Horace Campbell

INTRODUCTION

The intensified struggle in Southern Africa for political independence and human dignity is bringing to a close the South African form of repression in Namibia. The opposition to apartheid inside South Africa takes the form of daily insurrectionary violence against the apartheid war machine while inside colonial Namibia the liberation fighters have beaten back the combined efforts of the USA and South Africa to physically eliminate SWAPO, and at the same time remove the MPLA government in Luanda. This military campaign on the part of the South Africans was conceived of in the guise of defending the strategic interests of the West. Invoking the elements of East-West and the Cold War struggles, the South Africans had hoped to bind the Western capitalist states permanently to their particular form of racial exploitation.

This exploitation which segregated and humiliated the African majority challenged the masses to take up arms to resist and to remove colonial overrule. In the process of organizing armed struggles the oppressed peoples have gained significant victories – militarily, politically and diplomatically by successfully internationalizing the issue of decolonization. The Namibian question is now the central issue at many international meetings of the United Nations, the Non-Aligned Movement and the OAU largely because the freedom fighters continue to bear arms to challenge the continuing capitalist exploitation of Namibia. These freedom fighters have shown that the initiative for peace and stability now lies with the organized and struggling people.

At this period the questions of peace and security in the region can be posed from many angles, from the points of view of (a) South Africans, (b) transnational capital, (c) independent states of the region (especially the Front Line States), and (d) producing masses. All over the continent of Africa these masses yearn for food, security, and peace, as they are caught in militarized societies where force lies at the foundation of production. Inside South Africa the insecurity generated by the racial form of capitalism spreads war, terror, famine and harassment of the people on a day-to-day basis.

The prolonged struggles of the organized masses provides the scope for future forms of social organization which could end the present exploitative relations. Far-sighted elements from the international bourgeoisie have perceived this alternative; hence the incessant conferences, shuttle diplomacy and disengagement talks to search for some kind of settlement which could exclude working people from participating in the processes of reconstruction and development.

SWAPO, the principal political organization involved in the decolonization process in Namibia, now has the advantage of learning the positive and negative lessons of other experiences in the seizure of power in Africa. Throughout the continent the responses and machinations of transnational capital have sharpened to the point where even societies which proclaimed socialism have found they can be undermined by local elements allied with foreign capital. This fact has been brought into sharp focus by the Nkomati Accord between the South African regime and the Frelimo leadership.

Reversals of this magnitude abound all over the continent, with the question of food security and the fight against hunger claiming top priority. It could be said that the present international campaign to provide relief for famine victims in Africa is but one manifestation of the failures of present African leaders to develop self-sustaining economies which can guarantee the peace and security of the broad masses. Thus the food crisis as part of the crisis of capitalism imposes on those fighting for freedom a quest for emancipation which could be qualitatively different from the flag independence of the previous member states of the OAU.

There is no doubt that in Namibia there will be a transition period where there will be a sharing of power between the freedom fighters and the representatives of transnational capital. But the decisive question for the liberation movement will be to what extent the producing masses are drawn into democratic processes where they live and where they work in order to break the inherited structure of apartheid. Experience in Zimbabwe in the past five years has shown that freedom fighters can be seduced by the social

capital of the society to the point where they share power
with transnational capital to the exclusion of the broad
masses.

For the Namibians the questions of skill, competence and
administrative abilities to extract the minerals and
fisheries resources are being used to train a social strata
which would ally with international capital. The ideological
reference points of this thrust are modernization and
economic growth, ideas which in other parts of Africa have
foundered on the rock of petty bourgeois politics, regional
differentiation, and politicization of region and religion,
along with the militarization of society.

This chapter, written during a time of war,
destabilization and insecurity compounded by the crisis of
capitalism hopes to strengthen the cause of the exploited and
disenfranchised masses of Namibia and South Africa. It
cannot supplement the work done by the freedom fighters
themselves, the numerous support groups internationally and
the voluminous works of the United Nations Institute for
Namibia (UNIN). However, it hopes to raise questions which
could illuminate the path of the process of decolonization
beyond the simple seizing of state power.

THE WAR IN NAMIBIA

The vast territory of Namibia in the South Western part
of the continent has been the scene of a bitter struggle
between Europe and Africa, between labor and capital for over
one hundred years. This territory covering an area of over
824,925 sq. km. contains less than two million persons but
the level of extraction of wealth and the form of the
organization of labor have ensured that massive profits are
extracted from the society with a minimum return to the
people. The known resources of Namibia at present are the
basic natural resources of land, minerals, and fish,
including some of the richest inshore and deepwater fishing
zones in Southern Africa. A wide range of minerals is
extracted from the soil with the production of diamonds being
the most important for South Africa and transnational
capital. Large-scale uranium mining at the infamous Rossing
mines produces uranium under conditions which should be
prohibited if the miners had the minimum form of industrial
democracy.

It is the complete coercion and disorganization of the
working people whether on the farms, ranches, canneries,
mines or in domestic service which provide for the extreme
forms of militarization in this territory to the point where

there are over 100,000 South African troops – one military person to every twelve citizens. In challenging this militarization the Namibians have, first, organized into numerous organizations, cultural, religious, community and political, with the most widely-known being SWAPO. These people have also organized militarily in the Peoples Liberation Army of Namibia (PLAN) and have continued the long struggle which was initiated by the Namibian peoples who firstly valiantly resisted German rule.[1]

It is this rich tradition of resistance which strengthens the resolve of the peoples of Namibia as they daily toil to produce the surplus for South African and international capital. Part of the ability of the oppressors to have maintained their presence in its present colonial form stemmed from the thorough devastation which was wrought by the occupying German forces from 1884 to 1917. Long before fascism and mass genocide had taken root in Europe, German settlers and militarists had massacred more than sixty per cent of the population when they were seeking to institutionalize forced labor, forced destocking and plunder in Namibia. But even with its military superiority the imperial German state failed to subdue the people and when the South African-cum-British overrule sought to continue the oppression, the peoples of Namibia had developed new methods to resist colonialism both actively and passively.

The process of the entrenchment of South African rule and its extension of apartheid in all its forms have followed the requirements for the extraction of surplus profits from Namibia. This search for profits guarantees that South Africa would have the political and military support of the Western states in order to defy the numerous resolutions and statements of the UN on the question of Namibia's independence. It is part of the dialectic of the struggle of the oppressed peoples that they have been able to register this problem of Namibian decolonization as one of the foremost questions of the UN. But it is also the present strength of international capital which ensures that in spite of this international pressure Namibia remains colonized and illegally occupied by South Africa.

As part of the internationalization of the question of Namibia various groups and support organizations have documented the steps of South Africa's entrenchment of apartheid in Namibia and the scope of the militarization of the society. Three documents, in particular (a) Namibia-The Facts; (b) Apartheid's Army in Namibia, and (c) Namibia-The Ravages of War by Barbara Konig – have shed light on the massive military buildup inside Namibia and the ways in which over the past ten years the illegal occupation has been also used as a base for military assaults against Angola.

THE THREE PHASES OF THE WAR

The marshalled evidence shows that the war in Namibia has essentially gone through three stages:

a) the first phase, 1966-1975, where SWAPO set out to organize the challenge to South Africa's occupation of the territory;

b) the second phase, 1975-1981, where the South Africans undertook a massive build-up in Namibia subsequent to their defeat in Angola in 1976; and

c) the third phase, 1981-1984, where with the open support of the USA through the policy of 'constructive engagement' the South Africans sought to

(i)   crush SWAPO;
(ii)   build up the South West Africa Territorial Force (SWATF) as a purely Namibian army;
(iii)   remove the Angola government of the MPLA in Luanda; and
(iv)   build up UNITA as an alternative base of power to rule or share power in Angola.

The first phase of this war involved the determination of SWAPO to bear arms against the South Africans. In launching the armed struggle on 26 August 1966, SWAPO was in the process of developing its own ability to bear arms; to maintain a supply line from East Africa through Zambia to Namibia; and to develop communications and logistics for guerrillas in a sparsely-populated country.[2]

Industrial action by Namibian workers in 1971 had heightened the consciousness of the popular masses and in turn increased the repression and military build-up of the South African forces. A general strike by contract workers as an expression of proletarian opposition had been brutally suppressed with large police reinforcements flown in from South Africa. Through the expediency of a State of Emergency which had been declared in 1972, troops from the South African Defense Force (SADF) began to carry out police activities as well as extending its so-called counter-insurgency activities.

The low-intensity character of the South African war inside Namibia was rapidly transformed after the fall of the

Caetano regime in Portugal and the coming to power of the
MPLA in Luanda. The efforts of the Boers to reverse the
victories of the national independence movement in Angola led
to a massive three-pronged ground, air and naval invasion of
Angola by SADF. It is now recorded for history how the South
African and mercenary forces were routed in the war between
July 1975 and March 1976.[3]

The military defeat of the South Africans by the
Angolans with the support of the Cubans created a totally new
situation in Africa. Not only were the South Africans
defeated militarily in battle, exposing their myth of
invincibility, but a small socialist island – Cuba-
demonstrated its ability and its willingness to support fully
the African liberation struggle. This defeat in Angola
brought a rude awakening to the military strategists in
Pretoria and brought about the second stage in the war in
Namibia and Angola.

After blaming Washington and Henry Kissinger for
insufficient support in the advance into Angola, South
African strategists reorganized the politico-military
hierarchy under a State Security Council with greater powers
for the military. One of the immediate consequences of this
reorganization was the announcement of a grand policy of
destabilization under their conception of Total Strategy.[4]
This formula involved an increase in defense expenditure and
led to a rapid escalation of the war in Northern Namibia
between 1976 and 1977. By 1977 South Africa had increased
its troop strength from 16,000 at the beginning of 1976 to
over 80,000 by the end of 1979. Civil engineering works
transformed the whole territory into one massive battleground
with numerous military bases and airfields built across the
land to the point where by 1979 there were 40 military bases
along the Northern Namibian border with Angola and 35 in the
rest of the country, while the military base at Walvis Bay
and naval facilities in the harbor were expanded.

By 1979 all of Namibia was governed by the requirements
of martial law with over half of the country under the direct
control of the SADF. This military build-up also served as a
cover for intensified plunder of the mineral resources of
Namibia. Between 1972 and 1980 the principal mining
companies under the umbrella of the occupation forces carried
out extensive overmining. Evidence both inside and outside
Namibia exposed the levels of overmining, especially by the
Consolidated Diamond Mines (CDM), with all its negative
consequences for future generations of Namibians.[5]

In this militarized society the competing demand for
coerced labor from both the mines and the military led to
conscription. Conscription of able-bodied men and youths

over 16 ensured the flight of more refugees to Southern Angola and this in turn led the South Africans to carry the war further into Angola in an effort to destroy the bases of SWAPO. In one such foray the South African airforce bombed defenseless refugees at Kassinga in May 1978. Kassinga became imprinted in the struggle of Southern Africa as the place where the Boers massacred over 600 defenseless men, women and children.

Massacres and atrocities by the Boers in this phase increased the pressures on the UN to take up its role in the independence of Namibia. By September 1978 the United Nations Security Council passed resolution 435 which stipulated the stages for a ceasefire and a constitution for an independent Namibia. This resolution called for inter alia:

a) a ceasefire in Namibia;

b) the withdrawal of South African troops;

c) the demobilization of the command structures of the South African tribal armies;

d) that SWAPO personnel outside the country should return peacefully;

e) the setting up of a United Nations Transition Assistance Group (UNTAG) with military and civilian components to ensure observance of the aforementioned provisions by all parties; and

f) the holding of elections on the basis of universal adult suffrage.

Between 1978 and 1980 the South Africans were isolated diplomatically as the decolonization process in Zimbabwe further exposed the end of racial capitalism in Southern Africa. The formation of a 'Contact Group' of five Western nations - the US, the Federal Republic of Germany, France, Britain and Canada - served as a safety net for illegal South African activities. The South Africans sought more and more concessions from SWAPO and the Front Line States, while building up a new military force inside Namibia called the South West Africa Territorial Force (SWATF).

The creation of a SWATF was born out of the realization by the South Africans that they would have to give up Namibia. They thus set out to organize a defense unit which was supposed to be independent of the SADF. Large resources were transferred to the SWATF so that by 1983 it had moved into its massive headquarters at Windhoek with communications links to Pretoria, the British communications intelligence headquarters at Cheltenham in England, and to Washington. With a command structure based on the ideology of white racism, counter-insurgency and anti-communism, the SWATF was designed to serve the long-term objectives of defending Western military interests in Southern Africa.

Plans for a South African State Security Council (SSC) merged well with the policies of the US Administration of Ronald Reagan and served as a basis for the tactics of the third phase of the war. The State Department under Reagan had spelt out a policy of 'constructive engagement' as the basis for defending the growing link between US finance capital and South African capital. Under this policy the US administration overtly supported apartheid while opposing international pressures for a negotiated settlement in Namibia. Reagan's foreign policy simplified the struggle in Southern Africa into the narrow conception of East-West confrontation and the strategists in Washington poked the fires of war to provoke a confrontation between the Soviet Union and the West inside Angola. Using the presence of the internationalist Cuban forces in Angola as a pretext for delaying the independence of Namibia, the US and the South Africans dreamt up the idea of 'linkage'; that is the withdrawal of the South African forces from Namibia and Angola should be linked to the withdrawal of the Cuban troops from Angola.

This question of linkage has overshadowed the real issues in the decolonization of Namibia while with the open military and logistical support of the Pentagon the South Africans embarked on an all-out campaign between 1981 and 1984 (a) to crush SWAPO and PLAN and (b) to remove the MPLA government in Luanda. These objectives led to an unprecedented escalation of the war in Southern Angola as the South Africans invaded Angola in August 1981 with over 11,000 men in a massive bombing of the limited infrastructure of roads, bridges and telecommunications links. The South African troops occupied up to 200 km of territory in Angola. Documents which have already come to light reveal the extent of the collusion between the US Assistant Secretary of State for African Affairs, Dr. Chester Crocker, and the Defense Minister of South Africa, Magnus Malan.[6]

Namibia was portrayed as a key arena of the cold war where a settlement, favorable to the West, was necessary as a 'strategic gain' for Western interests against the Soviet threat. With this conception of strategic interest, the South Africans vowed that Namibia would never be independent until a pro-American government was installed in Luanda. Thus the question of Cuban troops became central to the bargaining position of the Americans in impeding the implementation of Resolution 435.

As the level of the war escalated in Namibia and Angola so did the demand for conscripts in South Africa and Namibia. In 1981, the South Africans introduced compulsory military service for all male youths between 16 and 25. Students became the targets of repression as the school system in Namibia joined labor, commerce, agriculture and mining where militarization governed the day-to-day life process. And yet even with this level of repression the Namibian people and the principal liberation movement continued to resist the South Africans.

In its failure to defeat the Namibian peoples the South Africans intensified repression to the point of creating a special death squad unit called Koevet. Learning from the examples of American-supported regimes in El Salvador and Chile, Koevet (which literally means 'crowbar') gained notoriety in its brutality, torture and murder of innocent civilians in the urban areas. And it is one symptom of the collusion between the Western news agencies and the South African regime that the atrocities of Koevet are only brought to international attention through concerned christians and church groups in Namibia.

FROM THE FAILURE TO CRUSH SWAPO TO THE MPC

The inability of the South Africans to achieve their objectives in the third phase led to the search for alternative strategies in the region. This strategy sought to reduce overt South African military forays in the face of the international outcry against its destabilization of the Front Line States. Thus the South Africans developed a posture where the regime in Pretoria would be seen as a peace-maker while at the same time giving more support to puppet armies such as that of Jonas Savimbi in Angola and the Multi-Party Conference (MPC) in Namibia. This represents the present stage of the war in Namibia and underscores the much-heralded peace agreement - the Lusaka Agreement of February 1984 - under which South African troops were supposed to have been withdrawn from Angola.

It was this same double-edged strategy which induced the now infamous Nkomati Accord of March 1984 between Mozambique and South Africa.[7] Up to the time of writing (April 1985) the South Africans had not totally withdrawn from Angola nor had the military establishment in Pretoria ceased support for the MNR in Mozambique.

The pressures of insurrectionary violence and uprisings inside apartheid society have led to a scaling-down of the number of troops in Angola. However, long-term plans to destabilize Angola are being reformulated with the opening-up of a northern front from Zaire. In this enterprise the renewed relationship between Israel and Zaire was to be strengthened with a military alliance which would also include rearmed batallions for Jonas Savimbi.

The questions of decolonization and self-determination for the oppressed majority in Southern Africa were never cold war issues. Thus SWAPO and the peoples of Namibia survived the machinations of the USA and South Africans to eliminate SWAPO as a political force. But even if the attempt to crush SWAPO failed there is still the attempt to create a political alternative. This now involves the creation of social strata inside Namibia which would carry out the same tasks that Muzorewa attempted in Zimbabwe between 1978 and 1980. However, the very ideas of racism, which had excluded a potential middle class from exercising any power, dictate that the process of creating black allies of Pretoria has started too late to be of any lasting political significance.

This explains the zig-zags and the formation of internal parties from the period of the Democratic Turnhalle Alliance in 1977 to the present internal government of 1985, which is called the MPC. In essence the parties of the MPC do not have a real political base in the society but are totally dependent on the repressive power of the South Africans. At the same time the South Africans have devolved power over the South West Africa Police to the MPC. But even before the MPC was installed dissension and disarray among the parties exposed the fact that the South Africans will ultimately have no alternative but to negotiate with SWAPO.

NEGOTIATIONS AND CONCESSIONS

Negotiations and discussions of independence for Namibia have been an integral part of the armed struggle for national liberation. The South Africans continue to flout international law long after they have lost the ability to control Namibia. Under international law South Africa illegally occupies Namibia as the legitimate authority over Namibia is vested in the UN. But if Namibia were ever to be independent on the basis of UN sovereignty it would already have been so, for after more than 900 meetings and over 75 resolutions the condition of South African control over Namibia has not changed fundamentally. It is for this reason that it needs to be reasserted that the principal force for peace and for decolonization in Namibia lies with the political and military struggles of its people, against SWAPO it has hoped to gain through what the South Africans have failed to win unlikely in the war to continuous process of negotiations and concessions wrung by the West from SWAPO and the Front Line States.

Part of the problem with documenting the concessions wrung from the liberation forces has been the way in which the West and the Front Line States have bounded together to deny information to the peoples of Africa on the process of the negotiations over Namibia. Proposals placed before SWAPO such as the complex and undemocratic electoral system – e.g. the 'one person, two vote' proposal of 1981–1983, the nature of the post-colonial constitution, the period of disengagement, and the question of Walvis Bay – are key issues which have not been properly discussed by the peoples of Africa either inside the Front Line States or even inside Namibia. Attempts to cut-off the broad majority of African peoples from discussion of the content of the negotiations over Namibia is but one expression of the demobilization of the masses in the region.

Since 1980 there have been constant meetings of the Front Line States with the masses only learning that there was a reaffirmation of the support for UN Resolution 435. The exact content of this resolution is not known to even the intelligentsia in the region, much less to the literate sections of the working class. Thus the concessions made by the Front Line States and SWAPO cannot be fully grasped or discussed at present. However, such a discussion is a necessary requisite for the strengthening of the popular masses in the region to withstand US/South African military and political onslaughts so that they can understand the real reasons why the US and South Africans would like to have the Cuban internationalist forces withdrawn from Angola.[8]

It is my view that the drawing-in of the people by progressive elements among the liberation movements is necessary in light of the extensive role assigned to the UN in the disengagement process which must precede any attempt to integrate the SWAPO leadership into an independent Namibian state. Because imperialism always attempts to recoup what it has lost in battle, the political-ideological struggle must be sharpened to strengthen the peoples of Namibia and the region. The experience of the UN in support for real decolonization in the Congo reinforces the point of the need for freedom fighters to be both politically and ideologically clear but also to be totally grounded in the masses.

Recent scholarship on the Congo - on the isolation, arrest and assassination of Patrice Lumumba in the presence of UN troops - has exposed the ways in which the Western capitalist states have been able to use the UN to further the interests of their mining capital. The chilling account in the Congo Cables, of how the US was able to manipulate the UN system, should be required reading for all Namibians.[9] Undoubtedly changes in the UN system since reversals in the Congo have weakened American domination, but the collective power of Western capital is still manifest in a number of ways in the specialized agencies of the organization. In this respect, the work of UNIN becomes important in the decolonization process.

SKILLED MANPOWER OR DEMOBILIZATION

The United Nations Institute for Namibia (UNIN) was started in Lusaka, Zambia in 1976 with the specific task of training public servants and administrators for an independent Namibia. Since 1976 an indeterminate number of Namibians have been through the Institute with the emphasis placed on the training of public administrators who would be capable of servicing the independent state. From the published documents of the Institute, the research and writings of the scholars and teachers of the Institute have gone a long way towards shedding more light on the social processes at work in present-day Namibia. These documents on constitutional options, language politics, sectoral analysis of the economy, economic development and administrative systems, mining, agrarian and manpower estimates seem to have as their central concern the ability of Namibians to determine their own destiny after independence.

But this documented evidence has also brought to light the dearth of really skilled personnel to participate fully in decision-making process after independence. A checklist of the technical, commercial and political-ideological skills necessary for the full participation of Namibians in their economy has shown that, apart from some of the technological skills being offered by socialist societies for young Namibians, the plan is for Namibia to depend on imported skilled personnel from the West to continue to operate the mines, the farms and the infrastructure required to speed the extraction of surplus.

Situated as it is in Zambia, UNIN has been uncritical of the recent experiences of this dependence on Western personnel in the decolonization process of the Front Line States. Thus many of the documents uncritically point to examples in Tanzania, Zambia or Zimbabwe of the role of educated administrators without drawing attention to the role that this strata has played in the process of class formation. After twenty years of independence in Tanzania and Zambia it is now possible to observe how this training has led to a new alliance between the ruling petty bourgeoisie and imperialism to the detriment of the popular masses.

More recently, it is possible to trace how a similar process has occurred in Zimbabwe when Britain and the US carried out a crash programme to train skilled manpower. So successful has this been that the assumption of power by Zimbabweans has led to a polarization in class terms under the present leadership in a manner which was not possible under Ian Smith. Using the measurement of Western education as the basis for recruiting administrators, those who were safely ensconced in Western universities now staff the Zimbabwean state while those who prosecuted the armed struggles have been marginalized because of their lack of formal bourgeois education.[10]

Such an experience of the demobilization of the freedom fighters in Zimbabwe is very relevant for Namibia. For in Zimbabwe the prosecution of the guerrilla war was quite widespread and had taken deep roots among the popular masses. Yet the British were able to integrate selectively the guerrillas into the armed forces of the Rhodesian security apparatus. This is an important precedent and it is partly for this reason that the South Africans and the Contact Group have since 1981 placed such emphasis on the autonomy of the SWATF.

These experiences are important also in that the ideological basis for the training of both skilled manpower and the future Namibian army is always to operate the system of repression efficiently and not to dismantle the system. It is for this reason that militants from the liberation movements in Namibia and South Africa critically need to study and analyze the decolonization process and the role of training in the experience of African states from Ghana to Zimbabwe.

THE INHERITANCE OF SWAPO

Already SWAPO as the principal liberation movement fighting in Namibia has proclaimed its political program as that of building a self-reliant and liberated society. Its published documents and broadcasts continuously reassert the need to build a classless society based on the principles of scientific socialism.[11] This sentiment towards socialist principles and the building of self-reliant economies has been behind the thinking of nationalist leaders in Africa from Nkrumah to Ghana in Nyerere in Tanzania and Sekou Toure of Guinea. But the reality has been that socialist declarations have been bereft of fundamental transformations in either the labor process or the relations of exploitation. Disparities between the rhetoric of socialism and the realities of the oppression of the popular masses remain one of the significant facts of the recent decolonization process in Africa.

For the Namibian peoples the tasks of social transformation have been compounded by the specific forms developed to exploit the mineral resources and labor power of Namibia. The extraction of minerals, diamonds and uranium which dominates the present colonial economy of Namibia creates specific relations of production. First, South Africa has formally imposed its apartheid policy of dividing the country into separate 'homelands'. And second, and more fundamentally, this homelands' policy ensures that the system of contract labor remains profitable for the capitalist companies. Without a stable and permanent workforce the capitalist class can superexploit labor by rewarding the workers below the cost of their own reproduction. Their families in the homelands are thus drawn into the web of exploitation. This fact belies the appearance of a dual economy.[12]

The specific form of the colonial economy of Namibia dictates that contract workers segregated without industrial or social rights are trapped in an economy where even the minimum of social amenities are denied.[13] So draconian are conditions for the reproduction of the labor power of Africans that an independent Namibian society will not only have to consider the question of the provision of social services but also to decide whether to carry out certain activities which are now central to the economy, such as the mining of uranium.

Mining represents one of the principal forms of extracting wealth and today Namibia ranks as the fourth largest mineral producer in Africa.[14] It is in part due to the significance of the minerals of Namibia that South Africa has been able to sell the idea to the West about the strategic importance of Namibia's control. The mining of uranium in Namibia has been carried out specifically under the logic of bolstering the energy needs of Europe and the requirements of the nuclear arsenal of the West. Numerous articles and pamphlets have documented how the Rossing mines, the largest uranium mine in the world, both exploits and permanently damages the ecology and health of Namibian workers while illegally exporting uranium to Western Europe.[15]

What the fact of the mining sector reveals is that the inheritance of an independent Namibia will be far more profound that whether SWAPO will or will not nationalize the mining sector to the legal forms of ownership and control to be instituted by Namibians. What the present conditions of the mines disclose is that SWAPO and Namibian militants will have to decide whether to continue to mine uranium or not. Corporations such as Rossing have no concern for the health and safety of Namibian workers, nor the protection of the environment. Lung and skin cancer, increased mortality rates and genetic damage are actual dangers associated with uranium mining anywhere. And the deplorable conditions of uranium mining in Namibia are not to be found anywhere else in the world.

Questions relating to the health, safety, education, housing and general welfare of the people are pressing issues which cannot be grasped with declarations of intent towards building socialism. Insofar as the ideological reference points in Africa, both socialist and non-socialist, can justify forms of economic expansion without taking into account the real interest of the masses, progressive militants need to place these questions on the agenda to move beyond the limited objectives of constitutional compromises or the formula for voting systems.

Imperialism has perceived that there are such fundamental questions relating to the decolonization process and the more farsighted sections of transnational capital would like to see a SWAPO government in Namibia before the real social questions are engaged in the society. Because of this perception those who seek to embark on a comprehensive programme of decolonization need to deepen their roots among the popular masses. This requires the strengthening of democratic forms and furthering the politico-ideological development of the people.

CONCLUSION

The struggle for Namibian independence has gone on for more than one hundred years. Armed struggles and worker protests in Namibia have placed this problem before the international community. Imperialism failed to crush the liberation movement and it is, therefore, now seeking new arrangements to integrate sections of the leadership of SWAPO into the circuit of exploitation and oppression inside

Namibia. Experience elsewhere in Africa, most recently in Zimbabwe and Mozambique, has shown that even the most strident nationalists or Marxists can be tamed by the power of international capital if there is not a process of politicization and mobilization of the masses after the achievement of political power. Thus the question of the decolonization process in Namibia must be posed while there is still scope for the further ideological development of those fighting for change.

Such a level of ideological development and clarity of political objectives needs to be articulated especially in the context of all class fronts such as that of SWAPO. Now that there is even greater consciousness among the masses in Southern Africa signified by the intensified struggles within the apartheid state, transnational capital is seeking ways to defuse the revolutionary potential of the organized workers and peasants.

It is the objective of the workers and segregated poor farmers to dismantle the present social system completely. These workers have seen concretely that the transfer of political power into the hands of a black ruling class will not fundamentally alter the relations of production. This is the concrete lesson of Zimbabwe.

Peace and security for working people in Africa, then, has to be conceptualized differently from peace and security for the West or the security of the aspiring ruling classes. The scope for subversion by imperialism remains immense but the African masses can learn many of the positive lessons of the Nicaraguan revolution: that, despite military invasion, the arming of opposition elements or the use of economic boycotts, the organized and politicized masses are the surest guarantors of security. SWAPO of Namibia needs to study these lessons to be able to further the cause of decolonization and social emancipation. For if the slogan "one Namibia, one nation" is to be meaningful in the future the question of social emancipation must be placed on the national and international agendas.

NOTES

1. H. Drechsler, Let Us Die Fighting, (London: Zed Press, 1980).
2. The principal ideas of the SWAPO programme can be found in: SWAPO, To Be Born a Nation: The Liberation Struggles for Namibia, (London: Zed Press, 1981) 171-183.
3. See John Stockwell, In Search of Enemies, (New York: Norton, 1978) and Michael Wolfers and Jane Bergerol, Angola on the Front Line, (London: Zed Press, 1983).

4. For two accounts of the conception of "Total Strategy" see Horace Campbell, "Total Strategy and Failure", Zimbabwe Herald, (Harare), 9 December 1983, and Robert Davies and Dan O'Meara, "Total Strategy in Southern Africa: an analysis of South African regional strategy since 1978", Journal of Southern African Studies 11(2), April 1985, 183-211. Reprinted as the conclusion to this volume.

5. Evidence given to the Thirion Commission into 'malpractices and maladministration of Public Funds' in 1984 and 1985 revealed that over a long period CDM carried out a policy of overmining at Oranjeund mine. See Namibia News Briefing, (London), August 1984.

6. Namibia: The Crisis in United States Policy towards Southern Africa, (Trans Africa: Washington, D.C., 1983).

7. Horace Campbell, "War, Reconstruction and Dependence in Mozambique", Third World Quarterly 6(4), October, 1984.

8. For an account of some of the changes to the original UN plan for decolonization in Namibia see "The Armed Forces in the United Nations Settlement Plan" in Apartheid's Army in Namibia, (International Defense and Aid Fund, London: Fact Paper on Southern Africa, November 1982).

9. Kalb, The Congo Cables, (London: Macmillan, 1982). Since the pacification of the Congo took place many former United Nations officials have written their own accounts of the infamy of the UN in the Congo. The Congo Cables has an excellent bibliography on this point.

10. Andre Astrow, Zimbabwe: a revolution that lost its way, (London: Zed Press, 1983).

11. SWAPO, To be born a Nation, pp. 255-296.

12. This thesis of a dual economy is present in many of the published works on the Namibian economy. See, inter alia, Namibia: the facts, (London: IDAF, 1980), p. 23; Towards Economic Development Strategy Options for Namibia, (Lusaka: UNIN Working Paper, 1982); and Robert Rotberg (ed), Namibia: Political and Economic Prospects, (Lexington: Lexington Books, 1983).

13. G. and S. Cronje, The Workers of Namibia, (London: IDAF, 1979).

14. For the importance of the mining sector to the economy see: Catholic Institute for International Relations, Mines and Independence, (London: CIIR, 1983).

15. Ibid.

3. Foreign Policy of Apartheid: From Settler Colonialism to State Capitalism and Neocolonial Corporatism
Timothy M. Shaw

A general (internal) situation of militant protest and
insurrection by blacks will make it more difficult to
achieve the class structuration of the conflict
envisaged in elite accommodation – a problem largely
created by the very limitations of South Africa's
ability to forge an effective neocolonial solution ...
It is upon the active involvement of the ordinary people
in the struggle against imperialism and its
representatives in Africa, a pre-eminently democratic
struggle, that the hope for any genuine or lasting
liberation can be founded.

- Sam C. Nolutshungu[1]

The destabilization policy ... has wide implications for
the economies of all African countries. However, for
those countries neighboring South Africa this is a very
critical issue of survival.

There are basically two forms: (a) direct
political and military intervention such as in the case
of Namibia and Angola, or through the military action
against the South African national liberation forces or
through the support of dissident groups, mercenaries and
subversive elements in independent African countries;
and (b) economic intervention through economic ties
involving critical economic sectors.

- UN Economic Commission for Africa[2]

South Africa carries little clout in world affairs.
Only recently has it become the object of serious great-
power concern. Yet, in thirty-five years of unbroken
rule by the Afrikaner-dominated National Party, its
leaders have never accepted the notion of South Africa
as a remote, third-rate power in the backwash of
international politics. Indeed, they have consistently
tended to think in strategic terms and to project an

image of South Africa as a regional power with a
significant role to play in global as well as regional
affairs.

-   Robert S. Jaster[3]

A number of ... (foreign policy) features are by no
means unique to South Africa, whereas others derive from
the Republic's oligarchic form of authority, its
international pariah status and the omnipotent threat of
perceptions ... A model of South African foreign policy
making will have to accommodate a diversity of features:
elements of foreign policy formulation in Western
states, in oligarchic states and in pariah states.

-   Deon J. Geldenhuys[4]

The second anniversary of the Nkomati Accord – the
supposed symbol of South Africa's regional hegemony – has
been marked by further difficulties and setbacks to the
apartheid regime's "total strategy". Regional security based
on relentless destabilization has been undermined by internal
insecurity: the 25th anniversary of Sharpeville and the
exponential increase of black alienation.   Neither limited
constitutional engineering nor marginal law reforms can
disguise continuing social cycles based on the ineluctable
intensification of social forces. The palpable presence of
essentially internal contradictions means that Nkomati has
led to the domestication of conflict not to its
internationalization or resolution. In short, the central
function of white South Africa's foreign policy – to keep
Africa and the world safe for apartheid[5] – is more
problematic than ever, forty years after the ending of World
War Two.

The seeming swings in South Africa's fortunes – which
reached their zenith in the early-70s dialogue and detente
exercises followed by their rapid demise in the Angolan
debacle of the mid-70s – disguise underlying structural
changes: from settler colonialism to settler then state
capitalism and the subsequent establishment of a "neo-
colonial" corporatism characterized by (in descending order
of importance):   (a) white bureaucratic-military alliance;
(b) black bantustan leaders; (c) regional puppets or
dependents; and (d) extracontinental metropolitan associates.
This transition into domestic neo-colonialism has occurred
against a global background of (a) increasing opposition to
apartheid; (b) inflation, recession and energy shocks; and
(c) changes in the global division of labor. In short, South

Africa's raisons d'etre in the international economy - gold,
minerals, profits, markets and the Cape Route - have declined
in a world of paper money, new technology, alternative
opportunities and strategic shifts. Hence the imperative of
new foreign relations and new domestic dispensations: total
strategy against total onslaught.[6] Yet the fundamental
feature of and flaw in South Africa's policy - apartheid-
remains.

This chapter seeks to explain white South Africa's
foreign policy by reference to changes in economic and social
structures - the national and international divisions of
labor - rather than to debates about ideology, diplomacy or
personality. It attempts to go beyond race and ethnicity as
factors to examine transformations in modes and hence
relations of production: the bases of the state, its power
and prestige. The demise of the South African reich lies not
only in the courage and persistence of black workers and
youths, but also in the structures of capital, production and
the state.

The paternalism and profitability of "settler
colonialism" in the inter-war years yielded after 1948 to
Afrikaner "state capitalism": anti-anglophone and-
transnational capitals. But with a quiet revolution in
Afrikanerdom, the demise of Afrikaner symbols of Reformed
Church and Broederbond, the global shocks of the 1970s, and
changes in the demand for, price and sources of black labor,
Afrikaner capitalism has been succeeded by "neo-colonial
corporatism": the State Security Council (rather than
tricameral legislature) at the center, Bantustans at the
periphery and dependents in the region.

In the ominous world of 1984, the signing of Nkomati in
Southern Africa and the recoronation of Reagan externally
were meant to reinforce and legitimize this neo-colonial
internal dispensation: white South Africa's reaction to the
demise of its cordon sanitaire and to international criticism
of racist structures. But the removal of the ANC's external
bases and relations served merely to accelerate the
inevitable domestication of South Africa's struggle; and, in
turn, "constructive engagement" has been replaced by
destructive disengagement as Reagan's second honeymoon has
been terminated by popular and congressional pressures
against apartheid. South Africa's unilateral withdrawal
(after more than a decade of resident armed intervention)
from Southern Angola in early-1985 did not safeguard its
further unilateral moves in Namibia. Likewise, repeal of the
mixed marriages act is almost irrelevant when the daily death
toll continues to mount from regime violence in the
locations. Sam Nolutshungu's insightful anticipation of five

years ago is now more relevant than ever: the essential powerlessness of South Africa once domestic contradictions explode, or implode, even if the causes of radicalization are more internal than regional:

> The radicalizing effect of the political transformations in neighboring countries has been felt within South Africa ... In this lies South Africa's gravest weakness: that popular revolt within its boundaries may deprive it of the Israeli option - of fighting in conventional terms against weaker states outside its own borders ... it will be more difficult for the major Western states to extend effective diplomatic and military support to South Africa and for African governments to acquiesce in Western and South African attempts to create new and more lasting forms of domination and exploitation in Southern Africa. It is in the absence of that mass involvement that South Africa's chief opportunities in Africa principally lie.[7]

Thus the impact of internal tensions are exported-South Africa requires regional diversions and global acquiesence while it pursues its total strategy - rather than regional transformations being imported - spill-over from Angola, Mozambique and Zimbabwe: the primary contradiction or generator is internal rather than regional or global. Indeed, unlike the euphoric mood at the end of the 1970s in Southern Africa - from Rhodesia to Zimbabwe and from Front Line States (FLS) to Southern African Development Coordination Conference (SADCC) - the combination of drought and destabilization has been disastrous. Regional regimes are quiescent and preoccupied while in the African National Congress (ANC) and United Democratic Front (UDF) are active and assertive. But the reason for such activism lies not so much in Nkomati (although it constituted a short-term catalyst) but in political economy: the neo-colonial corporatism of white alliance and black bantustans in a post-industrial world of new communications technologies, financial bases and strategic relations. The gradual and rational disinvestment of international companies is in response to the new division of labor rather than to either worker unrest or exchange-rate fluctuations.

The South African economy is a problematic Newly Industrializing Country (NIC) because of its mineral and agricultural rather than industrial and technological bases. Despite its head-start at the end of the nineteenth century, the Cape is not the Pacific Rim. South Africa can only aspire to NIC status along with Brazil, South Korea,

Singapore, and Taiwan if it can lay claim to a regional
market. But internal unrest and regional disengagement (let
alone drought and destabilization) make Southern Africa
problematic in terms of access, affluence and cohesion: not
yet ASEAN. So rather than economic entanglement, the white
regime has to rely on naked force: "total strategy" is not a
good economic instrument even if it momentarily enlarges the
local military-industrial complex. South Africa's defense
industry and establishment may be necessary for white
security but are no basis for white or black affluence.

This pariah status is ultimately counterproductive for
South African capitalism: labor and capital can at least
agree that apartheid is not good for business even if they
disagree about how to dismantle it. Meanwhile, the logic of
contemporary corporatism advances the prospects of national
fascism in South Africa as internal contradictions are hard
to contain and external pressures generate a laager
mentality. We may expect more repression before any
revolution.

FOREIGN POLICY AND/OR POLITICAL ECONOMY?

Ironically, the literature on South Africa's political
economy reflects this transformation in the character of
capitalism more than that on foreign policy. The critical
works of Heribert Adam, Dan O'Meara, John Saul and Stephen
Gelb, Stanley Trapido, David Yudelman, et. al. treat basic
features of substructure whereas James Barber, Geoffrey
Berridge, Deon Geldenhuys, Sam Nolutshungu, John Seiler, Jack
Spence et. al. deal insufficiently with anything but
superstructure.[8] There is now sufficient data and debate to
both juxtapose and integrate these perspectives; this is a
secondary goal of the present chapter.

Illustrative of the limitations of strategic analysis
divorced from political economy is the recent overview of
South Africa's defense strategy by Robert Jaster. He adopts
an unexceptionable periodization of "shifting threat
perceptions and response": (a) security and search for
allies, 1950s; (b) growing external threat and defense
buildup, 1960-74; and (c) toward fortress South Africa, 1975-
84.[9] Such a framework advances analysis of force structure,
size and function - the move towards a garrison state in
response to increasing regional threat and global isolation
along with the military's influence on policy - but these are
divorced from changes in national, regional and global
political economy. The crisis of apartheid, and hence its
strategic responses and constraints, cannot be separated from

shifts in relations of production at each level, notably, in
South Africa's post-war economic history, demand for and
prices of gold, oil, labor, capital and technology.

The very definition of security in an enforced racial
hierarchy is controversial. Hence the apparent contradiction
in the military's own positions, recognition of the
intractable domestic situation compared to the containable
regional context: "Although the military has taken an
extremely hawkish position on external matters, it has at the
same time taken a leading role in promoting domestic race
reform and non-white advancement."[10]

Jaster rightly notes the military's new assertiveness
after 1979 - destabilization in the region and reformism at
home - yet this is related only to strategic and not economic
issues: Zimbabwe rather than recession, Western diplomatic
distance rather than industrial decline. The social and
economic bases and interests of the military are ignored:

> ... only in the late seventies - following a dramatic
> shift in the balance of power in Southern Africa and a
> marked deterioration, both in South Africa's relations
> with the West and in its external security situation -
> has the South African military establishment suddenly
> emerged on the political scene to pursue and protect
> policy interests of its own. With the growing
> mobilization of the society in response to the concept
> of Total National Strategy, the military has come to
> exert a major, and at times decisive, influence on
> policy.[11]

The personal and institutional elements in the militarization
of South African policy are probed by Jaster as others-
"Botha's own hawkish inclinations and ... his close ties to
the military as defense minister for more than a decade ...
It was Malan who sold Botha on the ideology of the Total
National Strategy: an ideology that by definition implies a
leading role for the military"[12] - but the political and
economic dimensions are overlooked - the new military-
bureaucratic alliance which advances and legitimizes the
officers' inputs and status.

As indicated in the concluding preview below, it is this
corporatist coalition which is central to understanding,
projecting and confronting South Africa's future foreign and
security policy. Happily, not all students of South Africa's
external relations are so narrow in focus. One of the very
few extant attempts to link political economy and foreign
policy in this case is by Roger Southall who identifies three
periods in the relationship between "white survival" and

national economy:

> the consolidation of state capitalism, 1948-61; state
> partnership with monopoly capital, 1961-76; and fissure
> and crisis of the apartheid state, 1976 to the present
> ... this (admittedly arbitrary) characterization
> corresponds to three broad phases in South African
> foreign policy, namely: resistance and adjustment to
> Africa's decolonization; the Republic's emergence as a
> 'sub-imperial' power; and a transition from detente with
> neighboring black Africa to its destabilization.[13]

Southall's perspective parallels that proposed here until his
final period: the "turning point" of 1976 onwards. Clearly
the mix of regional political transformation (Mozambique,
Angola and Zimbabwe) and global economic shocks (dollar off
gold, oil price inflation, recession, post-industrialism)
mark the end of a 15-year period of South African-corporate
expansion in which both gained at the expense of (mainly
black) labor.

But whereas Southall reverts to the level of
superstructure to characterize the current dispensation-
"fissure and crisis of the apartheid state" - I would propose
further analysis at that of substructure - neo-colonial
corporatism. This is characterized not only by intensified
Bantustanization for blacks and cooptation of "Asian" and
"Colored" elites - the neocolonial elements - but more
importantly by a new "triple alliance"[14] of bureaucratic
bourgeoisie and national entrepreneurs along with
international capital. The centerpieces of this ruling
coalition are the State Security Council and corporatist
"Constellations" - the new "contract" between security,
administrative and business fractions - who in turn have
renegotiated links with foreign companies.

As we will see in the following sections, this national
state capital arrangement builds upon post-war Afrikaner
capitalism with its parastatal supports but widens it to
reincorporate local anglophone capital along with the
regional military-industrial complex: SSC and Armscor are
the anchors rather than the Dutch Reformed Church and the
Broederbond. Such a redefinition of the base of foreign
policy is bound to affect the policy itself: the increased
roles of the military as decision-makers (destabilization)
and of bureaucratic and entrepreneurial interests
(Constellation) are reflective of this. And in bureaucratic
terms, the previous hegemony of the Department of Foreign
Affairs has been yielded to the defense, intelligence,
economic and communications ministries. "Muldergate"[15] would

have been impossible in previous periods while the new
security blanket for business is indicative not only of
increased strategic dangers but also of corporatist
tendencies.

In short, the myth of (white) South African democracy is
ever more fanciful not just because of the racist legal
apparatus but also because power and decisions reside
elsewhere: the SSC rather than Parliament. The State
President is decisive because he chairs the former not
because he manipulates the latter. Corporatist imperatives
are repeated in the Bantustans with their military,
bureaucratic and intelligence, if not entrepreneurial,
fractions; and they underlie linkages with regional regimes
and movements. So, South Africa is increasingly a pariah
from the Western world as its neo-fascist tendencies are
revealed in the unacceptable direction and execution of
foreign policy: the external aspects of internal corporatism
with an emphasis on exclusion and repression along with
accumulation and reproduction. Before turning to consider
some of the implications of this perspective and condition, I
look first at the origins of South African corporatism.

CONTINUITIES: SETTLER CAPITALISM

The roots of apartheid lie, of course, in the
development of capitalism in Europe and its extension via
"explorers," traders, missionaries and administrators to the
"dark continent". In the South African case, the mix of
Afrikaners and Anglos, Boer and Bantu, minerals and maize
meant a dramatic increase in production, population and
accumulation in the nineteenth century, culminating in the
South African war. The evolution of settler capitalism in
the "Union" is instructive for the rest of the continent and
illustrative of Andre Gunder Frank's thesis; periods of
global contraction may be positive for economies at the
peripheries if self-reliance is an essential ingredient in
effective development. For the inter-war recession in Europe
encouraged industrialization in Southern Africa, notably in
South Africa and Rhodesia. In turn, this semi-autonomous
pattern of semi-industrialization laid the foundation for the
subsequent establishment of state capitalism after World War
Two: post-1948 National Party rule in South Africa and post-
1965 Rhodesian Front rule in "Southern" Rhodesia. The
precursor of both "apartheid" and "paternalism" was settler
capitalism.

South Africa's Department of External Affairs was
founded just ahead of the great depression and the rise of

fascism: 1927. But in the inter-war period it was preoccupied by the imperial connection and the interrelated white ethnic politics - British versus Boer. Despite the ambivalence of the Afrikaners towards fascism, the Smuts government emerged from the Second World War with enhanced status. Yet the United Nations which Smuts helped to found soon turned on one of its instigators as the post-war decolonization movement gained momentum. In the South African case, of course, the contrary nationalist movements of Africans and Afrikaners had many decades, even centuries, of antecedents. But the internationalization of African nationalism and institutionalization of Afrikaner racism generated contradictory agenda items for the UN.

Moreover, the industrialization and proletarianization of South Africa's economy accelerated in the post-war period of reconstruction in Europe and conflicts in Asia. The social bases of the ANC ensured continued vitality for its demand for majority rule despite the erection of racist legislation and superstructure. The character of the post-war polity and economy was symbolized by the conjuncture of the early-1960s: the ending of Commonwealth membership externally, of African connections regionally, and of vestiges of multiracialism and liberalism internally. Given white South Africa's twin preoccupations of (a) Western economic exchange and diplomatic respectability, and (b) African labor migration and security protection respectively, the early 1960s constitute a turning point. As Jack Spence indicates, from an orthodox perspective,

> South Africa's role in Southern Africa has passed through three phases since the victory of the National Party in 1948. Throughout this period relations with neighboring states and territories were perceived as having significance for the government's primary objective of foreign policy: the cultivation of close and mutually profitable relations with the major Western powers ... South Africa's rulers have tried to defend and assert a national interest in white survival ... (which) has been affected by changes in the Southern African region and the attitudes of the Western states.[16]

Spence proposes a periodization of South African foreign policy at the level of diplomacy and security; this could also be based on changes in substructure: relations of production. Foreign policy everywhere is the ideological expression of hegemonic bourgeois fractions; in the South African case it is the articulation of, successively, comprador (Anglophone), political and bureaucratic (Afrikaner), and now national (economic and strategic) fractions. This shift from settler to state capitalism coincides with the movement from intermediary (sub-imperial?) to regionalist roles and on to destabilization and militarization. According to Spence the first phase - the 1950s and early 1960s - was one of linkage between the West and Africa; the second period (1965-1974) one of "outward movement"; the third, short interregnum (1974-1978) one of detente, Soweto and their aftermath following the Portuguese coup; and the final fourth phase (1978 to 1980) that of "marking time".[17]

From a longer-term and more structural perspective, the post-1974 period may be seen as one of economic disorientation on the one hand and of regional dominance on the other: a mixture of economic change and political resistance. There is a growing divergence between South Africa's economic difficulties on the one hand and its strategic assertiveness on the other; these come together at the regional level in the distinctive mix of economic stagnation, especially for labor, and military aggressiveness. But this is to anticipate: post-war apartheid marked the coming-of-age of settler capitalism and the advent of state capitalism.

CHANGES: STATE CAPITALISM

The political victory of Afrikanerdom led ineluctably to economic nationalism and state intervention as well as to institutionalized racism: one white bourgeois fraction challenging established interests. The Nationalist Party used the state to rectify historical imbalances whilst laying the foundation for a more autonomous semi-industrial economy. With an ambiguous relationship to both English and external capital, the Afrikaner state set about modernizing both the economy and its ethnic associates. The multiplication of state and Afrikaner companies in mining, finance, manufacturing and military sectors laid the basis for a more autonomous capitalist system and for a regional military-industrial complex.[18] It also enabled South Africa to weather the coming shocks as the "winds of change" blew in unpredictable ways against the Boer laager.

But state capitalism generated its own contradictions; internally, the Afrikaners trekked off the land and into the cities and regionally, the apartheid regime needed non-white markets to survive in a protectionist and regionalist world order in which only Southern Africa was regarded as its market for manufactures, source of labor and sphere of influence. For a while (the decade of the 1960s) the white regime appeared to be almost impregnable: militarily invincible and economically inviolable. During the first decade of Africa's independence it seemed to weather any winds of change, in part because of its regional cordon sanitaire and in part because of its global economic good standing. As Thomas Callaghy noted:

> South Africa may be a political pariah state regionally and internationally because of the nature of its regime, but it is not an economic pariah – it is, in fact, well-integrated into the world capitalist system.[19]

This dialectic of political exclusion and economic inclusion was inconvenient for the South African regime but not too difficult to orchestrate. In fact, for the Afrikaner fraction it was even advantageous: social autonomy with industrial and financial cooperation whilst refashioning the domestic divisions of labor and property within the white state. And even if markets disappeared north of the Zambezi they expanded south of it because of the tenuous independence of BLS, Rhodesia's UDI and Portugal's colonial wars. In short, the post-Sharpeville dispensation was not unattractive for Afrikaner control and capital.

But if the 1960s were characterized by South African dominance in Southern Africa, "by permission" of extra-regional interests, the next decade witnessed great changes and challenges. From Soweto onwards, the 1970s were troubled: domestic strife and further repression, regional transformations and interventions, and global instability and uncertainty. South Africa's authority and assumptions seemed to be challenged at every turn.

Starting with the demise of the dollar gold standard, the decade of the 1970s undermined white South Africa's confidence and credibility: from the geometric progression in the price of petroleum to the independence of Zimbabwe, including the debacle in Angola and the institution of corporate "codes of conduct". The epitome of all this was the "Muldergate;" South Africa's information scandal with its non-Calvinist, desperate tones of intrigue and inexperience. Instead of being the regional industrial center, a self-proclaimed core of growth and stability, South Africa had become "the major destabilising force in Southern Africa"[20] – the "greening" of Afrikanerdom or the "modernization" of the "volk". The erstwhile NIC had become a regional militaristic power. As Callaghy remarks by reference to the literature:

62

> Kenneth Grundy entitled his 1973 book <u>Confrontation</u>
> <u>Accommodation in Southern Africa</u>. By early 1983,
> however, there was very little accommodation and much
> more confrontation then a decade earlier. South Africa
> has changed its mode of operation, its rules of the
> game. It is pursuing a sort of "Lebanonization" of
> Southern Africa.[21]

In response to the intensifying contradictions and
opposition, which South Africa's white regime characterized
as "total onslaught",[22] vestiges of liberalism were thrown to
the wind in domestic and foreign policies. The <u>laager</u> was to
be defended on the Limpopo through a variety of strategies.
The centerpieces of the total onslaught were regional
intransigence to ensure security as well as economic
cooperation, Bantustanization remodelled as Constellation,
and the State Security Council.

In the aftermath of Angola, Muldergate and Zimbabwe, the
military became an acceptable, central force in decision-
making: the militarization of South Africa. This process
was facilitated by the advent of Afrikaner capitalism and its
ownership or control over many of the means of production:
the beloved country could become a garrison state with its
own military-industrial complex. Ambiguities about Afrikaner
power were dispelled as the interlocking bureaucratic
military-industrial alliance assumed effective power. One
central element in this was the dissolution of formal power
to Bantustan leaders and then their incorporation into the
South African defense and intelligence networks: defense in
depth of the Zambezi salient.[23]

Internal colonialism was replaced by "neo-colonialism";
white power was succeeded by a corporatist structure in which
a few black leaders were incorporated but whose major feature
was an alliance between white bureaucratic, business,
political and military fractions. To be sure, the balance
within this grouping is never constant and it was marginally
moderated by tricameral reformism involving Colored and Asian
elites. But its major intent was to prosecute a "total
strategy" against myriad, interconnected opposition forces.
Apartheid prevented an orthodox international neocolonial
solution as in most of Africa; only a perverse internal neo-
colonialism was possible given the primacy of white power and
affluence.

CONTRADICTIONS: NEOCOLONIAL CORPORATISM

The late-1970s constituted a hiatus in South African

foreign policy both because of post-Muldergate changes in
leadership - accession of P.W. Botha to the premiership - but
also because of complex interrelated manoeuvres over Zimbabwe
and Namibia: successive South African-Zambian, Anglo-
American and "Contact Group" designs. These plus economic
stagnation generated a re-evaluation of policy direction,
instrumentation and coordination: constellation replaced
dialogue and detente, at least until the security pacts of
the Nkomati era, and Reagan succeeded Carter, even although
"constructive engagement" coincided with the new
protectionism. Moreover, as the examples of Mozambique,
Angola and Zimbabwe did inspire struggle, so the 1980s have
been characterized by almost continual popular pressures
culminating in the creation of the United Democratic Front
(UDF) and a succession of strategic explosions (e.g., Koeberg
and Sasol) and frequent demonstrations (e.g., Langa and
Uitenhage). And just as capital has become more national - a
combination of Afrikaner capitalism and international
divestment (itself a mixed reaction to codes of conduct, UN
debates and economic calculation) - so too has the freedom
struggle. African unions have played a growing role as
crucial elements in a cheap labor policy. But as workers
come more from within (including, of course, the
"Bantustans") than without and as the myths of modernization
and trickle-down - erode apartheid through growth - become
ever more apparent so the central dynamic has become
internal.

In a state capitalist system as advanced as South
Africa's it is to be expected that the core contradiction
will be capital versus labor. In settler society it was
between Anglophone and Afrikaner capital with considerable
migrant labor as a marginal factor; in the corporatist state
it is South African capital against local labor.
Notwithstanding the continued salience of regional,
continental and global pressures, the major contradiction is
internal: who defines and controls the corporatist state?

There are, to be sure, a variety of intra- as well as
inter-class tensions among fractions of the bourgeoisie,
petty-bourgeoisie, proletariat and peasantry; hence the
continued stand-off between ANC and UDF on the one hand and
PAC, AZAPO, Inkatha and Black Forum on the other, let alone
the intricacies of exclusivist white, colored, Asian and
Bantustan politics, as well as links between them. However,
in a post-Bretton Woods, post-expansionist period in a semi-
peripheral political economy with a history of
proletarianization (let alone alienation), any other outcome
would be surprising. Despite the prevalence of racial and
ethnic variables in debates about South Africa, the resilient

and reassuring feature is the salience of class.

Not that class relations are either simple or predictable. In any political economy there are likely to be complex patterns of coalition as well as contradiction.[24] Nowhere is this more true than in South Africa where capitalist and communal modes of production coexist and where race and ethnicity complicate solidarities. Nevertheless, the multiracial inheritance of ANC and UDF is indicative of potential interracial groupings just as the Bantustan and reform schemes peel-off thin layers of non-white elites into an unequal collaboration with the white state.

Likewise, although regional and global interactions remain important, the crucial dynamic is domestic, albeit with external supports and associates. Equally, as South Africa's international linkages have contracted so it has become ever more apparent that its foreign policy is an extension of internal relations and not vice versa. This is especially so over regional issues (e.g., Angola, Zimbabwe, Namibia, Nkomati, etc.) but it is also valid over global questions (e.g., energy, security, technology, etc.). In short, South African foreign policy continues to be the external expression of white bourgeois interests and ideology. And it will be so until the unpredictable, but not calculable, conjuncture occurs.

Hence the imperative in the short-term of SADCC as one collective Southern African response to South African policy: the mix of regional integration and destabilization. An indigenous and informed response to the difficulties of dealing with shifting South African fractions – the military's destabilization, the bureaucracy's disruptions and the entrepreneur's cooperation – SADCC affords some protection, reaction and alternatives. Yet, as Richard Weisfelder cautions, there are limits:

> SADCC can begin to serve as a safety net that can limit the damage to a member state exposed to serious South African economic or military pressure. This sort of role might prevent the "Finlandisation" of a weaker state like Botswana whose towns, population concentrations, and transportation links are especially vulnerable to South African actions. Stopping the "Lebanonization" of a state exposed to full use of force such as Angola would be less plausible. For states like Lesotho, Malawi and Swaziland, participation in SADCC is the best route toward a larger role in regional political and diplomatic transactions and a voice in the future of Southern Africa.[25]

65

It is to this future that I turn in conclusion, situating
regional strategies and global debates in historical and
social context: the political economy of white South
Africa's foreign policy to the end of this century.

BEYOND CRISIS: FUTURES FOR SOUTH AFRICA

South and Southern Africa have received more attention
from assorted futurists and prophets than any other region in
Africa. Unhappily, most liberationist projections have been
either inaccurate or premature; national repression has
coexisted with regional liberation. Kenneth Grundy's earlier
optimistic preview[26] may be contrasted with William Zartman's
alternative eventful and uneventful scenarios[27] and William
Clark's recent fictional anticipation in which Thabo Bokwe
becomes President of Azania which is (re) admitted into the
Commonwealth as part of the reconstruction of the world
economy after the great crash of 1987.[28]
Jaster's orthodox listing of "future constraints and
vulnerabilities" places most emphasis on military manpower,
economic sanctions, simultaneous internal uprisings and
external incursions, great-power intervention, and oil.
Together these constitute an expanded and intractable agenda:

South Africa entered the 1980s more concerned about its
isolation and the threats to its security than at any
time in the past. Its formerly close military ties to
the West had eroded and were proscribed by the 1977 UN
arms embargo. A similar falling-off had occurred in its
scientific and technical exchanges, which were
particularly valuable in such areas as nuclear fuel and
energy development. Botha's efforts to attract newly
black states into a defence alliance and a formal
economic grouping lay dead in the water, torpedoed by
the Mugabe election victory in Zimbabwe and by decisions
of the black-ruled states to try jointly to reorient
their economies away from South Africa.[29]

In response, Jaster anticipates that "South Africa's strategy
for the rest of the eighties is thus likely to be a
continuation of that developed by the Botha administration
since 1978"[30]:   (a) enhanced defense potential against all
possible contingencies, (b) initiatives to win black support
or acquiescence, (c) improved foreign relations, particularly
with the West, and (d) a combination of carrot and stick in
regional affairs.[31] Jaster cautions, however, that either
anti-white black violence or anti-black white resistance

could endanger Botha's reforms and balancing act leading
either to nuclearization (and?) or militarization,
respectively - apocalypse or repression:

> ... South Africa will be confirmed in the next few years
> to have a nuclear weapons capability. This will be
> Pretoria's ace in the hole, its insurance against
> external attack or blackmail, its ultimate club to back
> up a tough, go-it-alone stance in a hostile world.[32]

> ... it is not too farfetched to suggest that ultimate
> failure on the part of the government to accommodate
> non-whites could lead to a military takeover, with or
> without Botha, in which a military dictatorship would
> take the necessary steps to ram through a series of
> reform measures over the stubborn opposition of right-
> wing whites.[33]

By contrast to such essentially strategic, superstructural
projections, Roger Southall concentrates more on economics
and substructure, as well as on regional rather than either
internal or global forces:

a)   increasing militarization;
b)   increasing political confrontation between South
     Africa and neighboring states; and
c)   the increasing economic disengagement of black from
     white Africa;
d)   the increasing internalization of conflict within
     Southern Africa.[34]

To distinguish amongst these alternatives, Southall
identifies three alternatives for South Africa itself; given
its regional hegemony, these are likely to affect the whole
region of Southern Africa: "i) Ethnic exclusivist, ii)
reformist, and iii) revolutionary".[35]
      Southall dismisses the first option as essentially
domestic and short-term so the choice is essentially two-
fold, if not the over-drawn choice postulated by Samir Amin
between "socialism or barbarism".[36]   Yet Southall really
comes down on the side of a fourth option - repression-
which reinforces the notion of a corporatist state:

> In broad terms, the prospect for South Africa over the
> coming years would seem to be that of the much-predicted
> garrison state. Protected by her military might, the
> White Republic will experience growing political
> isolation within a context of declining regional

hegemony and a stalling economy, buffeted not only by the external forces of liberation fighters and an increasingly militant black workforce, but also by the Western powers ...[37]

This anticipated conjuncture would, in turn, lead to a reevaluation of assumptions and orientations, in the West as well as in Africa. For South Africa is decreasingly an outpost of monopoly capital and more a subcenter of national capital. The post-war contradiction noted in the literature may thus be resolved because of structural change. Reflective of this established argument, Southall has asserted an old-fashioned logic with its still relevant conclusion:

In contrast to its political isolation, however, the Republic is now much more closely integrated into the global capitalist economy, just as the Southern African peripheral states continue to exhibit a critical level of dependence upon South Africa. Yet ... these linkages are not determinate.[38]

And he goes on to argue, quite correctly, that as the balance of forces and difficulties changes so Western perfidy will grow:

... Pretoria's foreign policy will prove inadequate to the task of bridging the gap between the Republic's isolation and its increasing incorporation into the global capitalist economy. The Western powers, accepting that the writing on the wall for continuing racial domination, are likely to become more interventionist in South African concerns with a view to molding an eventual settlement which is favorable to their own needs.[39]

Such a perspective contrasts with the orthodox dependencia assumptions of the ECA which still sees MNCs as the major supports for apartheid and the primary sources of destabilization in the region, notwithstanding either their inclination to voluntary divestment or the Afrikaner's preference for national capital. Whilst it recognizes the destabilizing potential of regional exchange, infrastructure and labor, it emphasizes international capital which, despite evidence to the contrary, it sees as continuing "to expand steadily in recent years."[40] Thus the ECA's policy recommendations include action by home governments against MNCs operating in South Africa:

68

... to stop their TNCs from investing in the mining, military and commercial sectors which boost that country's morale and thereby directly or indirectly encouraging it to engage in subversive activities in neighboring countries.[41]

Such a prescription fails to note the rise of Afrikaner capitalism and the new alliance of national capital with bureaucratic and military fractions in South Africa. These now underlie the foreign policy of white South Africa. Any response, whether to regional destabilization or cooperation, needs to take into account such shifts in the political economy of apartheid.

NOTES

1. Sam C. Nolutshungu, "South Africa's situation and strategic opportunities in Africa" in Olajide Aluko and Timothy M. Shaw (eds), Southern Africa in the 1980s, (London: George Allen & Unwin, 1985), p. 292.
2. ECA, "The Destabilization of the Southern (Front Line) States: cumulative impact on the current economic and social crisis", Addis Ababa, 1 April 1985, E/ECA/CM.11, 11/66, p. 1.
3.Robert S. Jaster, "South African Defense Strategy and the Growing Influence of the Military" in William J. Foltz and Henry S. Bienen (eds), Arms and the Africans: Military Influence on Africa's International Relations, (New Haven: Yale University Press, 1985 for Council on Foreign Relations), p. 121.
4. Deon Geldenhuys, The Diplomacy of Isolation: South African Foreign Policy Making, (New York: St. Martins for SAIIA, 1984), p. 249.
5. See Sam C. Nolutshungu, South Africa in Africa: A Study in Ideology and Foreign Policy, (Manchester: Manchester University Press, 1975).
6. See Mafa Sejanamane, "The Crisis of Apartheid: South Africa and Destabilization in Southern Africa" Dalhousie African Working Paper, Number 9, 1985, and Geldenhuys, The Diplomacy of Isolation, pp. 99–100 and 100–149.
7. Nolutshungu, "South Africa's situation and strategic opportunities in Africa", pp. 291–292.
8. On this debate about South Africa's political economy and foreign policy see, inter alia, James Barber, South Africa's Foreign Policy 1945–1970, (London: OUP, 1973); Nolutshungu, South Africa in Africa; Christian P. Potholm and Richard Dale (eds), Southern Africa in

Perspective, (New York: Free Press, 1972) and J.E. Spence Republic under Pressure: A Study of South African Foreign Policy, (London: OUP, 1965). See also Gwendolen M. Carter and Patrick O'Meara (eds), Southern Africa: The Continuing Crisis (Bloomington: Indiana University Press, 1982, Second Edition); and International Politics in Southern Africa (Bloomington: Indiana University Press, 1982). For more critical perspectives see, for example, Kenneth W. Grundy, "Intermediary power and global dependency: the case of South Africa." International Studies Quarterly 20(4), December 1976, pp. 553-580; John Saul and Stephen Gelb, The Crisis in South Africa (New York: Monthly Review Press, 1980); and David Wiley and Allen F. Isaacman (eds), Southern Africa: Society, Economy and Liberation (East Lansing: Michigan State University, 1980).

9.   See Jaster, "South African Defense Strategy and the Growing Influence of the Military," pp. 122-141.

10.   Ibid., p. 135.

11.   Ibid., p. 122.

12.   Ibid., p. 134.

13.   Roger J. Southall, "South Africa" in Timothy M. Shaw and Olajide Aluko (eds), The Political Economy of African Foreign Policy (Aldershot: Gower, 1984), p. 222.

14.   For more on this formulation, with its considerable heuristic power see Peter Evans, Dependent Development, the Alliance of Multinational, State and Local Capital in Brazil (Princeton: Princeton University Press, 1979), especially pp. 11-12, 52 and 285-288.

15.   See Geldenhuys, The Diplomacy of Isolation, pp. 36 and 107-120.

16.   J.E. Spence, "South Africa, the World Powers and Southern Africa" in Thomas Callaghy (ed), South Africa in Southern Africa: the Intensifying Vortex of Violence, (New York: Praeger, 1983), p. 107.

17.   See Ibid. pp. 107-119.   Contrast with Southall at note 13 above.

18.   See Timothy M. Shaw and Lee Dowdy, "South Africa" in Edward A. Kolodziej and Robert Harkavy (eds), Security Policies of Developing Countries, (Lexington: Heath-Lexington, and Aldershot: Gower, 1982) pp. 305-327.

19.   Thomas M. Callaghy, "Introduction: the Intensifying Vortex of Violence" in his collection South Africa in Southern Africa, p. 9.

20.   Ibid., p. 5.

21.   Ibid.

22.   See Thomas M. Callaghy, "Apartheid and Socialism: South Africa's Relations with Angola and Mozambique" in his collection South Africa in Southern Africa, pp. 268-280,

70

especially 268-270.

23. See Kenneth W. Grundy, "South Africa's regional defense plans" in Callaghy (ed), South Africa in Southern Africa, p. 147.

24. For a general overview of this formulation see Timothy M. Shaw, Towards a Political Economy for Africa: the Dialectics of Dependence, (London: Macmillan, 1985).

25. Richard F. Weisfelder, "The Southern African Development Coordination Conference: a new factor in the liberation process" in Callaghy (ed), South Africa in Southern Africa 261. Cf. the more critical perspectives of Yash Tandon and Ibbo Mandaza in Timothy M. Shaw and Yash Tandon (eds), Regional Development in Africa and Canada (Washington: University Press of America, 1985).

26. See Kenneth W. Grundy, "Towards a more acceptable future in Southern Africa" in his Guerrilla Struggle in Africa: an analysis and preview (New York: Grossman, 1971): 153-188.

27. See I. William Zartman, "Social and political trends in Africa in the 1980s" in Colin Legum et. al., Africa in the 1980s: a continent in crisis, (New York: McGraw-Hill for CFR 1980s Project, 1979), pp. 109-119.

28. See William Clark, Cataclysm: the North-South Conflict of 1987, (London: Sidgwick & Jackson, 1984), pp. 167-173, 200-208 and 227.

29. Jaster, "South African defense strategy and the growing influence of the military," p. 145.

30. Ibid., p. 152.

31. Ibid., pp. 148-152.

32. Ibid., p. 152. See also J.E. Spence, "South Africa: the nuclear option" African Affairs 30(212), October 1981, pp. 441-452.

33. Jaster, "South African defense strategy and the growing influence of the military", p. 135.

34. Roger Southall, "Regional trends and South Africa's future" in Timothy M. Shaw and Olajide Aluko (eds), Africa Projected: from recession to renaissance by the year 2000? (London: Macmillan, 1985), p. 82.

35. Ibid. p. 96.

36. Samir Amin, "The Future of South Africa", Journal of Southern African Affairs, 2(3), 1977, p. 369.

37. Southall, "Regional trends and South Africa's future", p. 103.

38. Southall, "South Africa", p. 258.

39. Ibid., p. 259.

40. ECA, "The Destabilization of the Southern African (Front Line) States", p. 7.

41. Ibid., p. 14.

4. The State of the Economies of Front Line States and the Liberation Struggle in Southern Africa

Nguyuru H. I. Lipumba

INTRODUCTION

The economic performance of African countries during the 1970s has generally been poor. Per capita food production has declined.[1] The growth rate of agricultural output has not kept pace with the growth rate of the population.[2] Moreover, the decline in per capita food production has not been accompanied by an increase in export production. In many countries the volume of exports declined at a faster rate than the decline in food production. External factors such as bad weather, high oil prices, and deteriorating terms of trade have all contributed to this poor performance, given the high level of dependence of these economies on the world capitalist system that has been in a crisis since the 1970s.[3] The performances of African economies have in general been worse than more of other dependent economies, indicating that domestic factors have also contributed to the continent's economic crisis.

While the economic performance of independent African countries, including those bordering former Portuguese colonies was poor, liberation movements in Guinea Bissau, Cape Verde, Mozambique and Angola succeeded in dislodging Portuguese colonialism from Africa and at the same time contributed to the fall of the Salazar-Caetano dictatorship in Portugal.[4]

The establishment of a Frelimo government in Mozambique in 1975 intensified the struggle in Zimbabwe that forced the Smith regime to participate in the Lancaster House constitutional talks. Zimbabwe's formal independence was achieved in March 1980 and ZANU, the leading liberation movement, won the election with a clear majority and formed the first post-independence government. The independence of Angola was challenged by South Africa's invasion in alliance h UNITA and CIA-sponsored FNLA that attempted to prevent the MPLA from consolidating national independence. Thanks to Soviet-backed Cuban military assistance, MPLA prevailed, at least in the major cities and the western part of the country, including the strategic oil-rich Cabinda enclave. Angola under MPLA could be counted to support SWAPO's effort to liberate Namibia.

The fall of the Portuguese empire and the independence of Zimbabwe removed the buffer zone of South Africa. South Africa and Namibia now share a common border with independent African states. The armed struggle in South Africa could be intensified by allowing trained and armed freedom fighters to cross the border and enter South Africa. The ability to allow freedom fighters to cross the border and enter South Africa depends not only on the political will but also the ability to resist military and economic reprisals from the racist regime. The ability to resist reprisals from South Africa is related to the degree of dependence in trade, transport, finance, investment and employment. The higher the degree of dependence, the lower the ability to resist regardless of actual economic performance. Given the level of dependence, the ability to provide material support and to resist military and economic reprisals depends on overall economic performance, particularly in food production and foreign exchange operation. The latter is important in financing essential imports for defense and economic growth.

The objective of this chapter is to analyze the relationship between economic performance of the Front Line States and the liberation struggle in Southern Africa. Part I is the Introduction, and Part II analyzes the structure of the economies of the Front Line States and their performance. Part III analyses the ability of Front Line States to support liberation movements in Southern Africa, and economic strategies among them that will increase their ability to support the liberation struggle within South Africa.

THE ECONOMIES OF THE FRONT LINE STATES

The OAU Front Line States (FLS) are Angola, Botswana, Mozambique, Tanzania, Zambia and Zimbabwe. All, except Tanzania, share a common border with South Africa or South African-occupied Namibia. Compared to South Africa, the economies of the FLS are quite poor. The 1982 combined GDP of Botswana, Tanzania, Zambia and Zimbabwe was only twenty per cent of the South Africa GDP of $81.2 billion. South Africa has a sophisticated industrial base, of which manufacturing accounts for the largest share of GDP and includes basic industries and coal-petroleum converting industries. However, South Africa is not dominant in the export of manufactured goods, but still relies on primary exports. In particular, gold accounts for forty per cent of its net exports.

The majority of the population in the FLS depend on agriculture for their living. Mineral and agricultural commodities are the major source of foreign exchange. In general, all of the Southern African economies are dependent on the world capitalist system. In addition, the economies of FLS depend on South Africa to varying degrees.

Whilst the economic performance and potential of all these countries are not the same, all the FLS are underdeveloped and dependent upon the international capitalist system. Consequently, there are certain problems that most of these economies face. Table 4-1 illustrates some general economic indicators. Apart from Zimbabwe, none of these economies are self-sufficient in food production. In the 1980s, they all have faced balance of payments crises of varying intensity with the exception of Botswana. To understand each country's potential and ability to resist South African military and economic reprisals, it is necessary to have a brief account of each economy.

Angola

Geographically, Angola is the largest country among the FLS with an area of 1,247 thousand sq. km.; but with a population of only 8 million it is potentially the richest. Its climatic diversity allows the growth of a variety of crops, including coffee, cotton, sisal, maize, bananas and cassava. It also has a variety of minerals, the most important being petroleum, diamonds and high-grade iron ore.

During the colonial period the Portuguese dominated the modern economy. The indigenous population provided cheap labor for Portuguese-owned plantations. Ninety per cent of the African population depended on agriculture for their livelihood, and semi-skilled jobs were performed by the Portuguese. When Angola attained independence by November 1975, it was preceded by an exodus of 300,000 Portuguese who manned the modern sector of the national economy.[5]

In addition, since independence the people of Angola have not seen peace. South African-supported UNITA is terrorizing one-third to one-half of the country. The Benguela Railway that connects Zambia and Zaire to the Angolan ports has remained closed because of UNITA operations in the south-eastern part of the country. South Africa never really withdrew from Southern Angola after it was defeated by

MPLA and Cuban forces within the vicinity of Luanda. Rather, it continues to invade the Southern part on the pretext of destroying SWAPO bases.

The major cash crops of Angola were produced on large estates and plantations. As a result of the exodus of the Portuguese, there has been a sharp decline in production. Angola, which was the second largest African producer of coffee in 1974, with an output of 217.5 thousand tonnes, produced only 24,000 tonnes in 1981-82 and 13,000 tonnes in 1982-83. The same could be said of sisal and maize. Sisal output in 1974 was 66.7 thousand tonnes; it dropped to 20 thousand tonnes in 1979. And while this country was usually a net exporter of maize, with a marketed output of 700 thousand tonnes in 1978, it declined to 198 thousand tonnes in 1978. As a result, in 1981 Angola imported 200 thousand tonnes of maize. On the whole, per capita food production for 1980-82 was 77 per cent of 1969-71 level.

Since independence, Angola has become increasingly dependent on oil exports mainly produced by the Gulf Oil Company in the Cabinda enclave, which is well-guarded by Cuban soldiers. Oil exports account for 80-90 per cent of foreign exchange earnings. The United States purchases $600 million of Cabinda oil each year. The remaining portion is derived from diamond exports mined by Societe Generale. In 1971 Angola exported 5.2 million tonnes of iron ore but the reopening of iron ore mining has continuously been delayed because of South African invasions.

The economic potential of Angola cannot be achieved without achieving peace in the country, through the defeat of UNITA forces and the end of South African invasions. In an attempt to secure peace, the MPLA government signed an agreement with South Africa so that the South African force could withdraw from Southern Angola. In return, Angola would prevent SWAPO freedom fighters from crossing the border to fight South African troops in Namibia. However, the Lusaka Agreement has not led to the withdrawal of the South African troops. According to The Economist in early 1985 the effective border between Angolan and South African troops has been moved 40 miles inside Angola. South African support for Savimbi's UNITA has increased and indeed within the South African military there is a strong faction that favors a total onslaught to install Savimbi in Luanda, the only constraint being the Cuban and Soviet Union's presence. Furthermore, the linkage of Cuban withdrawal from Angola with Namibian independence that was proposed by the Reagan Administration and gladly accepted by South Africa is aimed to topple the MPLA government in Luanda and install a puppet regime led by Savimbi.

Unlike Botswana, Mozambique, Zambia and Zimbabwe, Angola is not economically dependent on South Africa. Therefore, the extent of support it can offer to SWAPO is only limited by South African military retaliation.

Botswana

A landlocked semi-desert country with an area of 582,000 sq. km. and a population of only 940,000, Botswana attained independence in 1966. This country was considered a worthless piece of territory with more cattle than people and little else. Before 1970, cattle accounted for ninety per cent of export earnings. A substantial proportion of adult males depended on employment in South Africa. After independence large deposits of diamonds, copper, nickel, coal, manganese, asbestos, common salt, potash, soda ash, and sodium sulphate were discovered. The most important mineral is diamonds, accounting for an average of seventy-six per cent of exports in 1980–84. As a result of the discovery of minerals, the GDP growth rate has averaged twelve percent since 1970 and per capita income in 1982 was US$900, one of the highest in Sub-Saharan Africa. However, the distribution of income is very unequal.

Only five per cent of Botswana receives adequate rainfall for crop production and even without the recent drought, Botswana depends on food imports mainly from South Africa. In 1981–84 Botswana was not only adversely affected by the drought but also the world recession which caused a sharp decline in prices of mineral exports. In 1981 there was a sharp decline in foreign exchange reserves to a level of less than three months worth of imports, but the balance of payments position improved in 1984 as a result of a partial recovery in diamond prices. By the end of 1984, foreign exchange reserves were sufficient to meet eight months of average imports.

While Botswana is mineral rich and does not face the balance of payment crisis that is common to other Sub-Saharan African countries, it is economically dependent on South Africa because of geography and history: Botswana is a member of the Southern African Customs Union, and thirty-five per cent of government revenue is collected by South Africa and handed over to Gaborone. Until 1976 Botswana was part of the Rand Monetary Area but since then it has introduced its own currency, the Pula. Most of its exports pass through South Africa which provides ninety per cent of its imports including over fifty per cent of food imports. Its diamond mines are owned by Botswana in which De Beers of South Africa and the Botswana government hold equal shares. De Beers, of course, provides the technology and the management and therefore controls the mining. Despite the return of migrant laborers from South Africa in recent years, there are still around 50,000 of Botswana's citizens working in South African mines and farms.

The economic dependence of Botswana limits its ability to support an armed liberation struggle in South Africa. Understandably, it does not allow armed freedom fighters to cross its border and enter South Africa. However, Botswana has one of the largest concentrations of refugees from South Africa who could possibly be airlifted for training in other countries.

Mozambique

Mozambique has an area of 799,380 sq. km. and a population of 16 million. Ninety per cent of its population is engaged in agriculture but only five per cent of the arable land is cultivated. Before independence 3,000 large-scale farms and plantations covering 1.6 million hectares were owned and operated by Portuguese settlers who depended upon cheap African labor. Marketed agricultural output originated mainly from these farms, in particular, sugar, tea, sisal and copra. The major export crop for Mozambique before independence was cashewnuts. In 1974 Mozambique produced 204 thousand metric tons of raw cashewnuts. By 1982, however, output had declined to 65 thousand tons. Sugar production reached 228 thousand tons in 1975 but declined to 120 thousand tons in 1982. Like Angola, the plantation and estate sector was adversely affected by the exodus of 200,000 Portuguese just before and after independence.

Before independence, manufacturing such as the processing of primary materials and simple consumer goods was concentrated in Maputo and Beira. Industrial production was also adversely affected by the emigration of the Portuguese. [The political economy of colonial Mozambique, like other Portuguese colonies, was characterized by complete domination of whites in all skilled and semi-skilled jobs.]

Frelimo was committed to establish a socialist society in Mozambique but was inheriting a structure that was a product of four centuries of Portuguese colonialism. Aware of the task ahead, on Independence Day, 25 June 1975, President Samora Machel stated that,

The state is not an external and immutable structure; the state is not the bureaucratic machinery of civil servants, nor something abstract, not a mere technical apparatus. The state is always the organized form through which a class takes power to fulfill its interests. The colonial state, an instrument of domination and exploitation by a foreign bourgeoisie and imperialism which has already been partially destroyed by the struggle, must be replaced by a people's state, forged through an alliance of workers and peasants, guided by Frelimo and defended by the People's Forces for the Liberation of Mozambique, a state which wipes out exploitation and releases the creative initiative of the masses and the productive forces.

In the phase of people's democracy, in which we are now engaged as a phase of the Mozambican revolution process, our aim is to lay the material, ideological, administrative and social foundations of our state. We need to be aware that the apparatus we are now inheriting is in its nature, composition and methods, a profoundly retrograde and reactionary structure which has to be completely revolutionized in order to put it at the service of the masses ... The new battle is only beginning.[6]

The task of totally destroying, breaking and reducing all aspects of the colonial state, to paraphrase Amilcar Cabral, may not be difficult, but building a workable new structure is a massive task requiring protracted struggle. Immediately after independence Mozambique, which supported ZANLA, the military wing of ZANU during the liberation struggle against the white minority regime in Zimbabwe, was involved in a war on its western border. The Rhodesian military forces invaded Mozambique and massacred African refugees and destroyed bridges and other infrastructure. The Rhodesian regime recruited former PIDE (secret police) agents and Portuguese soldiers and their African puppets to form the so-called Mozambique National Resistance (MNR) or RENAMO. The MNR was used by the white regime in Rhodesia to harass the masses in rural Mozambique and destroy the infrastructure to limit Mozambique's ability and will to support the liberation of Zimbabwe.[7]   After Zimbabwean independence, South Africa evacuated the MNR from bases in Zimbabwe and retrained and reorganized them to destabilize Mozambique. During Portuguese colonialism, the economy of Mozambique was integrated into that of South Africa. Mozambique provided cheap labor to the South African mines and in return Portugal was paid in gold valued at a fixed price that enabled the latter to earn foreign exchange by selling the gold at free market prices.[8]

Before independence the peak level of migrant workers from Mozambique was 115,000 workers. Independent Mozambique has continued to depend on revenues from the migrant workers. In 1985, it was estimated that 40,000 Mozambicans were working in South Africa. The decline in the number of workers is not the result of the policy of Mozambique to reduce migration to South Africa but has been caused by South Africa reducing the influx of such workers. After the Nkomati Accord, Mozambique expected that South Africa would double this quota.

The Maputo port depends on goods traffic to and from South Africa. The port is partly operated by the South African Transport Service. All the hydroelectric power produced by the Cabora Bassa dam is sold to South Africa yet electric power for Maputo is partly supplied by South Africa.

The economic condition of Mozambique in the 1980s has been very difficult. The drought in Southern Africa was particularly devastating in Mozambique. Thousands of peasants are believed to have died. The famine was worsened by the 'total strategy' of South Africa that concentrates on destabilizing the security and economies of Front Line States. The MNR sabotaged the railway and pipeline that link Mozambique and Zimbabwe. In December 1982 MNR destroyed huge fuel tanks that caused shortages not only in Mozambique but also in Zimbabwe, which was forced to sign an agreement with South Africa to supply fuel to Zimbabwe.

The combination of drought, MNR economic sabotage and poor management have caused a severe balance of payments crisis in Mozambique. By the end of 1983, the official debt was $1.35 billion of which $285 million were payment arrears. The 1984 the debt service ratio was 131 per cent. Even if all export earnings from shrimp, cashewnuts, cotton, tea, sugar and other exports were used to pay interest and mature debts, Mozambique would still not cover all of its external financial obligations. Mozambique has joined the IMF and the World Bank and is seeking financial assistance from these institutions.

In spite of the Nkomati Accord, and Mozambique's attempts to attract more tourists and investments from South Africa, South Africa still continues to support the MNR. In fact, just before signing the Accord, South Africa supplied the MNR with enough weapons and ammunition to last at least two years. Even when South Africa actually stops new supplies – a policy which the moderate verligtes support but the ultra-conservative verkramtes oppose – the security situation will continue to be a problem until Mozambique wins backs the masses.

Tanzania

Tanzania has an area of 945,087 sq. km. and an estimated population of 20 million in 1982. Ninety per cent of the population lives in the rural areas and agriculture accounts for 10-50 per cent of the GDP and employs 80-90 per cent of the labor force. In the past six years, Tanzania has experienced a worsening economic crisis. Per capita income as conventionally measured has declined at an average rate of 2.9 per cent per annum during 1978-82. Over the same period the annual decline in agriculture output was 2.9 per cent and in manufacturing output was 16.6 per cent. Production of major exports has stagnated or declined. Commodity terms of trade since the end of the coffee boom in 1978 have fallen sharply. These two factors have led to a worsening balance of payment crisis. Net foreign assets have been negative since 1978. Import payments arrears at the end of 1984 were $450-500 million - a figure that exceeds the recent annual value of exports.

Per capita food production declined by twelve per cent in 1982 compared to 1970. Dependence on food aid is now a dominant feature of the political economy of Tanzania.

The persistent balance of payments crisis has led to negotiations with the IMF. The last two-year standby arrangement was signed in August 1980 for a credit line of $250 million. However, this credit line was suspended early in 1981 after a single drawing because Tanzania failed to meet IMF conditions. Negotiations with the IMF have continued without reaching any agreement, and foreign aid and loans come mainly from official sources, financing fifty per cent of Tanzanian imports. The modern sector is dependent on foreign aid and loans.

Among the Front Line States, Tanzania does not share a common border with South Africa or Namibia. It is not economically dependent on South Africa, and there is very limited trade, if any, between South Africa and Tanzania. Diamond mining which had a South African connection has declined in importance. Tanzania can support the liberation movement without suffering economic reprisals, but freedom fighters in Tanzania are simply too far from the line of action. Tanzania can provide training facilities but there is a need to find a way of moving freedom fighters into South Africa.

Zambia

Zambia is another landlocked country with an area of 752,614 sq. km. and a population of 6 million in 1982. In the first six years of independence (1964-69), Zambia registered the average growth rate of GDP as thirteen per cent, the highest in Sub-Saharan Africa. Copper output which accounted for 95 per cent of export earnings increased from 5.5-6.0 per cent per annum while copper prices increased by 7.0 per cent. After the Mufulira Mines disaster of 1970, copper output never regained its 1969 level. Copper prices increased moderately until the mid-1970s but fell sharply during the 1975-76 recession. Prices were weak throughout the 1970s and fell drastically during the recession of 1980-83.

The cost of production of copper has increased as the easily accessible mineral has been depleted. Technological innovations have weakened the world demand for copper. This demand will further decrease as the use of optical fibre becomes widespread. The weakening of the copper sector reduced incomes of Zambians. In 1982 real per capita income was 23 per cent lower than in 1972. Attempts to diversify into agriculture and industry have not been successful, and Zambia is by and large dependent on food imports. A few hundred large-scale farmers, mostly white expatriates, dominate commercial agriculture and usually account for one half of the marketed output.

Since 1975, Zambia has faced a persistent balance of payments crisis. In March 1978 Zambia negotiated a stabilization programme with the IMF that involved a 10 per cent devaluation and a loan of $390 million. GDP fell by 10 per cent in real terms. The balance of payment position improved only for a short time and mainly due to exporting stocks of copper. Zambia went back to the IMF in May 1981 for a three-year Extended Fund Facility of $691 million which emphasized structural adjustment. As is common with IMF packages to Sub-Saharan African countries, this was suspended in mid-1982 because Zambia failed to meet IMF performance criteria, particularly government borrowing from the banking system.

External public debt was $2.4 billion and Zambia had to attend the Club of Paris meeting to reschedule its debt in May 1983. Another agreement with the IMF for $230 million was reached, but balance of payments have continued to be precarious and external payments in arrears have increased.

Though Zambia does not border South Africa it is still economically dependent on South Africa. Roughly 30-50 per cent of Zambia's external trade passes through South Africa, and South Africa is the second largest source of imports after Britain. The most efficient route to Zambia is through Zimbabwe to Beira followed by the Benguela Railway and TAZARA. However, security problems in Mozambique and Angola

have reduced the use of these routes and TAZARA and the port
of Dar es Salaam have not been efficient in handling Zambian
exports and imports.

Zimbabwe

Zimbabwe is a landlocked country with an area of 390,750
sq. km. and a population of 8 million in 1983.   At
independence, thanks to the trade embargo during the UDI
years, Zimbabwe inherited the most developed economy among
the Front Line States.   The economy is diverse with a
substantial industrial sector. Manufacturing output accounts
for 26 per cent of the GDP, including a developed iron and
steel industry.   In 1985 the Zimbabwe Iron and Steel Company
expected to export 600,000-700,000 tons of steel apart from
the 140,000 tons which it sold in the local market.   Under
peaceful circumstances Zimbabwe could easily be an industrial
center of SADCC countries.

Commercial agriculture in Zimbabwe is highly developed
and is still dominated by Europeans. The Land Apportionment
Act of 1930, replaced by the Land Tenure Act of 1969,
allocated the best half of the land - 181,900 sq. km. - to
Europeans who accounted for merely 3 per cent of the
population. Africans were allocated the remaining 50 per
cent.   The Land Tenure Act of 1977 allowed Africans to
purchase land in the 'white' areas, although after
independence in 1980 white farmers continued to dominate
Zimbabwean agriculture.   The exodus of whites was extremely
small compared to that in Mozambique and Angola.   In 1981
Zimbabwe had a bumper crop.   Marketed maize output - the
staple food of Africans - exceeded 2.8 million tons. Drought
reduced maize output to 2.0 million tons in 1982 and less
than one million tons in 1983, forcing Zimbabwe to seek food
aid. The improvement of weather in 1984 and 1985 is leading
to a recovery of the agricultural sector, and African peasant
agriculture has gained some foothold in commercial
agriculture.   Before independence 90 per cent of marketed
maize was produced by white farmers.   In 1984-85 African
farmers accounted for 40 per cent of the marketed output. As
economic discrimination against small-holder peasants is
reduced and more land is allocated to them, their
contribution to the monetary economy will increase.   Other
important products include tobacco, cotton, sugar, soybeans
and livestock.

Zimbabwe mines a wide variety of minerals.   The main
minerals in order of importance are gold, asbestos, nickel,
copper and chromium, totalling 34 minerals that are
commercially produced.   In 1979 minerals accounted for almost

50 per cent of exports contributing only 8 per cent of GDP and employing 6 per cent of the labor force. The world recession of the 1980s caused a slump in mineral prices that affected the foreign exchange earnings of Zimbabwe.

Foreign exchange reserves have been depleted partly because of the increase in imports, particularly in 1980–82, and partly due to a repatriation of capital by those whites who were leaving the country after independence. At the end of 1980 foreign exchange reserves were around US$280 million. By the end of 1982 and 1983 reserves fell to US$198 million and less than US$100 million, respectively. In 1983 Zimbabwe negotiated a standby arrangement with the IMF that involved a devaluation of the Zimbabwean dollar.

History and geography make Zimbabwe dependent on South Africa. Sixty per cent of Zimbabwe's external trade uses South African railways and ports. Twenty-five per cent of Zimbabwean imports originate from South Africa and 22 per cent of its exports go to South Africa. South African-based mineral companies such as Anglo American are quite dominant in the mineral sector of Zimbabwe.

The ports of Mozambique are closer to Zimbabwe than South African ports but the MNR sabotage campaign has increasingly made it difficult for Zimbabwe's external trade to be routed through Mozambique. The dependence of Zimbabwe on South Africa can be reduced if the security situation in Mozambique improves.

FRONT LINE ECONOMIES AND THE LIBERATION STRUGGLE

Each of the economies of the Front Line States is quite weak and generally dependent upon the world capitalist system. In addition Botswana, Mozambique, Zimbabwe and Zambia are directly dependent in different degrees on South Africa. Given South Africa's 'total strategy', actual or intended military support to any liberation movements in South Africa has and will lead to military and economic reprisals from its government.

The liberation struggles in South Africa and Namibia will be won by the people of these countries through a protracted struggle inside these territories. South Africa is a fascist state with a formidable coercive machinery that is mercilessly deployed against any opponents of the regime. Peaceful protests against the regime have been met with wanton killing of unarmed African demonstrators in Sharpeville, Soweto and Langa. Unarmed struggles inside South Africa have an important role in the liberation of South Africa but they are unlikely to lead to a fundamental change of the system. The liberation of Africans in South Africa requires a clear demonstration to the white population that they cannot maintain the status quo ante by military means. White supremacy fascism can only be removed by a politico-military defeat of the fascist state.

To facilitate an armed struggle in South Africa, Front Line States must provide training facilities and allow armed freedom fighters to cross the border into South Africa. While all Front Line States are ideologically opposed to apartheid, not all of them are willing to put the security of their own country at risk, nor are they convinced of the desirability of an armed struggle.[9] However, given the 'total strategy' of South Africa, the Front Line States have two major options: to become 'bantustans' and join the so-called Constellation of Southern African States or sacrifice and support the liberation movements for a free and peaceful Southern Africa.

Front Line States cannot be neutral in the struggle between the African masses of South Africa and their oppressors. The fascist system necessarily generates refugees committed to the overthrow of the regime. To accept refugees is considered by South Africa as harboring 'terrorists'. Thus, the Front Line States must make a choice of accepting and protecting the refugees and face retribution from South Africa or hand-over the refugees to the racist regime.

For Front Line States, supporting the liberation movements is in fact a move to enhance national self-determination in domestic and foreign policy. The ability to support freedom fighters in South Africa is constrained by dependence of the Front Line States on South Africa. It requires economic cooperation and integration.

The priority area is in transport and communication. As SADCC noted in the key policy statement, 'Towards Economic Liberation':

The dominance of the Republic of South Africa has been reinforced by its transport system. Without the establishment of an adequate regional transport and communication system other areas of cooperation become impractical.

Mozambique, which was given the role of coordinating transport and communication within SADCC, can provide the most economic outlet to the sea for landlocked countries. Establishing new and improving old transport and communication infrastructures require large investments that are just not available from the domestic savings of Front

Line States.

The irony of SADCC's strategy to reduce economic dependence on South Africa is to increase dependence on Western countries that also economically support South Africa through trade and investment. Armchair revolutionaries may ridicule the SADCC strategy as guaranteed to fail and call for complete disengagement from Western capitalism as soon as possible. However, the development of productive forces in the Front Line States is very low and economic dependence on the world capitalist system is likely to continue for the foreseeable future.

The viable policy option, therefore, is how to coordinate policies within independent Southern Africa states to increase economic independence over time. The struggle against the racist regime must include seeking support from democratic groups in Western countries to pressure their governments to reduce economic links with South Africa and at the same time assist SADCC in its efforts to reduce dependence on South Africa.

Internally, the Front Line States must improve economic performances and coordinate their policies. The agricultural sector is essential for the provision of food and employment for the majority of the population. Domestic policies should avoid alienating peasants by adopting policies that require the use of force. In many cases, socialist governments have neglected the role of incentives to peasants in encouraging production and generating political support for the government. Forced collectivization is likely to lead to a reduction of output and political alienation of the peasants who can be used by South African-supported saboteurs.

As a region, the Front Line States have a mineral base for establishing basic industries. To tap economies of scale, specialization should be based on each country's comparative advantage. Again, the major problem is inadequate domestic savings and technical know-how to finance large investments.

South Africa is sabotaging economic cooperation among SADCC countries by supporting MNR and UNITA in disrupting communication links among independent African countries. Economic cooperation is impossible without the security of communication links. To have economic cooperation, Front Line States must have security cooperation and therefore prevent South African-sponsored economic destabilization campaigns. Military cooperation requires closer political understanding but it is indispensable if Front Line States are to achieve economic independence from South Africa.

NOTES

1. See World Bank, World Development Report 1978, (Oxford University Press, 1978).
2. For details see USDA Food Problems and Prospects in Sub Saharan Africa: The Decade of the 1980s.
3. For a neo-Marxist analysis of the crisis, see Andre Gunder Frank, Crisis in the World Economy and Crisis in the Third World, (London: Heinemann, 1981).
4. For a discussion of the revolution in the Portuguese colonies, see John S. Saul, The State and Revolution in Eastern Africa, (New York: Monthly Review Press, 1979), pp. 23-107.
5. For a history of the Angola liberation struggle, see Basil Davidson, In the Eye of the Storm: Angola's People, (London: Longman, 1978).
6. Samora Machel, "The People's Republic of Mozambique: The Struggle Continues," Review of African Political Economy 4, November 1975, pp. 19-20.
7. For a detailed discussion of the origin of MNR see Horace Campbell, "War, Reconstruction and Dependence in Mozambique," Third World Quarterly 6(4), October 1984,
8. For a detailed analysis see Ruth First, Black Gold. the Mozambican Miner, Proletarian and Peasant, (Brighton: Harvester Press, 1983).
9. Colin Legum, "The Southern Africa Crisis," in his Africa Contemporary Record: Volume 12, 1983-84, (London: Africana, 1984).

PART TWO

Impact on the Front Line States'
Foreign Policy and Defense Policies

5. The Nkomati Accord and Its Implications for the Front Line States and South Africa
Colin Legum

Two forces are engaged in a warlike conflict in Southern Africa over the region's future political system; at the core of this problem lies the future political system inside South Africa itself. The one force seeks to establish a Pax Praetoriana, and the other a Pax Africana. The former envisages a security system imposed, maintained and supervised by South Africa as the dominant regional power, with the main purpose of defending and promoting its interests, and with the border states playing the role of dependency partners though maintaining their appearance of independent political states. The latter envisages a regional security system achieved through a voluntary alliance of equals committed to promoting the interests of all its members free from outside intervention.

The essential requirement of a Pax Praetoriana is the survival of a White-dominated regional power, whereas a prerequisite for a Pax Africana is the termination of the status quo of White supremacy within South Africa itself. So, the core issue in this conflict is the ending, not just of apartheid, but also of the political system of White supremacy. It is perfectly feasible to foresee the end of apartheid through reforms controlled from the top without, in fact, ending White supremacy. However, any abdication from the apartheid system must inevitably weaken White political power.

Viewed from the perspective of a struggle over two irreconcilable objectives, the champions of Pax Praetoriana achieved one major victory (the Nkomati Accord) and two smaller but nevertheless important victories – the agreement with Swaziland, which goes far beyond Nkomati, and the military stand-off with Angola between 1981-83. However, they failed to extend these advances along their borders with Botswana, Lesotho and Zimbabwe, besides sustaining two major setbacks over roughly the same period. The first of the setbacks was inside the Republic itself, where the stage was finally reached when it could be said, with accuracy, that apartheid was on the rocks and facing shipwreck. The second setback was on the international front where Pretoria failed in its bid to gain a more supportive role from the Western community and admission to the NATO club which was the aim of President Botha's mission to the capitals of Western Europe immediately after signing the Nkomati Accord. Although he was more or less courteously received, none of the European leaders, as he sourly remarked on his return home, were ready to respond positively to his demonstration of South Africa as a regional power.

Viewed purely in the short-term, this balance sheet of gains and losses comes out in favor of Pretoria; its policy of destabilization forcing three of its six closest neighbors to meet around the conference table and two of these included its principle bete noires, the regimes of Mozambique and Angola, so regarded because they had come to power through armed struggle, they had opted for Marxist systems and were bound by Treaties of Friendship and Cooperation with the Soviet Union. However, viewed in the medium-term, the balance of gains did not favor Pretoria for the following reasons of ascending importance.

First, its policy of destabilization was shown to have only a limited utility. It worked most effectively only in those border countries which were faced with serious internal political problems that could be exploited by Pretoria; attempts to create internal dissent by, for example, supporting the Lesotho Liberation Army failed to destabilize the regime of Chief Leabua Jonathan, its support for Super-ZAPU in Zimbabwe (admittedly limited, but potentially menacing) created difficulties for Prime Minister Robert Mugabe, but quickly failed; while the internal stability of Botswana was not even ruffled. Moreover, although the Luanda regime was anxious to negotiate over the departure of the SA Defense Forces (SADF) from its territory it did not yield on the major issue of support for Namibia independence or the withdrawal of Cuban troops as a prerequisites for the withdrawal of SADF. (In fact, SADF has now quit Angola before a single Cuban combat soldier has left.)

Second, it remained firmly on the hook of the U.N. Security Council Resolution 435 as the only basis on which the international community was willing to recognize Namibia's independence. None of the five Western Contact Group members could be shifted from that position; over the years even the Reagan Administration toughened its stand on this issue, despite its attempts to link Namibia's independence to Cuban withdrawal. While Pretoria can still continue to play games over Namibia, the final outcome can only be the full implementation of Resolution 435. SWAPO's position as the dominant challenger for power after independence remains unassailed.

Third, Pretoria has learned the lesson that while its military power gives it some temporary advantage, its army has no major role to play in promoting the kind of relations with its neighbours that are necessary for the fulfillment of its objective of establishing a Pax Pretoriana. Influential voices within the Afrikaner community have increasingly been heard to stress the fallacies of relying too heavily on military power.

And fourth, while the agreements with Mozambique and Swaziland have unquestionably affected the capability of the ANC to wage its armed struggle and have produced strongly negative feelings among politically articulate Black South Africans, this has not affected the struggle inside the Republic where Black and White opposition against apartheid has become better organized, more widespread and more militant in the last two or three years. Clearly, any number of agreements with border states cannot produce racial peace and security inside South Africa itself, which remains the hard core of the struggle over the future regional system in the sub-continent. The astonishing extent to which the present rulers in Pretoria have been compelled by the pressure of events to recognize and admit their growing inability to maintain either apartheid or an undiluted system of White supremacy is shown by the following statement made in parliament by Chris Heunis, the Minister in Charge of Constitutional Affairs:

It is necessary to recognize that the retention of White power in South Africa is untenable.

Such an admission, coming from a senior South African Minister, who speaks with the full authority of President Botha, is the clearest possible evidence that, however much Pretoria projects its military power and however fiercely it represses political demonstrations, the balance of power inside the country has begun to shift. While the final end of this struggle is not yet in sight, South Africa has entered upon a period of historic change.

THE ROAD TO NKOMATI

It is much easier to pass judgement, for or against, the FRELIMO government's decision to enter into its agreement with Pretoria than to analyze dispassionately the reasons for such a decision and to examine its consequences. Nkomati

came as a shock to most but, upsetting as it was, it was in
fact foreseeable. After a visit to Mozambique in 1983 the
author wrote that the disastrous economic and security
situation in the country left its leaders with only two
choices: either to risk complete immolation at the hands of
South Africa and the MNR for the sake of remaining true to
its principles, or to enter into negotiations with Pretoria
to establish a new code of good neighborliness. Even raising
the possibility of President Samora Machel coming to an
agreement with Pretoria was so surprising and disagreeable
that it bore a great deal of criticism.   In the case of
Mozambique, it is necessary to ask what other alternative was
open to President Machel, and whether anything was left
undone that might have softened the blow for the ANC.

The situation demanded a choice by South Africa's
neighbors between their State interests and their ideological
commitments. Angola could continue to allow the guerrilla
forces of the South West African People's Organization of
Namibia (SWAPO) to operate freely from its territory, and
Mozambique could continue to permit the African National
Congress (ANC) armed cadres to transit its territory only by
accepting further damage to their security and economies by
actions taken by Pretoria. The choice for these two
countries was made even harder than for the other border
states because both are ruled by movements which won power
through a liberation struggle during which they had relied
heavily on their border states. The MPLA and FRELIMO
leaderships might have made a different choice if it were not
for the terrible economic plight of their people and the fact
that the survival of both regimes was in some jeopardy. The
alternative to a stand-off agreement was to face the risk of
destruction on a scale previously accepted only by North
Vietnam in supporting the Vietcong; but there were two
crucial differences between their situations: first, Hanoi
was fighting for the unification of its own country; and
second, it could count on effective military and economic
backing from both the Soviet bloc and China. Mozambique and
Angola could not count on total support from any major power;
the Cubans in Angola were no adequate substitute for Soviet
power – even if they had been fully engaged in fighting the
South African Defense Force (SADF), which they were not. The
test was whether Moscow was willing and able to give its two
Marxist allies the kind of support they had produced for
Hanoi – or at the level sustained for Cuba, Syria and
Ethiopia. Once the Angolan and Mozambican regimes had
understood that Moscow was unwilling to make this kind of
commitment, their only available options were either to face
a period of virtual dictation by Pretoria, or to negotiate

stand-off agreements which would enable them to buy time to rebuild their economic and political bases. The only real surprise was that Mozambique decided to go as far as it did in signing a mutual security and economic pact with Pretoria unlike Angola which went for a much more limited, tentative agreement.

Angola and Mozambique were both in an extremely parlous condition in mid-1983. The Botha regime was determinedly asserting South Africa's role as a regional power, deploying the SADF across its border to any point required by its perceived security interests in keeping SWAPO and ANC insurgents at bay. For several years past, the SADF had occupied ever larger areas of Southern Angola and given increasing arms and logistic support to Dr. Jonas Savimbi's Union for the Total National Independence of Angola, whose range of military operations was growing almost by the month despite the efforts of the Angola national army (FAPLA) and the estimated 20,000-25,000 Cuban combat troops. The ruling MPLA-Labor Party was in a state of internal disarray, its regime having lost much of its popular base because of relentless economic hardship and conditions of insecurity; the country's economy was in ruins, and deteriorating even further; its system of internal communications was disrupted; and, despite its oil revenues (due to be doubled in 1984-85), it was unable to utilize its financial resources effectively to rebuild the internal economy. The situation in Mozambique was no less bleak. The South Africa-supported Mozambique National Resistance (MNR) was spreading havoc in the rural areas, and steadily expanding its field of operations. FRELIMO (though still in much better shape than the MPLA) had lost some credibility and a good deal of its popularity because of the security situation and desperate economic hardships suffered by most of the population. Their hardships were bitterly intensified by the worst drought of the century which had forced over 100,000 peasants to trek to Zimbabwe in search of food, and left an estimated 300,000 people either dying from starvation, or suffering acutely from dietary deficiencies; three million more were affected, though less acutely than those in the worst-hit areas.

It was against this somber background that the Angolan and Mozambican leaders - by then convinced that they could expect little effective support from the Soviet bloc - turned more urgently to the West. They sought economic, if not military, support and pressed them to take a tougher line over Pretoria's policies of destabilizing its neighbors, and to compel the Botha regime to implement the Security Council's Resolution 435 on Namibia's independence. Apart from offers to consider increasing their aid and expanding trade, the advice they received from the Western capitals was that they should enter into negotiations with South Africa to lower tensions in the region. Typical of such advice was that offered by Frank Wisner, the U.S. Deputy Secretary of State for African Affairs in December 1983:

> Our point of view remains that the situation in Angola can be solved only through political negotiations. There is no military solution for Angola nor for the conflict between South Africa and Angola, nor for the conflict between UNITA and Luanda Government. Since there is no military solution, the priority then is to find a political solution.

The advise proffered to the Mozambicans ran along similar lines. Denied effective Soviet help, counselled by the West to seek negotiated settlements, and faced with calamitous situations at home, both Presidents dos Santos and Samora Machel decided to explore ways of achieving stand-off security agreements on respectable terms which they could defend to themselves and to their people, as well as to the rest of Africa. They well understood that their greatest difficulty would be in persuading SWAPO, the ANC and the opponents of apartheid inside South Africa to accept that they were not being betrayed.

In October 1983, President Machel embarked on a European tour of the Netherlands, Portugal, Yugoslavia, France and Britain. He was hoping for European economic support and for a concerted Western policy of restraining South Africa; but the response was far from encouraging, and even during his European travels he began to indicate his willingness to contemplate security arrangements with South Africa. It might be asked why Samora Machel had decided to turn to the West for support and not to the Soviet bloc. The reason is that he had previously sought the support of his 'strategic ally'; not only was their advice to him to look to the West for the kind of economic aid that the Soviet bloc could not provide, but Moscow carefully counselled him on at least three separate occasions not to allow Mozambique to become involved in a serious military confrontation with South Africa since the Soviets were not logistically in a position to come to Mozambique's aid. (One is also entitled to assume that Southern Africa is a low priority on Moscow's present foreign commitments.) Machel, therefore, found himself strapped in a position where he could expect little from the West. The choice facing him, therefore, was between sacrificing his government and his country, or walking the long hard road to Nkomati. In either event, the ANC would be the loser.

The Angolan leaders were only slightly better off than the Mozambicans. The Soviet bloc and Cuba remained committed to providing substantial military aid, but very little economic aid.

REACTIONS TO AND IMPLICATIONS OF THE NKOMATI ACCORD

Of the Front Line and other border states, only Botswana and Lesotho were in any sense critical of Samora Machel's decision, and doubted its necessity or its wisdom. Nevertheless, they joined with all the others in saying that they understood and accepted Machel's reasons for doing what he did. However, they all disagreed with him over his style in making a great occasion of the signing of the Accord, and showed their disagreement by refusing his invitation to be present on the occasion. Machel's motive for wishing to make the signing ceremony into a great event was because he did not want to appear that he was walking to his Knossis; he wished to appear before the world as a proud and independent African who was scoring a victory for his cause. One of his closest presidential aides responded to this gesture by saying that it was always wrong to try and disguise a defeat and to dress it up as a victory. However, the Front Line leaders' main concerns were how to rescue the ANC from their new predicament; over whether the Pretoria regime could be trusted to carry out its side of the bargain (which they strongly doubted); and over whether the West, having encouraged Machel to take the road to Nkomati, would swing behind him in providing the kind of aid he needed to Pretoria if it seemed to be defaulting on its undertakings.

The ANC was caught between its obvious total rejection of the Nkomati Accord and the need not to appear in any way to offend Mozambique or the Front Line States. In the course of a carefully balanced statement, the ANC National Executive declared:

> Further accords, concluded as they are with the regime—
> which has no moral or legal right to govern our country
> – cannot but help to perpetuate the illegitimate rule of
> the South African White settler minority. It is exactly
> for this reason that this minority has over the years
> sought to bind independent Africa to such agreements.
>
> The ANC is profoundly conscious of the enormous
> political, economic, and security problems that confront
> many of the peoples of our region, but blame for many of

these problems must be laid squarely on the Pretoria regime, which has sought to define the limit of independence on the countries of our region through a policy of aggression and destabilization. We are convinced that this regime, which is dripping from head to foot with the blood of the thousands of people it has murdered throughout Southern Africa, cannot be an architect of justice and peace in our region. Neither can the ally of this regime, the Reagan administration of the U.S.A., with its so-called pro-apartheid policy of constructive engagement, be an architect of justice and peace in this region, while at the same time it is an angel of war, reaction and repression in other regions of the world, including the U.S.A. itself.

A just and lasting peace in our region is not possible while the fountain-head of war and instability in this area - the apartheid regime and the oppressive system it maintains in South Africa and Namibia-continues to exist. The Botha regime knows that no peace has broken out; it has resorted to other means to continue its war for the domination of South Africa. That commonly agreed position reaffirms the obligation of the people of South Africa under the leadership of the ANC to escalate their offensive using all means, including armed action, for the overthrow of the criminal apartheid regime and the transfer of power to the masses. We remain and shall remain loyal to this perspective.

Nkomati clearly struck a blow at the ANC's capability of waging its armed struggle, more especially in view of the collaboration between Swaziland and Pretoria. However, it did not affect the ANC's ability to intensify its political work inside South Africa itself. Some would even argue that by devoting more of its resources and efforts to political organization inside the country, the ANC would make an even greater contribution than it has already done. The ANC leadership like all the other opponents of apartheid have never doubted that the real struggle must be fought by a variety of methods within South Africa itself. As the founder of Umkhontowe Sizwe, Nelson Mandela, said at the time of its launching, an armed struggle was only one of many methods for combatting apartheid.

Finally, a question that needs to be addressed is what would have happened if Samora Machel had not signed the Nkomati Accord? What future would have faced his government and his country? Could the FRELIMO government have survived? Is it not better, taking a longer view of the struggle, that he should have bought time for Mozambique to recover from its parlous and vulnerable state in order to struggle on?

6. The Nkomati Agreement and the Future of the Second Phase of the National Liberation Struggles in Southern Africa

E. N. Maganya

INTRODUCTION

The "non-aggression pact" between the Republic of South Africa and the Peoples Republic of Mozambique was signed at the town of Komatipoort (hereinafter referred to as the Nkomati Agreement) on 16 March 1984. It is just a year since the agreement was signed but it is now clear that most of its important conditions have not been fulfilled and the pact itself is in danger of collapsing.[1]

The Republic of South Africa has not been able or willing to stop the destabilizing incursions into Mozambique by the Portuguese controlled bandit organization of the Mozambique National Resistance Movement (MNR or RENAMO) nor have organized struggles by the black population been eased by the expected control of the ANC's guerrilla soldiers crossing into South Africa. If anything, events that followed the killing of 17 unarmed people during demonstrations commemorating the 25th anniversary of the Sharpeville Massacre near Kitenge on 21 March 1985, show that the source of instability to the regime does not come from across the border.

What then went wrong with an Accord that was hailed particularly by the West as a success in the general world-wide Reaganite campaign to 'roll back communism' – a campaign that generally includes even genuine nationalist struggles to set up democratic institutions and self-reliant economies as the Nicaraguan case clearly shows?

Central to this chapter is the argument that, to be able to understand both the covert and overt aims of the Accord and why it has been such a weak agreement, it is important to situate all the events preceding and following the Accord within the context of the character of its epoch, which is that of the transition from capitalism to socialism.

Secondly, it is essential to consider both the general and cyclical crises of capitalism that explain this general movement.[2] This chapter further argues that this characterization of the present epoch is important in understanding the current efforts in Southern Africa to wage a struggle for economic self-determination through the formation of the Southern African Development Coordination Conference (SADCC) in 1980.

While SADCC involves nine countries of Southern Africa, it will be the argument of this chapter that the three countries that got independence through armed struggles in the 1970s are central to the success of what shall be called the second phase of the national liberation struggles; and that for reasons which will be mentioned shortly, Mozambique was identified as the weakest link in the chain of the most outspoken anti-imperialist countries in this part of Africa. Consequently, it will be argued that the Nkomati Accord was in the final analysis meant to paralyse all efforts to create self-reliant and self-sustaining national economies within the context of SADCC.

THE SECOND PHASE OF THE LIBERATION STRUGGLE

The success of the first socialist revolution in the world that took place in Russia in 1917 ushered in a new epoch in the development of mankind. For the first time in the history of the development of capitalism, a new process of effective struggle against imperialism through socialist and anti-imperialist nationalist revolutions began. The socialist revolution of Russia meant, at the same time, the first phase of the general crisis of capitalism (not restricted) to economic crisis - a phenomenon that had always been part and parcel of capitalist development.

This general crisis was deepened by the cyclical economic crisis of capitalism of the late 1920s and early 1930s that transformed state capitalism into fascism and led to the second struggle for the redivision of the World amongst major capitalist countries - World War II. The failure to "roll back communism"[3] in the first socialist state and victory against Nazi Germany led to the formation of a strengthened community of socialist states and the first effective and generalized challenge against imperialism. This success advanced the general crisis of capitalism into its second phase and laid a very firm foundation for a much more developed and deep going general crisis that was centered around the struggle for political self-determination amongst Asian and African countries.

Indeed, the presence on the world scene of a strengthened socialist system after the Second World War contributed to the first phase of the national liberation struggles that for Africa climaxed in which is often referred to as the 'Africa year of 1960' - a year in which 17 African countries achieved state independence. It was not accidental that the United Nations Declaration on Granting Independence to Colonial Countries and Peoples (Resolution 1514-XV) of 14 December 1960 was made on the initiative of the Soviet Union. Contrary to a number of radical analysts who dismiss the success of the struggle for political freedom as having brought about mere flag independence, this event was, perhaps second only to the 1917 Socialist Revolution, one of the few most important events of the 20th century.[4]

Let me here once more emphasize that the success of the nationalist struggles for political independence laid the foundation for a new form of struggle against imperialism- the struggle for economic self-determination. It was important that this semblance of political independence be there and under the nominal rule of indigenous people in order to lay bare the major contradiction between the exploited Third World people and imperialism (economic exploitation) - a fact that was hitherto hidden by the bilateral 'mother country'-colony relationship.

Indeed, the success of the first phase of national liberation struggles plunged capitalism into its third phase of general crisis which was to deepen as the people of the Third World countries awakened to the reality of the inadequacy of political independence and therefore began to demand real political independence - i.e. the objective necessity of going a step further in the struggle for national liberation.

The necessity of this transition began to be obvious to a number of Third World countries as the myth of the 'economic wonder' of capitalism of the post-Second World War period began to be questionable as signs of a deep going cyclical crisis - second only to that of the Great Depression of the early thirties - became clear, particularly after 1975. Increasing unemployment in the developed capitalist countries, unequal terms of trade for primary products coming from the developing countries accompanied by chronic foreign exchange deficits and a debt burden of unmanageable proportions all became common features of the post-1975 cyclical crisis of capitalism. The deterioration in terms of trade for many African countries by 1982, for example, was 50% since 1970 and over 67% since 1977 for coffee, tea and cocoa. Furthermore, there are no prospects of improvement during the whole of the 1980s.[5]

One of the most important and interesting aspects of the success of the national liberation struggles in the former Portuguese colonies of Sub-Saharan Africa and in Zimbabwe is that this took place when the combination of the cyclical and general crisis of capitalism had put the question of the necessity of the second phase of the national liberation struggles on the agenda. Thus, apart from the long war for national liberation in these colonies, that necessitated the formation of anti-imperialist and progressive liberation movements, it is to the credit of this 'historical' delay in the granting of political independence that conditions were created for these countries to have the two phases of national liberation follow one another immediately. The struggle for national political self-determination was objectively bound up with the struggle for economic self-determination precisely because the former was realized when objective conditions pertaining to the post-1975 period demanded that there be an immediate transition to the latter.

This, perhaps, is the most important single factor that explains why both those countries in Southern Africa that completed the first phase of the national liberation struggles in the 1960s and those that did so in the 1970s are interested in establishing economic links that can help make the second phase of nationalist struggle much easier. The geographical proximity of the former Portuguese colonies and the former settler economy of Rhodesia (now Zimbabwe) to South Africa and their historical economic dependency on South Africa (particularly in the case of Mozambique and Zimbabwe) and therefore the need to free themselves from this dependency, can only be concretely and scientifically comprehended by situating this objective within the context of the deepened third phase of the general crisis of capitalism. This is objectively bound up with generalized (although not necessarily coordinated) economic struggles against imperialism by the less developed capitalist countries.

While, therefore, the immediate aim for the formation of economic cooperation amongst Southern African countries within the context of SADCC was to stop increasing economic dependency on South Africa it would be strategically wrong- at least in the long-term perspective - to see it as the most important reason behind the ongoing efforts at economic cooperation in the region. In the short-term perspective, the success of economic cooperation within the context of SADCC has to depend on effective economic and political isolation of the racist controlled Republic of South Africa. In the long-term (a period that can only be determined by internal democratic struggles in South Africa), however, a democratically-ruled South Africa is absolutely vital to the survival and effectiveness of any economic cooperation in Southern Africa.

This is so not only because it would be impossible in the long-run to sustain any form of economic cooperation in the vicinity of such unprincipled and extremely reactionary neighbors, but more so because a democratic and rich South Africa would be a great asset to economic cooperation in Southern Africa. Present evidence suggests beyond any reasonable doubt that such a South Africa can only be created by the ANC in cooperation with other democratic and anti-imperialist parties and associations.

The Nkomati Agreement was, therefore, formulated by the United States as a means to block both the short-term and long-term preconditions for the successful economic cooperation in Southern Africa - i.e. short term political and economic isolation of racist South Africa and most important of all, the prevention of the realization of a democratic South Africa. Expressed in other words, it aimed at neutralizing or eliminating the most progressive countries in this region and ANC as the better-placed nationalist movement in the liberation of South Africa. As African Communist, the mouthpiece of the Communist Party of South Africa and the ANC, commented on the Agreement,

> Our position in regard to the Nkomati Accord is unique, not directly shared by others in the front line. Premier Botha undoubtedly hopes that the Accord will destroy our movement and our challenge to apartheid; undermining the Front Line States is only one aspect of it as far as he is concerned.[6]

And this is what has been partially achieved in the one year of existence of the Accord. It has been proved indeed that this was a destabilizing rather than a non-aggression pact-although it is Mozambique, much more than the ANC, that has been most affected. Thus it is in order that we go into the reasons that made South Africa identify Mozambique as the weakest link in the chain of anti-imperialist forces amongst the post-African decade[7] liberated countries in Southern Africa (Mozambique, Angola and Zimbabwe) before we can be in a better position to assess the Accord.

THE WEAKEST LINK

Apart from the little and stubborn Lesotho that has defied all attempts to coerce it into signing a 'non-aggression treaty' with South Africa, and the one signed secretly with the Kingdom of Swaziland way back in 1982, three important countries have been singled out for intensified destabilization: Mozambique, Zimbabwe and Angola. As I pointed out earlier, the three are unique in the region by having had the historically determined situation of having the two phases of national liberation struggles follow one another.

Apart from this important conjectural phenomenon, they are also economically important both for imperialism and for any effective economic cooperation in Southern Africa. Tanzania, Angola and Mozambique provide the best communication links to the remaining landlocked members of SADCC and the three are above all, the richest in terms of potential both agricultural productivity and mineral resources.

Indeed, as one study points out, Angola has 34 mineral resources, of which 14 are strategic: iron ore, coal, phosphates, uranium, titanium, copper, gold, manganese, bauxite, mica, nickel, cobalt, chrome, vanadium, beryllium, tin, lead, limestone, asphalt rock, rare earth and radioactive elements. And this is apart from oil reserves so important for industrial production in the region already being exploited and whose further development is dependent on conducive political and military conditions.

These reasons, and above all because of the importance of these countries in the liberation of South Africa and Namibia, make them central to any strategy to prolong the survival of apartheid in South Africa. One of the most recent tactics aimed at prolonging apartheid is "total strategy", first outlined in the Defence White Paper of 1977. According to M.H. Louw, former Director of the Institute of Strategic Studies of Pretoria University (ISSUP), the strategy has several implications at the level of foreign policy:

> National Security Doctrine is a trilogy of foreign policy, military and domestic policy ... We must mobilize through its mechanisms and resources a capability (power, leverage or violence) for effective resistance ... this means a capacity to withstand challenges to our territorial integrity and political and socioeconomic order as well as to exert pressure on other, mostly weaker states, to make their behavior consonant with out interests.[8] (emphasis added)

While, for reasons given above, all of the three countries have been singled out for intensive destabilization campaigns for both historical and conjectural reasons, Mozambique has been identified as the "weakest link" amongst the three most active anti-imperialist countries.[9]

There are two important reasons that can be advanced for this choice: economic and adherence to the traditional interpretation by Mozambique of the policy of non-alignment. Economically, pre-1975 Mozambique had forged strong economic links with South Africa. It was in the interest of imperialism that these links be maintained, particularly in view of the ambitious if not unrealistic indicative prospective plan of 1982 to 1990 - a period in which underdevelopment was expected to be defeated.

While this prospective plan was indeed unrealistic and led to a number of hurriedly formulated and badly implemented large- scale economic ventures (special reference is here made to the ambitious and highly mechanized Limpopo Valley rice scheme), it is nevertheless true that the years between 1975 and 1981 did show some gradual socioeconomic improvements that were not pleasing to those whose 'historical' function is to roll back communism and genuine anti-imperialist struggles.

It is perhaps significant to point out that even in the agricultural sector, which has been of late devastated by the combined impact of drought, floods and effectively organized bandits of RENAMO, the situation was not so desperate as it is usually made out to be - even as late as 1981.

Table 6-1
Mozambique: Marketed Agricultural Production
(in 000s tons)

Product	1980	1981
Cotton	63.9	73.6
Maize	65.0	78.3
Copra	37.1	54.4
Tea	94.7	99.2
Potatoes	9.0	73.9
Beans	9.6	14.9
Citrus Fruit	32.0	36.7
Vegetables	6.3	2.2
Rice	42.5	28.9

Source: Direccao Nactional de Plano, 1982

Apart from efficiency problems connected with the capital- intensive state farm based in the Limpopo which

negatively affected rice production, the growth in the volume
of marketed agricultural products between the two years did
indicate some positive shifts in productive, in spite of less
than spectacular growth rates. A better indication of
positive economic growth rates between the post-liberation
and pre-active bandit sabotage acts is afforded from the
following observations of the rate of change in GDP between
1974 and 1980.

Table 6-2
Mozambique: Rate of Change in Gross Domestic Production

Year	1974	1975	1976	1977	1978	1979	1980
GDP	-10.8	-13.1	- 4.8	0.8	0.8	2.5	3.6

Source: Various United Nations Statistical Sources, 1976,
1979, 1980 and 1981.

These modest economic achievements of the FRELIMO
government during this period counter hostile and incorrect
interpretations of the deteriorating political and economic
conditions after 1982. According to bourgeois academicians
and politicians, the poor performance is simply reduced to
the unworkable 'communist' economic strategies while radical
academicians characteristically trace these negative
developments one-sidedly to the increasing bureaucratization
process explained by the abandonment of mass politics of the
liberation struggles.
    Vice-President Bush, during a November 1982 African tour
which preceded and in many ways anticipated the Nkomati and
related agreements, made the following comments on 'old
ideologies':

    Now is the time for fresh thinking, an eschewing of old
    ideologies that have not passed the test of experience
    ... We are prepared to help give African governments the
    wherewithal and the international political and
    financial backing, to take steps where necessary to
    restructure their economies.[11] (emphasis added)

While Horace Campbell is miles apart ideologically from Bush,
his observation on the unworkable nature of too much 'statism
and leaderism' in Mozambique comes closer to the above
observation:

    For too long leaderism, statism, a fetishized concept of
    the development of the productive forces and commandism

of the working poor stifled the creativity of the
proletarianised masses in the name of Marxism-Leninism
and/or socialism.[12] (emphasis added)

This is, however, not to say FRELIMO did not make a number of
tactical errors both at the level of political and economic
strategies. It is true, as I have already pointed out, that
over-emphasis on state farms did mean less support to small-
holder cultivators who, in a country where they constitute
over 90% of the population, are bound for quite some time to
remain central to increased agricultural production and
productivity. This error was, indeed, recognized by the
FRELIMO leadership during the April 1983 fourth congress, in
a spirit of self-criticism and openness that is rare amongst
African political parties.

However, having agreed that this was a grave tactical
error, it would be inaccurate to attribute all the problems
of agricultural production and general productivity in the
post-1981 era to the `socialization' process. If we take the
case of agriculture, up to 1983 there were 1,350 communal
villages with 1,800,000 inhabitants only, and mostly
concentrated in the north where most of the liberation
struggles took place. The number of producer cooperatives
increased from 180 to 370, with 37,000 members during the
1977-1982 period.[13] Surely these figures do not suggest any
large-scale socialization of agricultural production. A
comparison with Tanzania's 1971-1977 villagization programme
which managed to settle something like 10 million people in
such a short time can, perhaps, help to minimize the
imaginary radical nature of Mozambique's `experiment.'

All said, it can be stated here that the fragility of
Mozambique's economy after 1981 can largely be attributed to
the devastating war of liberation and the post-independence
strict adherence to the United Nations economic sanctions
against Rhodesia. At least as far as the second aspect is
concerned, the economic consequences were very negative.
About 40,000 workers at the Port of Beira lost employment and
according to calculations made by the United Nations, the
total loss in financial terms amounted to $500 million.
After the independence of Zimbabwe, Mozambique was not given
enough time to consolidate her economic position and,
therefore, when full-scale organized sabotage set in after
1981, it was easy to create havoc in the economy.

While in the period between 1977-1981 total social
production grew by 11.6%, agricultural gross production by
8.8%, industrial by 13.7% and transport and communication by
a significant rate of 15.4%, this was turned into the
opposite as early as 1982. In this year, industrial

production was 2.2% lower than in 1977, transport and communication fell by 6.7% in 1982 after a healthy growth rate of 15.4% over the last four years. The gross value of domestic trade which was constant during the 1977-81 period fell by 4.2% in 1982.[14]

A quick look at the economic situation of both post-independence Angola and Zimbabwe on the other hand, shows that these were less dependent on South Africa than Mozambique. For Zimbabwe, the rather effective trade sanctions that were to a greater extent made possible by their strict implementation by Mozambique (almost singlehandedly!) forced the Smith regime to become more 'self-reliant' in both the industrial and agricultural sectors. As for Angola, it had more economic links with the traditional trade and economic allies of Portugal than South Africa, as the following table clearly shows:

Table 6-3
Angola: Direction of Trade

Imports from:	1979	1980	Exports to:	1979	1980
Western Europe	56.4	51.6	North America	21.4	31.8
Comecon (CMEA)	15.7	16.9	Latin America	35.1	28.9
Latin America	9.8	10.8	Western Europe	28.5	22.2
North America	5.6	7.7	Comecon (CMEA)	6.9	6.3
Africa	3.0	2.2	Africa	3.4	4.1
Other	9.5	11.4	Other	4.7	6.7

Source: M.R. Bhagavan, in Energy, Environment and Development in Africa: Energy and Development in Southern Africa. SADCC Country Studies, Part I, Stockholm and Uppsala: The Beijer Institute of Royal Swedish Academy of Sciences and the Scandinavian Institute of African Studies, 1984.

This economic factor that partly explains why Mozambique has been chosen as the 'weakest link' has been aggravated by FRELIMO's conventional understanding and implementation of the principle of non-alignment. The Mozambican government has consistently refused any outside military help either in the form of direct involvement of the Soviet Union or support by the same or of the Cuban forces as was the case for Ethiopia during the Ogaden War or still in the case for Angola. This rather dogmatist understanding of the policy of non-alignment has indeed deprived Mozambique of an effective counterweight to decisive US support given to South Africa.

Even the most consistent advocate of the conventional policy of non-alignment, J.K. Nyerere, former President of

Tanzania, has increasingly become convinced of the importance of the support of the Soviet Union in the complicated task of liberating South Africa. This is implied in a recent interview between Nyerere and Alfar Garhar, editor of Third World Quarterly, on the impact of the Nkomati Agreement on the liberation of South Africa and Namibia. Nyerere said, "We can explain Mozambique's former links would create a problem for us with countries who want to help us in our struggle against South Africa."[15] (emphasis added)

Perhaps even much more significant were Nyerere's most recent remarks on Nkomati in which he pointed out that "although UNITA was mainly African it would not succeed to overthrow the MPLA government." Alluding to the possible defeat of FRELIMO by RENAMO, he pointed out that "the situation was different in Mozambique where the MNR bandits were predominantly Portuguese. Even if they succeeded to topple the government, they would not form a new one to replace it ..."[16] Nyerere could most appropriately as well have said that the Cuban 'factor' has made all the difference and hence the American 'linkage' policy!

Having gone into the economic, political and military factors that made South Africa choose Mozambique as the weakest link in the chain of anti-imperialist neighboring countries, implications the future of Mozambique will be examined with reference to economic cooperation after the Nkomati Agreement.

AFTER NKOMATI: WHAT FUTURE FOR MOZAMBIQUE AND SADCC?

Contrary to the propaganda that surrounded the Nkomati Agreement, it really was never intended to increase the political and economic stability of Mozambique as has been the previous argument. Rather, in the one year of the existence of the Agreement, Mozambique has experienced more political and economic instability than in the previous years of its history. To the extent that this is so, it can be correctly pointed out that the agreement has been partly successful.

Emphasis is on partly for two reasons: first, the second aim of the Agreement - the elimination of the ANC and popular internal opposition to racist South Africa - has not been realized. If anything, South Africa has faced one of the most difficult years in terms of organized resistance by democratic forces inside it since the 1976 Soweto uprisings. The second reason is that even the strategy of weakening Mozambique by making her implement one-sidedly the so-called 'non-aggression pact' has not fully worked out. Mozambique now does fully realize that the agreement was never really intended to be a non-aggression pact, but indeed an aggression pact.

One of the possible positive results of the failure of Nkomati is to make FRELIMO realize three important issues:

a)   the importance and necessity of internal popular mobilization of the masses and the army on the one hand and economic stabilization through regional cooperation, not by increasing economic dependency on South Africa but within the context of SADCC;

b)   accept the reality that in the period of the deepened third phase of the general crisis of capitalism, imperialism is extremely aggressive and therefore that under certain unavoidable circumstances, direct military help from socialist countries is necessary; and

c)   the central role of ANC and active support to the liberation of South Africa as the only long-term effective solution to the political and particularly economic independence and prosperity of the countries of Southern Africa.

In conclusion, it can finally be pointed out that the failure of Nkomati has effectively frustrated the grand imperialist strategy of breaking the anti-imperialist chain (SADCC being the economic expression of the chain) at what was thought to be the weakest link.   Though Mozambique remains very weak both militarily and economically, the fact that it has now realized that Nkomati can't work will strengthen the collective spirit amongst the most anti-imperialist countries in Southern Africa which is needed for the more difficult second phase of the national liberation struggle - the struggle for economic self-determination.

NOTES

1.   Daily News, (Dar es Salaam), 12 March 1985, p. 7.
2.   Hartmat Schilling, "Colonial Downfall and Neo-Colonialism," Asia, Africa, Latin America, Special Issue 3, Akademie-Verlag Berlin, 1979, pp. 45-66.
3.   "Rolling back communism" is an important component of Reagan's foreign policy and is central in understanding the essence of the Nkomati Agreement.
4.   For the best representation of this position, see Y. Tandon, "Whose Capital and Whose State?", in Y. Tandon (ed), University of Dar es Salaam Debate on Class, State and

Imperialism: Tanzania, (Dar es Salaam: Tanzania Publishing House, 1982), pp. 154-170.

5. R.H. Green, "African Economies in the Mid-1980s: Naught for your comfort but that the waves grow higher and the storms grow wilder," in Jerker Carlsson, ed., Recession in Africa -Background papers to the Seminar Africa: which way out of recession? (Uppsala: Scandinavian Institute of African Studies, 1983), p. 176.

6. The African Communist, (London), 98, 1984, p. 11.

7. I take the 1960s as the decade in which well over a half of the former colonial African countries got political independence.

8. T. Sifunasoke, "Botha's 'Total Strategy': Crisis Management in South Africa," The African Communist, 94, 1983, p. 29.

9. This is not to belittle the position of Tanzania as the oldest and most consistent anti-imperialist country in Southern Africa. This choice takes into account geographical proximity to South Africa and therefore the strategic importance of these countries in the liberation of racist South Africa and Namibia.

10. New African, (London), (212), May 1985, p. 33.

11. W. Pomeroy, "Namibia's Independence and the Freedom of Africa," The African Communist (93), 1983, p. 54.

12. H. Campbell, "War, Reconstruction and Dependence in Mozambique," Third World Quarterly, 6(4), October, 1984, p. 865.

13. The African Communist, 95, 1983, p. 39.

14. Ibid., pp. 39 and 46.

15. J.K. Nyerere, "North-South Dialogue," Third World Quarterly, 6(4), October 1984, p. 833.

16. A talk given to District Party secretaries and chairmen by J.K. Nyerere at the Kivukoni Party Ideological College and paraphrased by the Daily News, (Dar es Salaam), 7 May 1985, p. 7.

7. Tanzania After the Nkomati Accord: Foreign Policy Restructuring in the Changing Strategic Balance in Southern Africa

Ibrahim S. R. Msabaha
Jeannette Hartmann

INTRODUCTION

Writing in 1977 on Tanzanian foreign policy one of the present authors had argued a) that Tanzania had found it difficult to translate the relative autonomy achieved in foreign policy in the 1960s into influence – a major component of such goals – because of its economic backwardness; and b) that any effectiveness it may have enjoyed with countries such as Mozambique and Zambia (for instance, in the formation of the Front Line States) was derived not so much from its influence but from Mozambique and Zambia's own position. Thus, the author was able to conclude that,

> Tanzania's effectiveness in foreign policy depends very much on her cooperation with other like-minded states. This in turn sets a limitation on the effectiveness of her foreign policy, especially with regard to Southern African Affairs. Mozambique and Zambia are more dependent on South Africa and their geographical situation makes them more vulnerable to military invasion than Tanzania, and should they adopt a conciliatory approach to the former because of their economic dependence and geographical vulnerability, Tanzania may well find herself isolated from both East and Central African Affairs.[1]

Seven years later, in 1984, Mozambique, a strategic member of the Front Line States (FLS) and Nyerere's good and solid friend, signed a non-aggression pact with South Africa at Komatipoort. According to this agreement, known as the Nkomati Accord, neither of the two countries would serve as a base for acts of aggression or violence against the other and that both countries undertook not to use the territory of a third state for this purpose.[2]

Other meetings in Cape Town and Maputo discussed economic relations, tourism between the two states, and the supply of energy from the Cabora Bassa hydroelectric scheme. A joint military commission was formed a week after the Accord. A similar agreement was signed in Lusaka a month before and Angola was expected to follow suit. Thus strategic members of the FLS and close friends of Nyerere have made a U-turn and embarrassed the enemy they had so strenuously fought against in the liberation of South Africa.

This development raises the questions of whether or not the Nkomati Accord defies the old patterns of Tanzania's foreign policy restructuring in the country's international relations. We argue that the Non-Aggression Pact does constitute a challenge that requires readjustment and restructuring in Tanzanian foreign policy if the country is to continue to pursue its interrelated goals of support for national liberation movements and drive for economic development. Thus, the present chapter examines why Tanzania must realign its foreign policy, and in which geographical and functional areas its foreign relations should not concentrate.

The basic premises for this chapter are drawn from a much more extensive and comparative work on foreign policy realignment by Holsti et. al.,[3] including one of the present authors, but with a difference. While Holsti's book centers on explaining foreign policy behaviors where governments sought to revise the total pattern of their external relations, the present chapter seeks to explain why transformation must take place; that is, through involuntary restructuring in that the Nkomati Accord has brought about new elements in the strategic balance in Southern Africa between the forces of liberation and the apartheid regime. And this alteration in the balance of power in favor of South Africa requires governments such as that of Tanzania to realign and establish new commitments, out of necessity rather than choice.

The objective of the present discussion is, then, twofold. First the chapter is based on the continuation of academic interest in the problem of foreign policy restructuring from the volume previously mentioned. Although Holsti's work was extensively theorized, the case study on Tanzania revealed that the country merely moved from classical dependence on the Western powers to

diversification. But while diversification might have
improved the country's capabilities in dealing with the
continuing problems of underdevelopment and liberation, the
extent of "change" was simply confined to establishing
relations with middle-power Western capitalist nations, and
Western-sponsored international financial institutions. It
is neither substantial nor significant enough to engulf other
geographic and functional areas such as the Afro-Arab circle
analyzed in the present essay. As such the results were
marginal. The question then is whether Nkomati-like Accords
provide the necessary momentum for embarking on much wider
and deeper diversification.

And second, this chapter is also intended for African
policy-makers, who must think through the implications of
South African diplomatic maneuvers. Upon talking to a number
of Tanzanian government officials, the overall impression is
that:

> Tanzania does not have to reorient its foreign policy.
> Mozambique is still a Front Line State but does not
> support the armed struggle. All that is left is how to
> deal with such a situation. If a split occurs in the
> Front Line States, South Africa will be happy.[4]

Honorable as the view may be, it mainly reflects the cautious
nature of statements by government officials or represents an
over-simplification of the whole situation. In either case,
officials cannot be expected to embark on open analyses of
major and sensitive policy issues. For us who can, by virtue
of our profession, it is necessary to initiate a scholarly
debate that may be beneficial to decision-makers as they
ponder the strategic implications of Nkomati.

Thus in terms of scope and time period, this is a case
study that looks at the pattern of Tanzania's foreign policy
over almost a quarter century: 1961-1984. During this
period, Tanzania displayed a range of types of foreign policy
reorientation and restructuring that could be distinguished
on the basis of intended changes in a) levels of external
involvement; b) policies regarding types and sources of
external penetration; c) direction or pattern of external
involvement; and d) military or diplomatic commitments.[5] It
was during this initial period that events in Tanzania's
domestic and foreign surroundings precipitated changes in
both domestic and foreign policies. These notable reactions
to the environment - from classical dependence to non-
alignment diversification - led to the present assumption
that similar changes in Tanzania's external millieu would
provoke rethinking about foreign relations.

Indicators for the bases of realigning foreign policy used by Holsti, include foreign policy statements, speeches, new treaties or commitments, degree of trade concentration, amount of trade and numbers of diplomatic missions abroad. These are important, and they have by and large been taken for granted here. But the single most important measurement which we apply is the effect of the Nkomati Accord on Tanzania's domestic and foreign relations.

In terms of organization of data, our chapter is divided into four sections. The first part is a review of the country's major foreign policy preoccupations since independence in 1961. The focus here is on Tanzania's contribution to the Southern African struggles; material support to liberation movements; and the politics of Southern African detente, including the Lusaka Manifesto, Mogadishu Declaration, Dar es Salaam Declaration and American diplomatic initiatives. Section two discusses the economic crisis that has engulfed the FLS and the impact of these problems on present political developments in Southern Africa. Part three looks at the implications of South African strategy for Tanzania. And section four concludes by identifying policy options that are open to Tanzania given that the country must adapt to the changing political environment in the region.

FOREIGN POLICY SINCE INDEPENDENCE

Since 196s, Tanzania's support for Southern African liberation struggles has been a continuing theme in its foreign policy.[6] And when, by 1964, all the nationalist movements resorted to guerrilla warfare as a means of pressuring the colonial powers to grant independence, Tanzania not only backed this strategy by providing training facilities and a rear base, it also became progressively more radical, organized and coordinated.

The greatest beneficiary of Tanzania's support was Frelimo. Tanzania and Mozambique share a common border. This geographical proximity to Southern Africa contributed to Tanzania's policy of militarization because it felt threatened; and it was in fact menaced in the 1970s by the "unholy alliance" of Portuguese, Rhodesian and South African regimes.[7] Moreover, despite the foreign policy crisis of 1964-65, the 1960s were by and large favorable to Tanzania, economically. This East African state enjoyed a healthy balance of payments, inflation was non-existent, and level of economic performance was acceptable.[8] These conditions enabled Nyerere to concentrate single-mindedly on the liberation struggles to an extent that the President's ideas came to play a major role in defining, structuring and implementing the decolonization process in Southern Africa, which logically should have been the prerogative of the OAU.

In 1969, Nyerere and other leaders of the East and Central African states met in a strategy session on Southern Africa and produced the Lusaka Manifesto. This document made a distinction between South Africa and other white-ruled states of Southern Africa (Angola, Mozambique, Rhodesia). Thus the Lusaka document stated:

> We would prefer to negotiate rather than destroy, to talk rather than kill ... But while peaceful progress is blocked by actions of those at present in power in the states of Southern Africa, we have no choice but to give to the peoples of those territories all the support of which we are capable in their struggle against their oppressors. That is why the signatory states participate in the movement for the liberation of Africa, under the aegis of the OAU.[9]

However, the overemphasis on negotiation dismayed the liberation movements of Southern Africa: that stress on diplomacy could lead to the abandonment of the armed struggle altogether.

Indeed, these reservations were to be vindicated by subsequent events within the OAU. By 1970, conflicts emerged among the OAU member states with regard to strategies which the Organization should adopt in the struggle against South Africa between the advocates of dialogue and those of confrontation. The original adherents of the former strategy were Malawi, Lesotho and Madagascar, which had been in a minority in the OAU. But by 1971, the Ivory Coast, Ghana and Uganda had joined the dialogue bandwagon as a possible means of bringing about changes within South Africa. There was also a possibility that these countries would bring with them the Francophone African states whose opposition to South Africa had always been somewhat muted because of France's bilateral link with the apartheid regime.

In response, in a document entitled The Organization of African Unity and the Freedom Struggle, Tanzania challenged the established OAU principles of universal membership and non-intervention. According to this position paper, a member who accepted compromises with South Africa should be expelled from the OAU and steps should be undertaken to overthrow any such leader in his/her own country. Tanzania asserted that there are certain matters, which concern the whole of Africa, on which individual members are obliged to formulate foreign

policies only on the basis of consultation with other states
- relations with South Africa were one such issue.
Therefore, by intervening in a particular African state's
foreign policy over South Africa, one was not meddling in
internal affairs but in pan-African matters. Further, the
document advocated collective intervention by OAU states on
such pan-African matters.[10]

Although Tanzania was unsuccessful with this proposal to
the OAU, in a move to nullify fears within the liberation
movements over the dialogue question, the Seventh Summit
Conference of East and Central African heads of states
adopted the Mogadishu Declaration in October 1971 which
stated:

> We ... therefore do declare ... that there is no way
> left to the liberation of Southern Africa except armed
> struggle to which we already give and will increasingly
> continue to give our fullest support; that the policy of
> dialogue advanced by a small group of African leaders
> which had already been rejected by the OAU is again
> rejected because it is a ploy to deceive the African
> peoples.[11]

War and Diplomacy   Despite OAU preoccupations, by 1975
Angola, Guinea Bissau, Mozambique, Sao Tome and Principe had
achieved their independence. The new post-1975 geopolitical
map of the continent heightened the specter of war and
diplomacy. For the first time, Western powers as well as the
remaining white-minority regimes in Southern Africa began to
take the new balance of forces seriously and to embark on
various attempts at negotiation with the liberation
movements. The change also necessitated a new appraisal of
the liberation struggles by the African states themselves.

At the 24th session of the OAU Liberation Committee in
Dar es Salaam in January 1975, Nyerere stated his call for
the independence of Rhodesia on the principle of majority
rule. His position was outlined in a speech to a Conference
of OAU Foreign Ministers in Dar es Salaam, which was adopted
as the Dar es Salaam Declaration on Southern Africa:

> ... We said clearly that Africa would conduct the
> struggle for freedom by peaceful means wherever and
> whenever that is possible. But if peaceful means are
> excluded by the actions of the oppressor, then an armed
> struggle by the people of that territory would have the
> full and active support of all the free states of our
> continent.[12]

Intense diplomatic undertakings took place between 1976
and 1980. The diplomacy occurred within the background of
guerrilla warfare and an escalation toward a major
confrontation with the white minority states. It was a
period in Southern Africa where the political fortunes of the
remaining white minority regimes hung in the balance.

South Africa was very quick to respond to this
situation. It began to revert to its 1971 policy of detente
and dialogue with African countries. Vorster visited Ivory
Coast and Liberia in 1975, and is reported to have conducted
fifteen meetings with President Kaunda in a bid to bring
about peaceful change in Rhodesia. The defunct United
African National Congress (ANC) was formed in these
circumstances. A major meetings, symbolizing these
diplomatic initiatives took place on 26 August 1976, between
Smith and his Rhodesian Front, Sithole, Nkomo, Vorster, and
Kaunda at the railway bridge across the Victoria Falls gorge.
Thus Smith and Vorster, in a bid to avert a radical black
government in Rhodesia, influenced the formation of a
'united' ANC, on the pretext that they could not negotiate
with four liberation movements: ZANU, ZAPU, FROLIZI and ANC.
Throughout this period, Kaunda was in full consultation with
the other FLS and a coordinated policy emerged to back up the
secret negotiations.[13]

Nevertheless, the South African invasion of Angola and
Ian Smith's continued intransigence brought about a change of
cohesion and tactics by the FLS. Thus in February 1976, the
four Front Line Presidents met at Quelimane, Mozambique and
came out with a joint communique in support of guerrilla
warfare. Mozambique closed its border with Rhodesia and
increased its training and support for Mugabe's guerrillas.

US and South Africa   Overall geopolitical changes in
Southern Africa compelled the United States to adopt a more
forceful interventionist policy in the region. It was
interested despite the fact it had no formal colonial links
with Africa. The major reasons for US involvement,
therefore, must be traced to its policy of containment of
"communism," to strategic interests in relation to the sea
lanes and the Persian Gulf, which fuel Western industries,
and to the need to expand its economic interests into Africa.
The Americans adopted a broader perspective: that is, to
maintain Southern Africa basically within the Western sphere
of influence - militarily, economically and politically.[14] A
system of consultation was established to coordinate
diplomacy with the FLS. In relation to Namibia, the Carter
Administration recognized that although the problem of the
territory was legally a matter of the UN, it should also

involve the US's Western allies.

The Reagan Administration introduced the policy of "constructive engagement" with South Africa. The theory behind this is that one can bring changes in Namibia and to the apartheid system by moving closer and by becoming friendlier to South Africa! The Reagan Administration has accordingly increased its political, military and diplomatic exchanges with the apartheid regime. In addition, based on the doctrine of the containment of communism in Southern Africa, the US has since 1981 linked the question of the withdrawal of Cuban troops from Angola with progress toward Namibian independence.

Although American involvement has not produced African liberation, the negative impact of this interference in Southern Africa would have been minimal if the economic stability of the FLA including Tanzania had been maintained at its 1960s and 1970s level.

Economic Crisis and Destabilization   Three years of drought, economic recession, depressed export markets, economic mismanagement in the countries concerned, lack of critical foreign exchange, and food shortages all began to threaten the economies of the FLS upon which their own political stability hung. For most, agriculture still forms the backbone of their economies. Over 80% of the population makes a living in this sector and the states depend on the exports of agricultural produce for over 70% of their foreign exchange. Yet, it was this very sector which was crippled throughout the region.

For instance, in 1979, Tanzania experienced its second major economic crisis, only four years after that of 1974-75, which also manifested itself in severe balance of payment problems. For example, the estimated volume of imports other than food grains and petroleum in 1979 was 16% lower than in 1978 and only 3% higher than six years earlier in 1973.[15] This severe balance of payments crisis had repercussions on all socio-economic sectors as practically every branch of its economy was dependent on foreign exchange for inputs. The economies of Mozambique and Tanzania were slowly grinding into a halt, symptomatic of the regional crisis induced by successive oil and other shocks.

Southern Africa Development Co-ordination Conference (SADCC)   Concern with intensifying economic problems and setbacks resulted in the creation of SADCC, which was conceived in 1979, as a logical development of the political struggles, now to be consolidated in economic reconstruction. The five FLS states - Tanzania, Mozambique, Angola, Botswana,

Zambia - joined by Lesotho, Swaziland, Malawi and Zimbabwe, met in Lusaka in April 1980 and adopted the Lusaka Declaration:

a) Reduction of economic dependence, particularly, but not only, on the Republic of South Africa;

b) Forging of links to create a genuine and equitable regional integration;

c) Mobilization of resources to promote the implementation of national, interstate and regional policies; and

d) Promotion of concerted action to secure international cooperation within the framework of our strategy for economic liberation.

Given the political diversity among these nine states and their varying degree of economic dependence on South Africa, this program was dependent on the coordination of mutually beneficial projects on which all nine could agree.

But even with the best estimates and evaluations, SADCC has its limitations. Although political mandate of SADCC is to lessen dependence on South Africa, its Transport and Communications Commission predicts that trade to and from South Africa will increase by 28% by the year 2000, while intra-SADCC trade will increase by 44% by that year. Thus, trade with South Africa will still be almost four times as great as trade inside SADCC. Furthermore, SADCC will continue to depend on aid from the West because processes of internal capital accumulation and technical expertise are slow.

Just as these constraints impose limits on the scope of action by the FLS, other changes have compounded the political equation in Southern Africa. On the one hand, the independence of Mozambique, Angola and Zimbabwe and their consolidation into the FLS enabled them to coordinate foreign policies and security. But on the other hand, these very achievements posed a threat to South Africa. The latter was now surrounded by governments whose seriousness, maturity and statesmanship were becoming internationally recognized. From the perspective of the strategists in Pretoria, Mozambique and Angola were outright enemies and Lesotho was being influence by the FLS to the extent of forgetting its hostage status. Further, the new geopolitical situation in the region was being taken seriously enough by the Western countries to the extent of even pressuring South Africa to modify its internal policies and to terminate its continued illegal occupation of Namibia. International condemnation of the occupation of Southern Angola was also growing.

What was perhaps even more frightening for the white minority was that the situation was inspiring mounting opposition against the regime internally and creating within South Africa a strong base for ANC support as witnessed by the increasing and successful acts of sabotage which were taking place; e.g. in mid-March 1984 a petrol depot at Ermelo was blown up. This was precisely what South Africa wanted to avoid. For its own self-preservation the government had to alter the new geopolitical environment in its own favor. New conditions had to be created to reverse perceived threats to the apartheid system. The apartheid regime adopted two methods in response to FLS and SADCC.

The first formula South Africa applied was economic sanctions against Mozambique. A document prepared by the Mozambican National Planning Commission[16] has outlined some of the economic embargoes which South Africa has imposed on that country. South Africa was able to do this by merely withdrawing the support which had previously kept the Portuguese territory financially viable. South Africa reduced traffic passing through Mozambique/Maputo. Whereas in 1973 Maputo handled 6.8 million tons of South African imports and exports, by 1979 the figure dropped to 4.3 million tons and then down to 1.1 million tons in 1983. Based on 1973 traffic levels, the report calculates that the diversion of South African traffic has cost Mozambique R310 million in lost revenue. The traffic flows most affected were those which attracted high tariffs such as chrome shipments, which dropped from 980,000 tons in 1980 to 450,000 tons in 1982; also steel declined from 107,000 tons in 1980, to none at all by 1982.

There was a further 60% cutback in the recruitment of Mozambican labor for the South African mines. While in pre-independence days there were, on average, 120,000 Mozambican miners in South Africa, by 1977 this number had dropped to slightly more than 41,000; thus more than 70,000 Mozambicans were out of work. Accompanying this huge increase in unemployment was also the loss of the miners' unremitted wages, which was estimated to run at R710 million a year. The South African government also annulled the agreement signed in 1928 between Portugal and Pretoria whereby the miners salaries were remitted to the colonial authorities in gold at a set rate per ounce. This represented a subsidy to the Portuguese Government from Pretoria. In April 1978, the fixed gold price subsidy was scrapped unilaterally and between 1978 and 1983 its elimination cost Mozambique R3.25

billion.[17]

The second technique was more direct: destabilization
in Mozambique. South African financed, armed and trained the
Mozambique National Resistance (MNR) to destabilize the
countryside. The MNR destroyed railway locomotives, tracks,
bridges, farms, factories, communications lines, and
vehicles, totalling about R416 million. In 1982, the MNR
destroyed 140 villages, leaving 110,000 people homeless, and
forced the closure of 489 primary schools, which had catered
for 90,000 children. More than 100 health clinics were also
rendered useless. Between 1982 and 1983 it destroyed 900
rural shops. The National Planning commission document
estimates that the combined effects of the Rhodesian war, the
activities of MNR guerrillas and "sanctions imposed by South
Africa" have cost Mozambique a staggering R6.9 billion over
the past nine years.

The South African policy of destabilization had become
part and parcel of its overall defense policy and is designed
to present the FLS with enough strategic and economic
problems to preoccupy them so that they will no longer be
capable of functioning as effective rear bases for the
liberation movements:

a) to create a buffer zone in Southern Angola against
    SWAPO's operations in Namibia, and in Mozambique
    against ANC-PAC guerrilla activities;

b) to promote a situation whereby the FLS are occupied
    with the invasion/occupation of their territories
    rather than supporting the liberation movements;

c) to establish conditions for internal opposition
    forces to destabilize and therefore neutralize the
    FLS;

d) the shift military operations from inside Namibia
    and away from South African borders, and in to the
    FLS, to destroy the military infrastructures of
    these host countries and the liberation movements
    as well as to make these states suffer war
    devastation; and

e) to enable South Africa to maintain a good posture
    with the major Western powers by exaggerating the
    linkage between the presence of Cuban troops in
    Angola and the specter of Soviet domination in
    Southern Africa, which is seen to be a threat to
    Western interests.

124

Together with domestic defense measures, South African
destabilization is an aspect of what is popularly known as
"total strategy" that stretches from the factories, mines,
farms and bantustans inside South Africa, to the neighboring
states, Indian and Atlantic oceans, and up to the Cabinda
strip in Angola. As Horace Campbell explains:

> In essence, the ideas of total strategy emanated from
> the defeat of the South African army in Angola in 1976
> and the shock of the massive rebellion/strikes in Soweto
> in the same year.[18]

The precise shape of this defense policy was contained
in the South African Defense White Paper of 1977, in which
the process of militarization was outlined to combat threats
to the regime's security. The exact tactics to accomplish
the strategy are divided on a 80% political:20% military
ratio to encompass political action, psychological warfare,
scientific and technological work, religious and cultural
functions, intelligence services, transport and communication
activities, and production, distribution and general supply
services. In all these areas, Angola, Mozambique, Zimbabwe,
Botswana and Lesotho are the immediate targets.

The Nkomati Accord. South Africa's Nkomati Accord with
Mozambique, negotiations with Angola and security deals with
Swaziland should be understood in this context of South
Africa's politico-military strategy.[19] They are intended to
enable South Africa to turn some of the FLS from enemies into
allies; or at least to coerce them into a "constellation of
states" around Pretoria, thus creating a cordon sanitaire
around the apartheid heartland, as in pre-1974 days, in which
the ANC would be emasculated. In this way, too, South Africa
hopes to reduce pressure for diplomatic isolation and to gain
legitimacy as a major partner with one or two of the
strategic African governments. The most realistic assessment
of the significance of the Nkomati Accord, has come from
Pretoria itself, in a White Paper on Defense presented to
parliament:

> Forceful military action by the South African security
> forces during the last decade or more has provided
> sufficient time to allow Africa to experience the
> dangers of Russian involvement in their countries, as
> well as the suffering and retrogression that follows
> upon the revolutionary formula. South Africa's
> neighbors had their eyes opened to the dangers of
> Russian imperialism. By taking firm action the SADF had

created a successful strategy of deterrence. As a result of this overall situation, it will be possible to conduct future negotiations in a calm and relaxed atmosphere, thereby gaining more time in which the negotiating process can develop.[20]

Implications for Tanzania. What are the consequences of South Africa's strategy for Tanzania? First, South Africa has been successful in isolating Tanzania from the FLS, especially from Mozambique, Tanzania's closest friend and ally. By creating conflicting goals within Mozambique between her radical/progressive ideals and the barest economic survival, South Africa has forced Mozambique to see that the key to the country's future prosperity lies in Pretoria not Dar es Salaam. The Accord stipulates that there will be economic assistance in terms of finance. This means that if "peace" prevails over a long period, Angola and Mozambique will become increasingly integrated into the South African economic orbit – in terms of infrastructure, finance, markets, labor, technology and managerial capacity – making it difficult to reorient them and if the case should arise.

Second, since most of the strategic members within SADCC are themselves heavily dependent on South Africa (with the exception of Tanzania), South Africa indirectly becomes a member of SADCC. Tanzania's long-term interests may now be at logger-heads with most of the SADCC countries, whose dependency on South Africa may force them increasingly to cooperate with that regime and to redefine the objectives of economic cooperation, as Maputo has done with respect to the liberation struggle, calling it an "internal problem." This could further isolate Tanzania both from Mozambique and eventually from other Southern African countries, which have constituted Tanzania's major area of foreign policy activity for the past twenty years.

Third, the Nkomati Accord stipulates cooperation on security and defense as well as economic matters. For instance, the Cabora Bassa is now to be guarded by both South African and Mozambican troops. This means that South Africa's presense and threat have been brought closer to Tanzania than ever before. Mozambique had been a security buffer state for Tanzania when it was allowing the ANC to operate on its territory. With the Nkomati Accord, this buffer has become a reverse "corridor" through which South African agents can easily pass to gather intelligence and security pertaining to the ANC, who have been offered a base in Tanzania, as well as on Tanzania itself. Depending, of course, on how the situation in Southern Africa develops, Tanzania may well find itself bordered by weak countries who may pose a security threat to its southern flank.

Fourth, the consolidated form of voting bloc which the FLS were able to muster in the United Nations and other international forums will have been compromised. Tanzania can no longer bank upon Mozambique, for instance, for support over sanctions on South Africa; at most, Mozambique may abstain.

Fifth, the Nkomati Accord represents a major setback in Tanzania's attempts to pursue a "dual strategy" within the OAU. Tandon has described this:

> On the one hand, she has been working for the building of a revolutionary wing of the OAU to deal with the problem of the liberation of Southern Africa; and on the other, she has been trying to coexist in the OAU with members who are anything but revolutionary.[21]

Indeed, Mozambique now constitutes a quandary for Tanzania. In the late 1960s and early 1970s the dialogue strategy "opened up the possibility that many more states in Africa might join in."[22] Three choices were then open to Tanzania: a) to continue membership with a divided OAU; b) to quit the organization; or c) to seek to deny membership to states that advocated dialogue. Tanzania not only followed the latter course, it was instrumental in making the OAU prevent such states from getting access to documents that dealt with sensitive questions about the liberation movements lest these should fall into enemy hands.[23] More than a decade later Tanzania may not only have lost the battle to create a tightly organized group of revolutionary states; but it also faces the prospect of the defection of Mozambique from the FLS 'Club'. Over a dozen years ago, a leading African scholar in international relations foresaw such a gloomy prospect:

> There may well be good arguments for creating a tightly organized group of revolutionary states within Africa which would undertake the task of liberating the countries which are now under the control of racialist or colonialist governments. But such a revolutionary club ... must be prepared occasionally to get into conflict ... The oldest parallel would be the present situation in the Middle East which is a perpetual battleground of internecine violent conflicts among the Arabs themselves.

> Perhaps Africa is moving in a similar direction ... with respect to the Southern African problem, so that in a

few years from now states in Eastern, Central and Southern Africa may begin to fight against each other ...24

THE SEARCH FOR A STRATEGY

In short, the recent Non-Aggression Pact has introduced challenges to Tanzania's foreign policy. A new strategy must be chosen to reincarnate the stability of the country's foreign policy and the prospects for economic development. This strategy must operate in geographical and functional circles to adopt to an historic conjuncture in Southern Africa.

Nothing is inherently new in this. Since the achievement of its legal independence in 1961, Tanzania has participated actively in African and global diplomacy. Further, Tanzania has traditionally based its international conduct on the assumption that statesmen in Third World nations have some scope to develop their nations and to shape the international environment to suit national development objectives.[25]

What is new, however, is the call for reorganization of national domestic and foreign policies, to concentrate the latter in those geographical and functional circles (discussed later) that enhance national security and development, and in turn, effectively support national liberation movements. The latter's success depends upon the continued progress of Tanzania and other FLS.

In a traditional conception, national security is usually regarded as the condition of freedom from external or internal physical threats. Although moral and ideological threats are no less significant, it is physical violence that is generally perceived to be the ultimate leverage against a state and which constitutes the real danger to its survival. It is this conception of national security which has been predominant in Tanzania's perceptions.

However, economic growth and prosperity are also important components of national security yet these have received less attention in practice. The overwhelming preoccupation with security in terms of eliminating physical threats was brought about by specific conditions which prevailed then in the region. During the 1960s and 1970s, Portuguese colonialism in neighboring Mozambique, South African racist aggression and the remnants of British imperialism in Rhodesia threatened in a real way the national security of the Republic. As a consequence of this,

128

Tanzania's primary objective was to push South Africa's borders as far south as possible. In this way, foreign policy issues and specifically the liberation struggle became intricately related to problems of national security. The independence of Mozambique and Zimbabwe achieved this purpose.

But this single-minded commitment to foreign policy issues deflected attention from a wider and more comprehensive understanding of national security, a conception which would incorporate an idea of economic growth and prosperity. Indeed, the destabilization of Mozambique and the Nkomati Accord exemplified in a crucial way the link between weak economic structures and security threats. The reverse argument can be made of South Africa: Nkomati was possible because of South Africa's superior military capabilities and economic strength. As the economic giant of Southern Africa, South Africa has used its powers to destabilize its neighbors.

This argument is not intended to rank economic concerns above valued political and security problems; but rather, to view economic development as an integral process of consolidating national security. A strong economic base provides the most effective barriers against both internal and external threats of destabilization. Had a more comprehensive conception of national security prevailed since the 1960s, Nkomati might not have occurred. For then Tanzania and other progressive African states would have gone to the assistance of the Frelimo government caught in a trap of hunger, economic doldrums and destabilization. In the post-Nkomati context, the long-term strategy for Tanzania must be to realize an internal and external environment in which it can advance its external domestic plans to procure specific goals.

THE DOCTRINE OF CIRCLES AND FOREIGN POLICY

Nasser's doctrine of circles can help us understand the present arguments for Tanzania's restructured policies. In his "Philosophy of the Revolution"[26] Nasser spoke of the ties that made Egypt and the Arab and African "worlds" an integral and indivisible whole. This philosophy was in part a response to the British colonial attitude of treating the Sahara as a barrier between the Arab and African worlds. Nasser conceptualized Egyptian foreign policy in terms of three circles: the Arab, the African and the Islamic. Egypt's foreign policy under Nasser was able to operate effectively in the three circles and attempted to weld them together towards the achievement of its national interests. Whether he was successful or not is for history to judge. But the notion of circles at least provided Egypt with a conceptual framework through which to operate simultaneously and consistently in various regions.

Like Egypt, Tanzania could conceive of its international relations in terms of circles as a basis for foreign policy orientation. The country's rich historical past and fairly diversified economic, political and social interests should give it the flexibility to operate simultaneously in various regions. Here, we identify major circles and within each circle we also identify sub-circles within which Tanzania could develop associations.

First the African Circle: The African system as a subordinate system within the international system is important for a number of reasons. First, a united Africa would constitute a fairly powerful sub-system within international forums and its power could be felt at different levels of negotiations and on issues ranging from such problems as the IMF and debt rescheduling to military bases and commodity prices. Indeed, such a situation would compensate for the powerlessness of individual states and it would minimize the tendency of foreign powers to deal with issues on a bilateral basis, taking advantage of the weaknesses of individual states. Second, some bilateral relations and foreign policy goals of African states are being negated by those of others. Thus bilateral relations could be enhanced by the unity prevailing within a broader African circle. we do not argue that Africa should strive for harmony and a situation where no conflicts occur. Such a position would be utopian. There are bound to be conflicts and tensions prevailing within the African circle as a whole, but such problems should not prevent an attempt to reach a consensus over a small range of vitally important issues, especially vis-a-vis international relations, which affect most African countries. These issues can range from the problems of debt rescheduling and foreign military bases to those of apartheid. Nyerere had always placed grater emphasis on Africa as an important area of promoting good relations and cooperation. As he stated: "Events in Africa are of even greater and more direct relevance to us."[27] Tanzania's conception of African interests has become a strong factor in its foreign policy. For instance its independence address to the UN on 14 December 1961 contained four aims, which were:

a)   A recognition of the fundamental importance of the UN in for a peaceful world.

130

b)   Our basic and continued opposition to colonialism
      anywhere in our continent and in any other part of
      the world.

c)   The attainment of African unity to avoid conflicts
      between independent states as well as to strengthen
      the continent in the war against poverty, ignorance
      and disease. And

d)   Internationally, we believe that we have entered a
      world driven by ideological dissensions. We are
      anxious to keep out of these disputes, and anxious
      to see that the nations of our continent are not
      used as pawns in conflicts which very often do not
      concern them at all.[28]

These aims covered issues of peace in the world, support
of liberation struggles throughout the world, the promotion
of African unity based on consensus and of promotion of
developmental goals, and the principles of non-alignment.
These policy aims, however, could only be fully and
meaningfully implemented if other African states were also to
implement them and if they were to be adopted by the whole
continent. Bilateral implementations of such policies become
ineffective if neighboring countries do not adhere to the
same principles.   It is necessary to divide the subsystem of
the African subordinate state system (circle) into more
manageable sub-circles for purposes of operations.   Also,
events taking place in these sub-systems affect, in turn, the
African subordinate state system (the circle).
      Second, the East African sub-circle: Relations with
other African states cannot substitute for the necessity of
East African cooperation. Tanzania is closely affected by
the events taking place in these neighbors. The 1960s scene
of peaceful co-existence, and cooperation which characterized
these east African states turned nasty in the 1970s, creating
conflicts throughout the region.   Tanzania's physical
security was invaded by Uganda, leading to war, after which
Tanzania suffered economic dislocation as the result of the
manner in which the East African Community was broken.
Ideological conflicts between Kenya and Tanzania continued
through the late-1970s.   These problems created political
tensions and feelings of perceived threats.[29] In the 1980s
the East African states have attempted to reestablish
dialogue and cooperation to maintain regional stability and
cooperation.
      East Africa had been historically developed as one

region, with countries sharing a number of common features including joint economic ventures such as the railways and harbors, language, and the people were (and remain) close ethnically and intellectually. These characteristics can be used to strengthen other ties and create strong identity and pride among East Africans. Within this context Tanzania is well placed as the geopolitical fulcrum of East Africa. From North to South, Tanzania is geographically located as a transit center. The country also has the necessary infrastructure of roads, sea, air and rail links. In terms of trade, Tanzania is also strategically located as the center from the Preferential Trade Area (PTA), as well as for SADCC. These factors lend it additional advantages which could be used to enhance foreign policy and economic development.

Third, the Horn of Africa as a sub-circle is equally important because of its proximity to East Africa. In particular, Kenya is more directly affected by events in the Horn than other East African states. It borders Somalia with which it has been involved in a war of attrition over the North Eastern Province, and it entered into a military treaty with Ethiopia in 1964 aimed primarily at Somalia. Because of its close proximity and border conflicts with Somalia and potential border difficulties with Ethiopia, Kenya, in the mid-1970s, perceived itself to have been surrounded by pro-Russian socialist regimes – Somalia, with which it had been having a constant war of attrition over the North Eastern Province; Sudan of 1969 under Numeiri announced socialism; and the overthrow of Haile Selassie in 1974 who was replaced by a socialist government – which led it, among other reasons, to allow the US a military base in Mombasa. Thus, Kenya's response to these events in the Horn can also affect Tanzania's attitude.

Second, the events taking place in the Horn of Africa, the war between Ethiopia and Somalia, and foreign involvements in that region introduced a process of destabilization which weakens the bargaining position of Africa and creates tensions in the region.

Third, the Horn is important because it holds a strategic position in air space in relation to East Africa. Planes from the Middle East or Europe to East Africa have to fly over the Horn of Africa. Horn states can intercept these planes. For instance, Israeli planes involved in the Entebbe raid could have been intercepted. Sudan intercepted Libya's planes which had gone to assist Idi Amin's regime. This makes the Horn of Africa very strategic and creates a vital link with East Africa, especially in times of crisis. Its position in relation to the Red Sea is also important, since it gives it a critical ocean. Again, in times of crisis, the role the states at the Horn may play, would be crucial for East Africa.

Fourth, the Southern African sub-circle, has been, as we have seen in this chapter, an important area of operations for Tanzania. The post-Nkomati period does not diminish its significance. SADCC has introduced a new dimension of economic cooperation, which needs to be further developed as a means of enhancing greater economic cooperation. Despite the present crisis, it is imperative that the Front Line States do not lose momentum and that periodic meetings to discuss the foreign economic and security issues within the Southern African sub-circle continue to take place. Areas for joint action, though limited, could be pursued and joint policy statements in international forums should not be given up.

Fifth, the West African sub-circle: It is important in diplomacy and negotiations to enhance the position and bargaining power of the Eastern and Southern African states in international relations. However, within this circle, Nigeria appears to be the sleeping giant; an attempt to involve it increasingly in this region, as has been happening, is a positive step towards increasing the bargaining positions of these states vis-a-vis the international community. Of the African states, Nigeria's voice carries more weight with Western countries because of its strategic position in West Africa, economically and politically. Since most of the events in the Southern, Eastern and Horn do not bear directly on Nigeria's own internal politics, it is advisable to increase Nigeria's participation and action in these regions.

Sixth, the Afro-Arab circle: African integration with Arab countries is a historical fact. In East Africa, this interaction resulted in the emergence of Islam, Swahili, civilization, architecture and law.[30] Tanzania is potentially well placed to develop this circle. It has the largest Muslim population in East, Central and Southern Africa, which is a constituency for Arab-Muslim interest in the country. In Egypt, Kuwait, Yemen, Saudi Arabia, Oman and United Arab Emirates there are a significant number of people of Tanzanian descent and nationals who could be cultivated as lobbying groups for Tanzanian interests.

In addition to these advantages, there are common interests which bind the Afro-Arab circle, namely the liberation struggles of both Southern Africa and Palestine. Despite a number of historical and contemporary interests which unite Tanzania with the Arab world, the former has instead chosen to promote greater forms of activity with the

Western countries. For instance, Shaw and Msabaha's study of Tanzania's pattern of student enrollments abroad, international treaties, foreign aid, arms imports, foreign trade and foreign investment, reveal that it has been heavily dependent on Western capitalist nations.[31] Thus, despite Nyerere's pronouncements on and encouragement of South-South dialogue, linkage with the North has been more pronounced.

Over the last decade, Arab countries have become an important source of foreign aid. In 1974, Tanzania received a total of $48,355m commitments, of which $14.2 million was concessional. In 1983, Tanzania received 200,000 barrels of oil from Libya alone, worth about $55m in loan form. Both oil and foreign exchange are in high demand in Tanzania and the Arab world can provide them.

Tanzania would need to develop more strenuously the Afro-Arab circle in the OAU, the Arab League, and the Afro-Arab Bank and work out a programme for bilateral and multilateral relations as well as activities. Such cooperation could cover political, diplomatic, economic, financial, commercial, educational, cultural, scientific, technical and information fields.

Seventh, the Indian Ocean circle: This is another circle which needs to be conceptualized in its totality. Again, history, trade and migration have always linked the people of East Africa with those in the Indian Ocean states. The Western Indian Ocean stretches from the Horn to Southern Africa, and includes the islands of Seychelles, Comoros, Mauritius and Madagascar. The Eastern Indian Ocean encompasses India, Sri Lanka and Western Australia. Problems of economic development and the militarization of the Indian Ocean by foreign powers have introduced new dangers and concerns which the Indian Ocean community needs to consider seriously, as well as explore areas for cooperation in various fields.[32]

And finally, eighth, the European Circle: Tanzania has always maintained relations with the governments of Western countries. Here we call attention to the need to develop relations with political parties which may be more sympathetic to the problems facing the continent and region, especially in relation to the liberation struggles of Southern Africa. Another important avenue to explore is the increasing number of mass-oriented organizations such as the anti-apartheid and anti-nuclear movements which have sprung up throughout Western societies. These movements can be linked to similar concerns in our region and can be vigorously supported because, given the democratic structures of Western Europe, mass oriented organizations can have an effective role to play in the voting patterns as well as in support of specific political parties. Thus, in the long run, progressive political parties, as well as progressive mass movements could be useful actors for diplomatic and economic support.   Another important actor is the EEC. Attention could be given to consolidating relations with the EEC.

Tanzania needs to operate in all these circles simultaneously and try to weld them together.   One advantage which Tanzania has is its relative stability in the continent and its strongly identified position as a no-aligned nation. It could use these two factors to try and promote goals which would be acceptable to a number of these circles because of their mutuality of interests.   While in the 1960s, when Tanzania was often prepared to break from the group and 'go it alone', so to speak, in the 1980s Tanzania could become the spokesman for consensus. More emphasis could be given to intraregional development schemes, so that more countries become integrated into Tanzania, making her a central focus. However, to achieve this frontal approach towards integrated regional political, economic, diplomatic and strategic interests, Tanzania would have to develop her own economic base strenuously and introduce a work and moral ethos which would regain credibility and legitimacy.

CONCLUSIONS: RESTRUCTURING FOREIGN POLICY

Recent events in Southern Africa should compel Tanzania to attempt to restructure its entire foreign policy, especially on the problem of decolonization and racism.   As mentioned earlier, such a foreign policy review is not without precedent. In Why Nations Realign[33] it was suggested that states reorient their foreign policies when old patterns no longer serve their national interests.   Bhutan, Canada, Burma, China, Chile and Tanzania were used as case studies to support this thesis. Indeed the factors which accounted for Tanzania's attempted foreign policy reorientation then-regional conjuncture – are quite similar to the present situation in terms of the threats they posed to the country's national security, stability and economic development.

Between 1961 and 1966 Tanzania was faced with economic and diplomatic pressure from its major economic mentors. These problems precipitated its determination to recast external ties. In the post-Nkomati period the non-military threats implied in the possible isolation of Tanzania from the rest of SADCC and the FLS are compounded by direct military and security threats posed by South African policies of destabilization.   Foreign policy restructuring in this instance is even more inevitable. For, in the previous period, one of the decisive factors in reviewing foreign policy was the concern of the primary policy-maker (Nyerere) about the extent of foreign penetration, vulnerability to outside economic preserves, and lack of autonomy in government decision-making.[34] By 1966, Nyerere became convinced that if Tanzania were to overcome underdevelopment and pursue an effective foreign policy there had to be a major and radical redefinition of the country's development objectives and strategies for pursuing them. The Arusha Declaration of 1967 was a product of this search for a viable strategy in Tanzania's foreign and development policy.[35]

Thus Nnoli aptly contends:

> The crisis of the first diplomatic phase fundamentally undermined Tanzania's general orientation to the external environment. A new approach was imperative. Although after each crisis the nation made relevant but specific changes in its external relations, it was necessary to rationalize these reforms within a broader framework ... Such a framework would provide a more comprehensive and structured national participation in international affairs. Obviously, in the light of the close interrelationships between external conditions and domestic relations was necessary if the projected alternations in external relations were to yield the desired results.[36]

In the post-1967 period, the government sought to reduce vulnerability by diversifying foreign trade, but the data over a ten year period indicate only marginal improvement. To date, Tanzania remains firmly within the Western economic orbit. Where the country may have achieved some success is in the area of political and cultural autonomy. Tanzania has been able to maintain political autonomy, including the ability to direct its meager resources towards nationally-determined priorities.[37] However, this is all that can be said. The country's general economic record is a disaster. It is in these circumstances that Tanzania's foreign policy must now operate within a more complex and difficult regional environment. First, economic difficulties and constraints create a more complex situation in regional politics, making foreign policy goals more difficult to achieve. And second, the increasing participation and domination of South Africa in regional politics also adds to the complexities of economic cooperation, trade, security, and defense matters as mentioned earlier.

In appraising the present situation, Tanzania must

recognize historical conjunctures in international diplomacy
and the efficacy of certain techniques in this regard.   In
the 1960s and 1970s, Tanzania enjoyed a high intellectual and
philosophical profile.   The assumption was that the
liberation of Mozambique and other Southern African states
would create a bandwagon effect advancing the freedom of
Namibia and South Africa, as well as the economic development
of Tanzania and the FLS.   South Africa and the major Western
powers were then largely on the defensive.   The Nkomati
Accord regains the initiative for these countries.   By
bringing Mozambique and possibly Angola into a negotiated
non-aggression pact, South Africa has forced these countries
to focus attention on the narrow conception of the survival
of their regimes, and has exposed Tanzania's fundamental
weakness - economic mismanagement and lack of contiguity to
South Africa and Namibia, the present theaters of liberation
struggle.

The implication of the Nkomati Accord for the liberation
process and development objectives is that this entente makes
old techniques historically transient.   In turn, this
constitutes the motive force for the restructuring of foreign
policy in Tanzania.

NOTES

1.   J. Hartmann, "Economic Dependence and Foreign
Policy: the case of Tanzania," African Review 7(3 and 4),
1977, p. 70.
2.   Agreement on Non-Aggression and Good Neighbourliness
between the Government of the Republic of South Africa and
the Government of the People's Republic of Mozambique, 16
March 1984.
3.   K.J. Holsti (ed), Why Nations Realign: foreign
policy restructuring in post-war world, (London: George
Allen & Unwin, 1982).
4.   Confidential interview with a high ranking
government official, Dar es Salaam, June 1984.
5.   Holsti, Why Nations Realign, p. 4.
6.   See Catherine Hoskyns, "Africa's Foreign Relations:
the case of Tanzania," International Affairs, 44(3), July
1968, pp. 446-462; Julius K. Nyerere, Freedom and Unity, (Dar
es Salaam: Oxford University Press, 1966), The Arusha
Declaration, (Dar es Salaam: Government Printer, 1967), and
"Non-Alignment in the 1970s", (Dar es Salaam: Government
Printer, 1970); Nnoli, Self Reliance and Foreign Policy in
Tanzania; Jeannette Hartmann, "Economic Dependence and
Foreign Policy: the case of Tanzania"; and Timothy M. Shaw
and Ibrahim S.R. Msabaha, "Tanzania: from dependence to

diversification, 1967-1977" in Holsti Why Nations Realign, pp. 47-72.

7. George T. Yu, China's African Policy: A Study of Tanzania, (New York: Praeger, 1975), p. 102.

8. See Jeannette Hartmann, Development Policy Making in Tanzania, (Ph.D. Dissertation, University of Hull, 1983).

9. The Lusaka Manifesto on Southern Africa, 1969.

10. See, "The Organization of African Unity and the Freedom Struggle, A Document presented by the Government of Tanzania at the OAU Summit Conference at Addis Ababa, June 1971." For a critical discussion of the Tanzanian position paper see Yash Tandon, "The Organization of African Unity and the Principle of Universality of Membership," African Review, 1(4), April 1972, p. 52-60.

11. The Mogadishu Declaration, Mogadishu, 20 October 1971, para 13.

12. President Nyerere's Opening Speech to the OAU Conference of OAU Foreign Ministers in Dar es Salaam. Reprinted in Daily News (Tanzania) 8 April 1975; also in, Nathan Shamuyarira (comp.) Documents and Speeches on the OAU Strategy for Liberating Southern Africa (University of Dar es Salaam, Mimeo, 1975), p. 53. See also Shamuyarira, "African Strategy in Southern Africa," Tanzania Position Paper, pp. 56-84.

13. "Economic Dependence and Foreign Policy."

14. See the American National Security Memorandum on Southern Africa prepared by the National Security Council Interdepartmental Group for Africa, under the direction of Dr. Henry Kissinger, 1969.

15. See Amon Nsekela (ed), Southern Africa: toward economic liberation, (London: Rex Collings, 1981).

16. Report of the Mozambican National Planning Commission, Maputo 1984.

17. Ibid.

18. Horace Campbell, "Total Strategy and the Total Failure of White Supremacy in South Africa," (University of Dar es Salaam, Mimeo, 1983).

19. See Simon Jenkins, "Regional Stability in Southern Africa," Optima 32, July 1984, pp. 52-55.

20. Solidarity News Service, 27 April 1984.

21. Tandon, "The Organization of African Unity and the Principle of Universality of Membership," p. 53.

22. Ibid.

23. See OAU Resolution, CM/Res. 175-XII, p. 2, Addis Ababa, February 1969.

24. Tandon, "The Organization of African Unity and the Principle of Universality of Membership," pp. 59-60.

25. See Ibrahim Msabaha, The Anatomy of Tanzania's

138

Diplomacy in the Third United Nations Conference on the Law of the Sea: seabed EEZ Negotiations (unpublished Ph.D. Dissertation, Dalhousie University, 1982), pp. 1–4.
26. See Gamal Nasser, "The Philosophy of the Revolution" in Paul E. Sigmund (ed), The Ideologies of the Developing Nations, (New York: Praeger, 1969. See also Jeannette Hartmann, "Nasser's Africanist Policy," (University of Dar es Salaam, Mimeo, 1979).
27. J. Nyerere, Policy on Foreign Affairs. 1967, 8, Dar es Salaam.
28. J. Nyerere, Freedom and Unity, (Dar es Salaam: OUP, 1966), pp. 153–4.
29. Katele Orwa, "From Disequilibrium to Equilibrium: Kenya inter-state relations in Eastern Africa." (Nairobi University, Department of Government, Mimeo).
30. Saleh Abu-Osba, Afro-Arab Centricity: A model for Development Communication, (Ottawa: Jerusalem International Publishing House, 1982).
31. Shaw and Msabaha, "From Dependence to Diversification: Tanzania, 1967–1977" in Holsti et. al., Why Nations Realign.
32. Jeannette Hartmann, "The Nkomati Accord and the Littural states of the Western Indian Ocean." Paper presented at the International Conference on Indian Ocean Studies 11, Perth, Western Australia, 1984.
33. Holsti et. al., Why Nations Realign.
34. Ibid., p. 212.
35. Cranford Pratt, The Critical Phase in Tanzania. 1945-1968: Nyerere and the emergence of a socialist strategy (Cambridge: Cambridge University Press, 1976), pp. 3–4.
36. Nnoli, Self-Reliance and Foreign Policy, cited in Msabaha, The Anatomy of Tanzania's Diplomacy, p. 22.
37. For details see Shaw and Msabaha, "Tanzania: From Dependence to Diversification."

PART THREE

Regional Integration:
SADCC and PTA

8. Regional Economic Integration and the Liberation Struggle in Southern Africa

D.A.K. Mbogoro

INTRODUCTION

... The independent states of Southern Africa have chosen to go forward in solidarity and to coordinate their efforts towards economic liberation. This is a momentous decision with consequences which stretch far into our future.[1]

Regional economic integration of adjoining national economies is generally believed to be a powerful means of promoting economic development besides leading to other desirable ends like peace and security. In general regional economic integration is credited, on a priori grounds, with facilitating industrial development and technical progress, expansion of trade leading to better use of existing productive capacity, greater bargaining power in negotiations with third parties and an improvement of political relations among nations. Regional economic integration among developing countries helps to attract foreign capital, which is essential for easing foreign exchange bottlenecks.

Regional economic integration may take many forms ranging from a very loose form of economic integration, whereby member countries agree to cooperate in trade matters by giving preferential treatment to each others' products, to tighter arrangements under which countries agree to have a supra-national body which manages the economic affairs of member countries. The strongest form of regional economic integration involves, as a matter of necessity, political union. In between these two extreme forms of regional integration there is a plethora of regional schemes. The most notable forms are: a) a free trade area under which

The paper was written before the author was appointed Minister of State for Finance and Economic Planning in Tanzania in November 1985.

member countries abolish all import duties on goods trade with one another but each member country retains its import duties against non-members; b) a customs union whereby member countries establish common import duties on products emanating from third parties in addition to having a free trade area; c) a common market whereby members of a customs union also agree to allow free movement of factors of production from one member country to another; and d) an economic union under which members of a common market agree to harmonize their monetary and fiscal policies.

Regional integration in the above forms is generally regarded as 'market based' economic integration. Economic development is attained by unleashing market forces in member countries forming the scheme. This is the classical view of regional economic integration; and it is based on the experiences of arrangements among developed Western economies.

Experiences of regional economic integration schemes among developing countries show that such schemes can take other forms, but with the same objective of promoting economic development. The most notable form is what is known as 'integration by projects.' Under this arrangement member countries agree to implement certain projects which would enhance their economic capabilities and facilitate economic development. In this case, trade is not considered to be the primum mobile of economic development. Another form of economic integration by projects involves rationalization of the productive capacities of member countries so as to reduce unnecessary duplication of capacity (in a situation of scarce resources - particularly foreign exchange) and establish complementarity. Integration by projects is sometimes described as the planning approach to economic integration mainly because it is similar to that adopted by the CMEA (Council for Mutual Economic Assistance) member countries of Eastern Europe and the USSR.

The general conclusion arrived at by a good number of scholars[2] on regional economic integration among developing countries is that the market, or trade liberalization, approach has had a very marginal impact on the economic growth of member countries; it has actually resulted in serious distributional problems which have finally contributed to the collapse of such integration schemes. Evidence cited in this respect includes the East African Federation among many others. The general thrust now is that if regional economic integration schemes among developing countries, particularly in Africa, are to bring about economic development the project approach to regional integration should be adopted. As Reginald H. Green aptly makes the point:

> ... the Common Market approach to developing country
> economic integration has a poor track-record; therefore
> the identification of a series of common interests and a
> network of coordinated national and regional initiatives
> to achieve them has a stronger analytical and practical
> justification than absence of feasibility of a customs
> union ...[4]

This chapter addresses the issue of modalities of
regional economic integration schemes among Southern African
countries which will enhance the chances of successful
liberation struggle. Although it focuses on the form of
regional schemes, which stand a better chance of bringing
about economic liberation of the already politically
independent countries in Southern Africa, it will also
discuss the 'spill-over effects' of this economic liberation
on the political liberation struggle being waged against
South Africa in respect of both Namibia and apartheid South
Africa itself.

The rest of the chapter consists of four sections.
Section II deals with the nature of economic dependence of
the independent Southern African countries; Section III
outlines regional economic integration arrangements already
in existence in Southern Africa; Section IV discusses the
role of regional economic integration in the liberation
struggle in Southern Africa; and Section V consists of
concluding remarks and recommendations.

THE NATURE OF DEPENDENCE OF SOUTHERN AFRICAN COUNTRIES ON SOUTH AFRICA

Among African countries South Africa has a highly
industrialized and diversified economy. It is well-advanced
in energy production, transport and communications,
agricultural and industrial goods, research and development,
and military hardware. There are the facts confronting
independent Southern African countries; and there is very
little that can be done about them at the moment.

Some of the economic performance figures, which do not
include those of the "homeland" republics, are as follows:
a) by 1981 South Africa employed about 300,000 workers from
Southern African states (excluding Tanzania); b) in 1980
South Africa accounted for 77% of total Southern Africa
region GNP (excluding Tanzania) - this translated into a per
capita income which was about eight times that of Mozambique,

four times that of Zambia and 3.6 times that of Zimbabwe in
the same year; c) in 1980 South Africa accounted for 77% of
electricity generated in the region, 97% of coal mined, 98%
of iron ore mined, 70% of maize grown, 87% of wheat grown,
39% of cattle stock and 80% of sheep stock reared in the
region.[5]

South Africa's links with the Southern African states
vary from country to country depending largely on proximity.
Botswana, Lesotho and Swaziland (BLS) are closely linked
because they are members of the Southern African Customs
Union (SACU). Malawi, Mozambique, Zambia and Zimbabwe have
economic and other links with South Africa, which vary in
degrees. Tanzania and Angola, largely because of the
distance factor have very limited links. Of the many
regional economic links with South Africa, the most important
ties are trade, transport and communications and labor.

Labor Dependence

For many years South Africa has been a major source of
employment for countries in Southern Africa. In 1980 there
were 360,000 workers from the Southern African states.
Foreign labor constituted about 44% of total labor in the
mining sector. By June 1981 there were 301,178 workers from
Southern African states.

Table 8-1
South Africa's Trade with African Countries

	1973	1977	1980	1981
Exports (%)	14.1	5.6	5.7	5.7
Imports (%)	5.8	5.6	2.0	1 . 7

Source: Africa Insight, 13(1) 1983, 75-76.

Dependence on Transport Network

The transport system in Southern Africa is dominated by
the South African Transport Services (SATS). Six of the nine
independent Southern African states are landlocked (Botswana,
Swaziland, Lesotho, Zimbabwe, Zambia and Malawi). These
countries rely on intra-regional transport facilities to
reach overseas markets. Countries like Lesotho, Zimbabwe,
Botswana and Swaziland and, to a significant extent, Zambia,
rely heavily on South African transport networks.

It may be argued that South Africa in this sense
relieves the Southern African states of an unemployment
problem. It may also be argued that these migrant workers

provide their home countries with foreign exchange through home remittance of their earnings (estimated at R315 million in 1981). The issue, however, is the dependence that is created for the independent Southern African states on South Africa, whose apartheid policy constitutes a serious crime against humanity. It is comforting to note that the Southern African states have decided to tackle this problem. At a meeting in Gaborone in 1980, seven of the SADCC states (excluding Tanzania and Angola) agreed to form the South African Labor Commission (SALC) to harmonize and coordinate policies and practices with regard to the supply of migrant labor to South Africa. The aim of SALC is to reduce and ultimately eliminate the supply of such labor to South Africa.

Trade Dependence

Many of the Southern African states have strong trade links with South Africa. The strongest are between the BLS countries and South Africa because they are members of the Southern African Customs Union (SACU). Table 8-2 below shows the dependence of the Southern African states on South Africa.

Table 8-2
Trade with South Africa as percentage of
total trade – various years

Country	Year	Exports to SA	Imports from SA
Angola*	----	----	----
Botswana	1980	6.6	87.0
Lesotho+	----	----	----
Malawi	1980	3.3	37.3
Mozambique	1977	6.2	19.5
Swaziland	1976	19.8	90.3
Zambia	1981	21.6	27.5

*It is estimated that about 80% of Angola's trade with African countries in 1980 was with South Africa.
+At least 90% of Lesotho's imports originate from South Africa.
Source: Africa Insight, 13(1), 1983, 78.

In recent years, South Africa has been handling a large proportion of foreign trade with Zaire, Zambia and Zimbabwe. About 70% of Zambia's rail cargo, about 60% of Malawi's exports, and about 70% of Zimbabwe's traffic goes through

South Africa.

Moreover, the railway administrations of the adjoining independent Southern African states are linked to the SATS through longstanding business agreements. These agreements aimed at: regulating and facilitating the flow of traffic and the interchange of rolling stock; provision of rolling stock, common accounting procedures, clearance of credits and debits, repair and maintenance of equipment and hire charges thereon plus other related matters.

Dependence in other areas

South Africa interacts with the Southern African states in energy supply, water supply, monetary issues and marketing of products overseas. Mozambique and South Africa, for example, sell each other hydropower; Lesotho has a plan to sell water to South Africa; Swaziland and Lesotho are members of the Rand Monetary Area (RMA); and some South African based companies (like de Beers) market overseas most of the diamonds mined in Southern African countries.

In conclusion, it is worth noting that the dependence of the independent Southern African states on South Africa is a well-established fact. Both the Southern African states and South Africa are aware of this. Because of the antagonistic political philosophies of the two groups of countries, a situation of dependence of one group on another puts the dependent group (the Southern African states) on a very weak footing. Dependence in this case must be reduced to the bare minimum.

REGIONAL ECONOMIC INTEGRATION SCHEMES IN SOUTHERN AFRICA

Several regional economic integration arrangements are in operation within the Southern African region. These integration schemes have come into being at different times during the 20th century. The Southern African Customs Union (SACU) and the Rand Monetary Area (RMA) are the oldest. Other regional integration groups which have come into existence in recent years are: a) the Constellation of Southern African States (CONSAS); b) the Southern African Development Coordination Conference (SADCC); and c) the Preferential Trade Area (PTA).

Southern African Customs Union

SACU is a regional economic integration scheme which brings together South Africa and the BLS countries. It dates from 1910. This customs arrangement was renegotiated in 1969 after BLS had attained independence. At present the customs area includes Namibia and links the three economically small and weak BLS countries to South Africa. The potential negative effects of such an arrangement (polarization effects) have been recognized. South Africa has agreed to an arrangement of fiscal compensation to the losing member countries. Revenue collected on imports from non-member countries is divided up among members on the basis of the relative importance of imports into each of the BLS countries, as well as the amount of dutiable goods produced and consumed. In addition, the share of the revenue is increased by 42% to compensate the BLS countries for the fact that the common external tariff is largely decided upon by South Africa and is geared to protect South African industries. Moreover, the treaty allows the BLS countries to protect their domestic industries by imposing tariffs on manufactured products from the industrially strong South Africa.

Because of the political differences between South Africa and the BLS countries the latter have recently questioned the usefulness of the customs union. The main advantage is the substantial revenue they receive annually: in 1982-83 Botswana received 120m, Lesotho 77m and Swaziland 118 million rand. On the other hand BLS membership in SACU affects their external relations. Although the BLS countries have been able to join PTA and SADCC they are prevented from granting tariff preferences.

Rand Monetary Area

SACU member countries have also been members of the Rand Monetary Area from 1910 to 1974. Since 1974 only Lesotho, Swaziland and South Africa are members as Botswana left it in 1974 and established its own currency, the Pula. Lesotho and Swaziland have their own currencies too - the Loti (1979) and Lilangeni (1974), respectively - which are at par with the rand, which remains legal tender in those countries. The monetary union entails free transfer of capital within the region with the proviso that Lesotho and Swaziland may impose restrictions if there is a detrimental outflow of capital to South Africa.

Constellation of Southern African States

The idea of a "Constellation" of states was first raised by the South African Minister of Foreign Affairs in March 1979, and was announced as a formal "CONSAS" proposal by the

148

South African Prime Minister that November. The CONSAS proposal includes any country in Southern Africa wishing to expand relationships and regional cooperation. Countries which were mentioned in the proposal are independent homelands, members of SACU and, in due course, other countries in the region.

The CONSAS concept embodies both economic and political objectives; it is a direct outcome of the policy of separate development which has resulted in the creation of independent homelands. Other factors which have contributed to this concept include: the deterioration in South Africa's relations with the Western allies, the so-called threat of communism in Southern Africa, the need to harmonize economic policies, and the desire to find solutions to problems facing the region.

The idea of CONSAS does not seem to have taken off the ground. The reasons are obvious. In the case of the independent homelands they are already members of a very close relationship; and so are the BLS countries. It would be embarrassing to the BLS countries to enter into a special CONSAS treaty when their existing links are questioned by other independent African countries.

Southern African Development Coordination Conference

The first steps to establish SADCC were taken in July 1979 at a conference in Arusha, Tanzania. At the conference the five Front Line States - Angola, Botswana, Tanzania, Mozambique and Zambia - decided to establish a new economic alliance in Southern Africa, particularly to:

a) reduce economic dependence, particularly but not only, on the Republic of South Africa;

b) forge links to create a genuine and equitable regional interaction;

c) mobilize resources to promote the implementation of national, interstate and regional policies; and

d) to secure international cooperation within the framework of a concerted strategy for economic liberation.

SADCC was formed in March 1980 with the Lusaka Declaration by Heads of State and Government of Angola, Botswana, Lesotho, Malawi, Mozambique, Swaziland, Tanzania, Zambia and Zimbabwe. The organizational structure of SADCC is as follows: i) the Summit is the supreme body consisting of heads of state and government; ii) the Council consists of one minister from each member country; iii) sectoral Commissions - established in specific functional areas; iv) Standing Committee of officials, consisting of members from each country; and v) a Secretariat, established in July 1982 to service SADCC and to coordinate SADCC activities.

Each member country has been assigned a specific sector to coordinate: transport and communications (Mozambique); energy resources i.e. coal, oil and hydroelectricity (Angola); harmonization and trade (Tanzania); food production and distribution (Zimbabwe); agricultural research (Botswana); manpower development and training (Swaziland); fisheries and wildlife development (Malawi); soil conservation and land utilization (Lesotho); and Southern African Development Fund and mining (Zambia).

The SADCC approach to regional economic integration is that of "functionalism" i.e. start with concrete projects on a limited scale and then expand areas of interaction. SADCC is based on pragmatism, decentralization and consensus in decision-making. SADCC has tried to avoid establishing massive bureaucratic institutions, the way the EAC was run, for example. This has the objective of improving efficiency and reducing expense.

The SADCC concept has indeed taken root among the member countries and as a project it has taken-off the ground and could be said to be air-borne. Notable success has been recorded in the transport sector where several projects have been or are in the process of being implemented. SADCC has also been able to improve the region's bargaining power; witness the many donors who show up at the donors' conferences. SADCC has been able to register such successes largely because of starting with clear and well-articulated objectives. Professor Green aptly summarizes this point:

> ... SADCC does have two central strategic themes: reduction of external dependence, especially on South Africa (a goal not seen in terms of autarchy); and building up their economies along lines which meet the basic human needs of their citizens more fully. The strategic operational principle applied to relating these goals to SADCC's work has been that of critical common interests i.e. areas in which all participating (which can be less than all SADCC member states) see a clear benefit to acting jointly rather than severally.[7]

Even the enemies of SADCC have admitted that so far the integration scheme is definitely a success:

There can be little doubt that SADCC is shaping up to be a much more formidable organization than South Africa's confederation of black ruled states. That said, dependence on South Africa will continue for the foreseeable future.[8]

And again, another South African scholar confirms SADCC's success:

Compared with most other African regionalization schemes, the objects of the SADCC are fairly realistic, and given political will in the leadership of member states, they might succeed in establishing and running some common training and research facilities ...[9]

In spite of these notable successes SADCC has problems: a) historical inheritance of structurally deformed economies since colonial times; b) South Africa's destabilization, particularly in Mozambique, Angola and Zimbabwe; c) impact of international economic crises on fragile national economies; and d) problems related to establishing an effective functional regional integration scheme. The task is made more difficult because of lack of adequate funding and skilled indigenous personnel. Indeed one of the objectives of SADCC is to enhance the capability of member-countries to deal with these problems.

Preferential Trade Area

The PTA is a brainchild of the UN Economic Commission for Africa (ECA), which has acted on OAU resolutions calling for an African common market by the year 2000. An economic community for the Eastern and Southern African region would finally lead to the formation of an all-African economic community. PTA potentially includes 20 countries – Ethiopia, Djibouti, Somalia, Kenya, Uganda, Rwanda, Burundi, Madagascar, Seychelles, Mauritius, Comoros and the nine SADCC countries. Countries which have signed the treaty establishing PTA by now are Ethiopia, Djibouti, Somalia, Kenya, Uganda, Rwanda, Burundi, Tanzania, Zambia, Zimbabwe, Lesotho and Swaziland, Mauritius and Seychelles.
The objective of PTA is to

... promote cooperation in the fields of trade, customs, industry, transport, communications, agriculture, natural resources and monetary affairs with the aim of raising the standards of living of its peoples' of fostering closer relations among its member states and to contribute to the progress and development of the African continent. (PTA treaty article 13). Article 12 of the same treaty states that a common market within which customs duties or other charges will be progressively eliminated and a common customs tariff established is the final objective.

The treaty was concluded in 1981 and became effective in June 1982. Among the achievements of PTA to date include the establishment of the PTA headquarters in Lusaka, Zambia and a clearing house in Harare, Zimbabwe, using a special unit of account – the UPTA (1 UPTA = 1 SDR).

The PTA approach to regional economic integration is the market approach. PTA brings together about twenty countries which differ not only in geographical, demographic and economic aspects but also in socio-political backgrounds. When relatively industrialized and economically diversified countries like Zimbabwe and Kenya are lumped together in a common market with impoverished countries like Somalia and Ethiopia one should expect that polarization effects will be strong. Redistributive measures through fiscal compensation must be entrenched in the common market treaty to safeguard the interests of the economically weak. Otherwise it will not take long before such a common market faces disintegration.

PTA covers a vast area from Djibouti in the North to Lesotho in the South. The poorly-developed transport and communications networks among African countries may mean serious administrative problems for the common market. Such issues must be tackled first if a common market is to function at all. Moreover, as I have argued in Section I, an economic integration scheme among developing countries based on trade liberalization produces marginal benefits by way of economic development to its members.

REGIONAL ECONOMIC INTEGRATION AND THE LIBERATION STRUGGLE

In Section II I discussed the nature of the Southern African states' dependence on South Africa. Section III analyzed the objectives of the various regional schemes already in existence in Southern Africa. This part discusses the role of economic integration in enhancing the liberation struggle in Southern Africa.

The word "liberation" is used to refer to economic as well as political liberation. In Southern Africa, the liberation struggle has two major fronts: the political and

the economic. All SADCC and PTA member countries have
already attained political independence, in the sense that
they have their own national flags and other symbols. For
these countries the liberation struggle is now to achieve
economic independence. In Section II we saw how most of the
SADCC countries are dependent on South Africa, a country
which pursues policies which are inimical to independent
Africa so the liberation struggle is primarily a struggle for
political independence for SWAPO in Namibia and for genuine
democracy based on racial equality in apartheid South Africa.
Once political independence is achieved in South Africa and
Namibia, the liberation struggle in these countries will also
come to focus on economic independence.

Can regional economic integration among Southern African
states improve the chances of successful liberation in
Southern Africa? In Section I, I pointed out that regional
integration can take many forms. I also argued that the form
of such integration of substantial benefit to members is that
which involves joint planning. In Section III, I outlined
the main integration schemes in existence in Southern Africa
with their main characteristics. Of the five schemes I
showed that three are based in South Africa and two are based
in the independent African countries. The objectives of
these two sets of schemes are thus at cross-purposes.

On the one hand, integration schemes whose members are
the independent Southern and Eastern African states aim at
isolating South Africa economically because of its crimes
against humanity. And, on the other hand, integration
schemes which are based in South Africa aim at expanding its
economic influence northwards to the independent African
countries. South Africa is interested in "rolling back"
(northwards) the frontiers of the liberation struggle. While
the independent countries are interested in "rolling forward"
(southward) the same frontiers. In both situations, regional
economic integration arrangements have been adopted. I argue
that the success of either independent Africa or South Africa
in rolling forwards or backwards the frontiers of the
liberation struggle will depend in both cases on the form of
regional economic integration adopted. In the following
penultimate part, I briefly review the contribution of each
of the integration schemes to the liberation struggle.

SADCC

SADCC and CONSAS came into being at the same time. Some
writers have argued that SADCC was established in response to
CONSAS while others would argue the reverse. We should
remember that the frontiers of the liberation struggle have

been changing over the years. When the Portuguese were in Angola and Mozambique and Ian Smith was in Rhodesia, South Africa was safe. The frontiers of the liberation struggle were then the borders between Tanzania and Mozambique, between Zambia and Southern Rhodesia, and between Angola and Zaire/Zambia. Angola and Mozambique under the Portuguese and Southern Rhodesia under Smith formed a "constellation of states" with South Africa. They held back the liberation struggle up to the time Portugal and Smith were defeated. On the other side, the Front Line States, mainly Tanzania and Zambia, were staunch supporters of the struggle.

The fall of Portugal in Angola and Mozambique and the fall of Smith in Southern Rhodesia (Zimbabwe) set the frontiers of the liberation struggle rolling south. The frontiers are now the following borders: Angola/South Africa, Botswana/South Africa, Zimbabwe/South Africa and Mozambique/South Africa. The Front Line States are now Tanzania, Zambia, Zimbabwe, Mozambique, Botswana and Angola. There is no doubt that the liberation struggle has gained in strength.

Having achieved political independence, the Southern African states have now turned to the struggle for economic independence, particularly from their arch-enemy, South Africa. SADCC was formed and comprises the nine independent African states. Three of these nine are very closely linked to South Africa through SACU. SADCC has deliberately avoided forming a regional scheme which is based on mere trade liberalization. Two reasons explain this: a) experience has shown that any regional economic scheme which is formed by developing countries and which is based on trade liberalization is likely to be short-lived; and b) the three BLS countries which are members of SACU would not have been able to join. SADCC has instead decided to concentrate on key areas of dependence on South Africa like transport, energy, food, etc. So far it has proved feasible for SADCC to implement projects in these areas. The argument here is that once the basic infrastructure has been laid cooperation in other areas like trade will be easy.

That SADCC is succeeding is proved by the reactions from South Africa. Destabilization measures directed at transport and energy networks in Mozambique, Angola and Zimbabwe are aimed at frustrating the SADCC countries in their efforts to break away from dependence on it. The frantic efforts made by South Africa to win friends from among SADCC members through accords, like Nkomati, show that its economic isolation, which is being achieved through SADCC, has begun to bite. SADCC is threatening to pull from right under South Africa's nose its longstanding trade partners like Zimbabwe,

Botswana, Lesotho and Swaziland.   SADCC is the regional
economic integration scheme which will greatly enhance and
accelerate the liberation struggle.

PTA

PTA is a very recent creation and from the start it has
suffered from two major shortcomings. First, it has no clear
set of priorities.   And second, it faces a serious
credibility gap.   Countries like Tanzania hesitated to join
it partly because of past experience with integration schemes
based on trade liberalization.   What will prevent PTA from
collapsing just as the East African Community did in 1977?
Further, the PTA is likely to enhance the economic power
and to reduce the economic isolation of South Africa.   So
far, South Africa is happy about the formation of PTA
because: i) BLS countries joining PTA are not required to
leave SACU (this is because provision has been made in the
PTA treaty to the effect that though BLS countries' products
will get preferential treatment in PTA member countries, BLS
countries need not reciprocate); and ii) South Africa is
known to have substantial investments in BLS countries and
Zimbabwe which are likely to benefit from PTA.   As far as
economic interests are concerned, PTA may end up being an
ally of South Africa and fit very well into the concept of an
"outer constellation" of states.

CONCLUSION

... A movement has begun which, if sustained, could in
time fundamentally change the economic direction of our
continent.[10]

In this chapter I have looked at the role of regional
integration in the liberation struggle in Southern Africa.
In Section I, I tried to establish the nature of a regional
economic scheme in developing countries which can bring about
development.   In Section II, I established the extent of
dependence of the Southern African states on South Africa;
major dependence is in transport and communications, trade,
labor and energy.   In Section III, I outlined the integration
schemes in existence in Southern Africa and their objects.
And in Section IV, I looked at the role that the existing
schemes in Southern Africa can play to strengthen the
liberation struggle.   I argued that SADCC and not PTA stands
a better chance of being a more effective instrument in this
struggle.

To end this chapter I would like to offer the following suggestions:

a) SADCC should be given all the support which liberation-minded peoples and nations can muster; and

b) regional economic integration schemes like PTA should be reviewed from time to time to make sure that they do not unwittingly frustrate the liberation struggle.

NOTES

1. From the late Sir Seretse Khama, SADCC's founder Chairman, in his introduction to "Southern Africa: Towards Economic Liberation, 1980".

2. See economists like Peter Robson, Economic Integration in Africa, (London: Allen and Unwin, 1968), p. 159; C.V. Vaitsos, "Crisis in Regional Economic Cooperation and Integration Among Developing Countries: a survey," World Development 6(6), June 1978, p. 746.

3. R.H. Green, "In praise of SADCC: from dependence and poverty towards economic liberation," in Colin Legum (ed), Africa Contemporary Record: Annual Survey and Documents 1981-82 14, (New York: Africana Publishing House, 1982), p. A98.

4. Southern African countries include Angola, Botswana, Lesotho, Malawi, Mozambique, Swaziland, Tanzania, Zambia and Zimbabwe. By South Africa I mean the so-called Republic of South Africa itself plus the so-called homeland republics of Bophuthatswana, Ciskei, Transkei and Venda. Figures related to economic performance, however, exclude these homelands.

5. These comparative figures do not include figures from Tanzania.

6. African Insight 13(1), 1983, p. 75 shows that in 1981, 64.8% of South Africa's exports of artificial resins and plastic materials and products, rubber, etc.; 60.3% of total exports of machinery and equipment; and 50.3% of total exports of articles of stone, glass, etc. went to African countries.

7. Green, "In praise of SADCC", p. 108.

8. Financial Times, (Johannesburg), 1981.

9. Theo Malan, "Regional Economic Cooperation in Southern Africa," Africa Insight 13(1), 1983, p. 50.

10. Khama, "Southern Africa".

9. The Implications of the Preferential Trade Area for Economic Integration in Eastern and Southern Africa

Hawa Sinare

INTRODUCTION

The Preferential Trade Area for Eastern and Southern Africa (PTA) was established in 1981 (after nine member states ratified the treaty), and started operating in July 1982.[1] Today, the PTA has about 15 members, including Burundi, Comoros, Ethiopia, Kenya, Lesotho, Malawi, Mauritius, Rwanda, Somalia, Swaziland, Tanzania, Uganda, Zaire, Zambia and Zimbabwe.[2] Tanzania is the newest member, having ratified the PTA treaty on 11 April 1985. About four potential members have yet to ratify it, namely Angola, Botswana, Mozambique and Seychelles. The PTA encompasses an area of 5,013,087 sq. km. with a population of more than 114 million.[3]

As a regional trade grouping, the PTA is not the first one. There have been many such groupings long before it was established. For instance, such organizations as the Southern African Customs Union, European Economic Community (EEC), African Caribbean and Pacific (ACP) countries associated with the EEC, European Free Trade Area, Latin American Free Trade Area, Australian New Zealand Free Trade Area, Arab Common Market, the defunct East African Community, West African Economic Community and Southern African Development Coordination Conference (SADCC), as well as the PTA, can be categorized as regional economic and trade groupings.[4]

These groupings derive from the concept of free trade area and custom unions, entities within which trade is freer than trade among countries outside them. Thus trade preference is accorded to members while non-members face higher tariff rates. This basically is contrary to the spirit of the General Agreement on Trade and Tariffs (GATT), to which many of the customs entities are parties, because it discriminates positively in trade.[5] Yet customs unions and free trade areas have been accepted by GATT as one of the exceptions to the rules of conduct of trade on the grounds that they are trade-creating.[6]

Article 24 of GATT permits the formation of either a custom union, a free trade area or an interim arrangement pending the establishment of either of the two. A customs union is an arrangement creating a single customs territory so that "substantially all" internal trade is free from duties and restrictions, providing for a common external tariff and uniform regulations.[7] The common external tariff must not be higher than the general incidence of the duties and regulations applicable in the territories before the formation of a union.[8]

A free trade area is also a customs territory in which duties and regulations on trade are reduced on "substantially all" trade, but more exceptions are permitted as specifically provided in Articles 11 to 15 and 20 of GATT. Thus a free trade area encourages an increase in the movement and volume of goods within it.[9] It is different from a customs union because there is no common external tariff, no intention of a closer economic integration, nor desire for a well coordinated commercial or industrial policy.[10]

The common goal of a custom union or a free trade area is to increase the volume of trade among members. This is good for trade because it raises the competitiveness of imports from within the wider territorial market against similar imports from outside. Therefore, preferential tariffs act as catalysts for the expansion of the industrial sectors of the members of the union or free trade area. However, this expansion is rather selective. Accordingly, a custom union or free trade area tends to develop the already more advanced of its members and underdevelop those whose economies are less advanced. But this is what competition is all about, only that it is harmful to any young industries of the lesser advanced members. Thus, in intra-regional trade, the less advanced members tend to face constant trade deficits while the more advanced members tend to get trade surplus. As such any expectations of "mutual benefit" in the literal meaning of the phrase are bound to be dispelled by the operations of the economic laws of motion.

Distinguished from customs unions and free trade areas is a preferential trade arrangement. Such an arrangement is reached between one country and another or several. Internal duties, restrictions and regulations remain the same;[11] no measures are taken to liberalize trade. Such preferential trade arrangements are frowned upon by GATT because they monopolize and restrict trade. For example, the Ruvuma Free

Trade between Tanzania and Mozambique is more of a preferential arrangement than a free trade area.

The PTA falls within the exceptions outlined in Article 24 of GATT. It is still too early to assess the implications of this preferential trade area but an examination of its performance so far may be sufficient for realizable projections. Examining the provisions of the treaty, it is difficult to conclude whether the PTA is a free trade area or a customs union as defined by Article 24 or whether it is an interim arrangement for both.[12]

This chapter starts from the premise that any genuine economic integration will depend largely on the degree and extent of common economic policies, rather than the political willingness of PTA members. The rules of origin intended to confine preferential treatment to indigenous enterprises and exclude the influence or direct participation of multinational corporations can succeed if they are backed by indigenous technology. The experience of the Latin American Free Trade Area should convince PTA members to give priority to working out a common foreign investment policy.

THE NATURE OF THE PTA

The treaty shows that the PTA is both a free trade area, a custom union and a development coordination entity.[13] It can be both a trade and development organ but certainly not a free trade area as well as a custom union. Provisions in Article 3(1) and (4) reflect the PTA as entity with an amalgam of functions. In fact the term PTA is a misnomer.

The objectives of the PTA can be divided into two. First, it is aimed at the growth and expansion of trade through the trade liberalization provisions to be found in Articles 12 through 20 of its treaty, bringing these countries into closer trade integration. And, second, it is intended to promote closer cooperation and integration in all fields of economic activities other than trade. Of high priority are the fields of industry, transport, communications, agriculture, natural resources and monetary affairs.[14] Consequently, the PTA deals with more than trade.

It is clear from the preamble and from Article 3, that the purpose for the establishment of the PTA is not simply to foster closer economic integration but also to lay the foundation for the economic development of its members and thus improve the living standards of their peoples.

First PTA is to develop gradually from a free trade area into a common market and finally into an economic community.[15] The members have set year 1992 as the year by which such an economic community will have been established. The Customs and Trade Committee has suggested that member states should states should further reduce their PRA (original reductions varied from 70%-10%) tariff rates if 25% original tariffs every two years starting from October 1986 and bringing them to zero in October 1992.[16] To achieve this goal, the treaty provides for the gradual reduction and eventual elimination of customs duties and non-tariff barriers to trade.[17] Further, within a period of 10 years members are prohibited from imposing new customs duties or increasing existing ones on intra-PTA trade. Member states are obliged under Article 16 to relax and remove existing quotas or prohibitions on goods originating in the other member states.

And second, the achievement of this regional economic community is expected to be a step towards the fulfillment of the African Declaration on Cooperation, Development and Economic Independence made by the 10th Assembly of Heads of States and Government of the OAU in Lagos in April 1980 - the Lagos Plan of Action - that there should be an African Common Market established by 2,000.

Rules of Origin

Preferential treatment is accorded only to products originating from within the member states which appear on the common list.[18] The members negotiated an initial list of products included in the first common list that covered 132 products.[19] Then, in April 1985, the Customs and Trade Committee met to negotiate products to be included on it.[20] A casual examination of this reveals that the bulk of products listed are consumer goods. The member states exchange what they already produce; the products reflect their level of development. Yet in expanding trade through trade liberalization, industrial and agricultural production will generally be stimulated, albeit at different levels in each member state. The decision of the member states to cooperate at the level of production could be an attempt to increase the quality and type of products traded.

Tanzania has a list of products it is interested to sell to and import from PTA members. The list of exports includes products which are scarce in the domestic market,[21] which has capacity to absorb consumer goods from other members.

It is possible to understand the Tanzania government's reluctance to join the PTA, particularly on the points of mutual benefit and the effects which intra-PTA trade might have on domestic industries. Industries producing similar products as those imported from PTA members will have to

improve the quality of their products if they do not want to
be outflanked. However, the effect of intra-PTA trade could
be devastating to some of the domestic industries, if not
done selectively. However, protection of domestic industries
is meaningful only if strict quality standards are enforced,
or if protection is accompanied by monopolies.[22] Yet some
Tanzanian industries have had both monopoly and protection
for years while the quality of their products has remained
poor. Intra-PTA trade may force an element of
competitiveness and quality into trade.

In PTA intra-trade relationships, Tanzania is bound, for
the foreseeable future, to pay for outstanding balance
deficits if items to be traded are not unduly restricted.
The implications of a trade deficit is that any outstanding
balance must be settled in convertible currency. So the list
of imports is kept short to avoid outstanding deficit
balances while that of goods to be exported is longer. Is
this a plus for Tanzania?

Tanzania will definitely suffer loss of revenues on
duties and transit dues which it would get if it were a non-
PTA member. So will all other members. But if each member
considered this element negatively, there would be no
economic communities. Each member loses something while it
gains another; it is a give and take exercise. Of course,
the size of what is given and taken differs.

Not only must a product be in the common list and
originate from the member state but also it must satisfy the
Protocol on the Rules of origin for products to be traded
between the member states (Annex III, Rule 2).[23] The goods
must be:

a) directly consigned to a member in another member
state, and produced in the member state by an
enterprise which is subject to management by a
majority of nationals and at least 51% equity of
holding by the nationals of the member state or a
government or institutions of the member state; and
b) wholly produced in the member state.

Rule 3 specifies goods which are wholly produced in a
member state to include:

a) mineral products extracted from the ground or
seabed of a member state;
b) vegetable products harvested within the member
state;
c) live animals born or raised within the member
state;

d) products and by-products from animals born or raised within the member state;

e) products from hunting or fishing;

f) products obtained from the sea and from rivers and lakes within the member state by a vessel of a member state;

g) products manufactured in a factory of a member state exclusively from the products referred in (f) above;

h) used articles fit only for the recovery of materials provided that such articles have been collected from users within the member state;

i) scrap and waste resulting from manufacturing operations within the member state;

j) goods produced within the member state exclusively or mainly from either products referred to in a-i above or materials containing no element imported from outside the member states or of undetermined origin.

or under Rule 3:

a) they have been produced in the member state and the c.i.f. value of materials imported from outside the member states or of undetermined origin which have been used at any stage in the production of the goods does not exceed 60% of the total cost of materials used in the production of goods;

b) they have been produced essentially from imported material and value added is at least 45% of exfactory cost. Exfactory is defined to be the value of the total materials required to produce a given product;

c) they do not satisfy the rules of origin but they have been designated in a list by the Council to be goods of particular importance to the economic development of a member state, provided they contain not less than 25% of value added;

d) they do not satisfy rules but are produced in the member states and are consumed in large quantities throughout the member states and are approved by the Council as goods in short supply in the member states provided value added must not be less than 80%.

e) they have been imported into the member state and have undergone a process of substantial transformation such that they are classified under a CCCN tariff heading other than the tariff heading under which they were imported; or

f) they have been imported into the member state and are deemed by the Council to have undergone a process of substantial transformation.

Special provisions are provided for the Comoros, Djibouti, Mauritius, Swaziland and Zimbabwe whose shareholding in enterprises of which products become eligible for preferential treatment is less than the 51% required of other states but is raised gradually.

Thus complete freedom of intra-PTA trade is not envisaged, at least for the next decade. Freedom of trade is limited to the common list which can be varied by members. Also preference is directed to indigenous industries.[24] The rules of origin deliberately disqualify products produced by subsidiaries of transnational corporations.[25] They are strict so as to seal off the preferential market from the influence of such corporations. This constitutes a noble step and plausible reasoning, yet its success will not depend on the rules, but rather on the organizations of the economies of the member states.

The rules may well apply to countries like Tanzania, especially on the equity, but other countries will find it hard to satisfy them. In making the rules of origin strict to guard against transnational corporations, members are suffering from the effects on themselves. Already, Malawi and Kenya have complained that the rules are too narrow and impair trade. Malawi seeks to have the provisions relaxed for 3 years while Kenya has called for a review of the rules in respect of ownership, and is seeking a reduction of equity ownership to 30%.[26] It can safely be forecasted that Botswana, Swaziland and Zimbabwe, despite the special favorable provision will also support this claim that the rules are too narrow. Responding to this, the PTA Secretariat has initiated a study on whether Rule 2 of the Protocol on rules of origin impairs trade. The ITC and UNCTAD are conducting this research. Kenya will provide the data.[27] The rules of origin debate may determine the success or failure of the PTA. These have to be flexible enough to accommodate the different interests of its member state.

Clearing House

The PTA has established a payments Clearing House to enable members to trade in their national currencies and thus reduce the use of scarce foreign exchange.[28] Members exchange their currencies for the UAPTA (Unit of Account of the PTA), the PTA currency through the Clearing House. Trade between a member and another is cancelled without actual payment. Only the outstanding deficit balance is paid in convertible currency. Therefore, only the member whose balance of trade is in deficit will be required to make payments equivalent to the margin of the deficit. Since the Clearing House was launched in 1983, a few members have used it. There is resistance by the monetary authorities of some members towards the use of the Clearing House; instead they will insist on settlement in convertible currencies.

For the period February to March 1984, the total volume of trade through the Clearing House of UAPTA 5.6 million of which a balance of US$1.3 million, accounting for about 23% of the total, was paid in convertible currency. By July, the volume settled through the Clearing House was UAPTA 9.7 million, of which a balance of US$9.1 million was settled in convertible currency accounting for 93% of the total. This is due to some members insisting that certain trade transactions/goods must be settled in convertible currency. The purpose for which the Clearing House was established will be defeated if members continue to insist on trade in convertible currencies, because foreign exchange will not be spread out. Further, the number of members using the Clearing House is so far limited to Ethiopia, Malawi, Mauritius, Swaziland, Zambia and Zimbabwe.

As if these problems were not enough for the fledgling Clearing House, some member countries have withheld their products in the common list and sold them outside the PTA to earn convertible currency.[29] These problems are undermining the very foundation upon which the Clearing House was built and, to some degree, affect the attainment of overall PTA objectives.

The Eastern and Southern African Trade and Development Bank

The PTA Treaty provides for the establishment of an Eastern and Southern African Trade and Development Bank (the Bank).[30] Initial capital stock is proposed to be UAPTA 400 million (1 UAPTA equals 1 SDR, the value of which will be determined by current prices in the exchange market). 1 SDR is composed of a basket of currencies,[31] dominated by the US dollar which carries about 42% of the total weighting in the basket.

The capital stock will be paid in by members' subscriptions. The total allocation of capital to member states is equal to 66.67% of the total capital stock which is UAPTA 266.8 million.[32] Subscriptions are assessed on the basis of a member's share of the entire PTA population, share of GDP, share of volume export and services, etc.[33] Thus the

less advanced a member the more likely that its quota will be
smaller, but this does not affect decision-making since this
is made by consensus.[34]

A scheme of payment has also been proposed that 10% of
the payment be made 30 days after the date of deposit of the
instrument of ratification by a member, 10% within the first
year and the remainder in 4 yearly installments of 20% each,
(equal to 20%) of the payable capital.[35] The initial form of
payment of subscriptions will be initially in convertible
currency and thereafter it will be in the member's own
currency.[36]

The Bank will have two main functions. First, it will
promote trade by providing credit to members with outstanding
balance of deficit. And second, it will promote economic
development in the member states by financing PTA joint
projects.[37]

Economic Development

In an attempt to stimulate production in their
countries, PTA members undertake to cooperate in industrial,
agricultural and service sectors. Several study reports on,
inter alia, interstate road projects, railway projects,
harmonization of flight schedules and optimum utilization of
air passenger travel between countries, utilization of air
cargo services, interstate telecommunication and the
establishment of a PTA international shipping company are
under discussion.[38] These projects reflect the realization
by PTA members of the crucial role transportation and
communication play in the movement of goods and services.
Alongside these projects is the desire by members to adopt
one transport document. A study has been initiated by the
Secretary General to find out which one of the documents TIA
(carnet PTA or an Interim Transit Document) will be
adopted.[39]

In agriculture joint projects to be recommended will
include projects designed to improve their production and
quality of livestock, staple food crop production, manpower
training, and development of forests and forestry related
industries.[40]

In industry, cooperation will be on metallurgical,
chemical, petro-chemical geared towards the development of
basic and heavy industries. On the priority list are also
intermediate goods industries, food and agricultural
industries, consumer goods industries for the purpose of
obtaining the economies of scale, reducing external
dependence for the supply of industrial products and
achieving greater complimentarity of the economies of the

member states. Members intend to create multinational
enterprises, joint industrial supporting institutions and
other infrastructural facilities, including joint development
of industrial research, skills and modern technology.[41] From
the treaty provisions it is clear that as much attention is
paid to trade as to economic development.

Multiplicity of Similar Institutions

One of the setbacks to effective economic integration of
the Eastern and Southern African countries is the
multiplicity of institutions dealing with the same issues.
This arrests both attention and degree of cooperation.

Within the region there are the following cooperation
and integration arrangements:

a) The Organization for the Planning and Development
    of the Kagera River Basin
b) The Ruvuma Free Trade Area
c) The Multinational Programming and Operational
    Centres for East and Southern Africa (MULPOCS)
d) The Preferential Trade Area for Eastern and
    Southern Africa (PTA)
e) Southern African Development Coordination
    Conference (SADCC)
f) Bilateral cooperation arrangements in the form of
    Joint Commissions

Three of these are of interest to us: namely, the Joint
Commissions, the PTA and SADCC.

The Joint Commissions are typically bilateral, and
encompass Burundi, Mozambique, Rwanda, Uganda, Zambia, and
Zimbabwe. Joint Commissions are responsible for the
initiation, coordination and supervision of cooperation
programmes in economic, scientific and technical fields,
trade, industry, transport and communication, and finance.

With the exception of trade, the PTA and SADCC compete
in the same fields of cooperation. The Lusaka Declaration
provided for a sector on trade in SADCC but a trade sector is
yet to be established.

The objectives of PTA and SADCC are similar. It is not
unusual for members in a wider organization to be members of
a smaller organization. A good example is the UN and OAU.
The PTA can be said to be the wider organization and SADCC
the smaller, but the activities of such organizations as the
UN and OAU are complementary. While the UN deals with world
peace, the OAU deals specifically with Africa. The
relationship between PTA and SADCC is not complementary.

Table 9-1
Comparative PTA and SADCC Goals

PTA Agenda   SADCC Action Programme

i.   Transport Communication   i.   Transport Communication

      road transport   road transport
      air transport   air transport
      railway transport   railway transport
      inland waterway   shipping
      shipping ports
      freight bookings

ii.   Telecommunications   ii.   Telecommunications

      postal communication

iii. Agricultural Cooperation   iii. Agricultural Development

      food security   food security
      agronomic research –   agricultural research
      crop production   in the semi-arid tropics
      livestock, fisheries
      forestry, livestock   fisheries, forestry
      production and disease   and wildlife, animal
      control   disease control, soil
      regional agricultural   conservation and land
      trade   utilization

iv.   Industrial Cooperation   iv.   Industrial Development

      industrial development   industrial manpower
      multinational industrial   development, investment
      enterprises, industrial   laws, security printing
      manpower training,
      investment and marketing

v.   Customs and Trade   v.   Development Fund

      trade liberalization   energy conservation and
      customs cooperation   security
      transit trade facilities
      rules of origin

vi.   Clearing and Payments

      Clearing House
      Trade and Development Bank

They duplicate their fields of operation; their sectors overlap.

It would be ideal for the region to concentrate on one regional organization, say an economic community, and work more towards the attainment of that goal than the establishment of so many organizations dealing with same fields and involving the same members. With the exception of Burundi and Rwanda, all members of SADCC are members of the PTA and its Joint Commissions.

CONCLUSION

The future of the PTA will depend on the political climate in its member states, which in turn is mainly determined by the state of their economies. The establishment of SADCC, which seems to grow faster and stronger compared to the PTA, may affect the future of the latter. There are possibilities of some PTA members mistaking it as an institution dealing with consumer or trade integration rather than with economic cooperation in all fields, whereas SADCC is seen to be an organization that works to foster production. This may make some members of the PTA give priority to SADCC and less to it on the argument that production precedes trade.

Further, the success of PTA in fostering closer economic cooperation and integration will depend on its flexibility. For the moment its rules of origin are too rigid and do not take into consideration the diversity of interests to its members.

Any closer integration requires a common economic policy. The economic structures and organizations of all the members must be the same. As such there can be no economic cooperation without political integration. Nor can there be genuine economic integration of indigenous industries without indigenous technology.

The establishment of a free trade area or a customs union or an economic community in the Third World is different from earlier processes of integration (e.g. the European Economic Community) because the exclusion of third party products does not mean the effective exclusion of foreign economic agents. For instance, about half intra-regional exports of the Andean Pact in 1974 were made by foreign firms. Keeping this fact in mind, then, the PTA countries should adopt, as the very <u>first measure</u>, a common policy on <u>foreign direct investment</u> to define the role of external capital integration policy and process.

NOTES

1. Progress Report to the Third Summit of Authority on the Implementation of PTA Work Programme from January to December 1984, p. 1.
2. "Africa's newest common market," Daily News, 23 July 1984, p. 4.
3. Total sq. km. for PTA countries was 4,068,000 before 11 April 1985. Now Tanzania has joined its total sq. km. is 5,013,087.
4. Most of these are customs of free trade areas, with the exception of SADCC.
5. One basic principle of GATT is the liberalization of trade based on non-discrimination and most-favored nation clause. Therefore if this basic spirit was to operate without exception, no room would be left for custom unions or free trade areas. But like any basic principle, GATT has permitted exceptions. One of the exceptions is the formation of customs unions or free trade areas.
6. Articles 1, 2 and 24 of GATT.
7. Article 24 8 (a).
8. Article 24 5 (a).
9. Article 24 8 (b).
10. H. Jackson, World Trade and the Law of GATT, (Ann Arbor: University of Michigan, 1969), pp. 580-587.
11. Ibid.
12. It seems as if the parties intended to establish first a free trade area, then a common market and finally an economic community. 1 The treaty provisions included an Economic Community Treaty and this is supported by the sectors of cooperation on the PTA committees agendas.

Nor is the PTA merely a preferential trade area. The provisions on industrial agricultural and transportation and telecommunication show that the PTA is also an economic development institution.
13. The Preamble and Article 3 of the PTA treaty.
14. Article 3 of PTA treaty.
15. The Preamble and Articles 12 and 13 of PTA treaty.
16. Article 12 of treaty and Annexes I and II to the treaty.
17. Annex I - Protocol on the Reduction and Elimination of Trade Barriers on selected commodities to be traded within the PTA.

Annex II - Protocol relating to Customs Cooperation within the PTA.
17. Ibid.
18. Article 15 and Annex III on Protocol on the Rules of Origin for products to be traded between the member states of

PTA.

19.   The initial list was published in the PTA Official Gazette 3(1), January 1984.   It has 132 products.   This list is subject to variations and additions of new products as and when decided by the members.

20.   Agenda accompanying notice of meeting of the Customs and Trade Committee of 15-19 April 1985.

21.   Products such as sugar, natural honey, batteries, electric lamps and bulbs, bicycles, cement, wine, cigarettes, etc.

22.   Some of the services of Tanzanian enterprises could improve if strict standards were enforced.   An example is the National Bank of Commerce.   Customer services are slow and bad.   If the Bank was to face the competition of other banks it would be compelled to improve the quality of its services. In the absence of that, close supervision of services would help.

On protection of infant industries, such protection is bad if it is done for the sake of it.   Our industries have enjoyed protection for almost 20 years.   They have not improved the quality of their products.   They have been allowed to sell such products that sell simply because consumers have no alternatives.   This is not protection.   It is the ruin of the economy of the country.

23.   Annex III - Protocol on the Rules of Origin for products to be traded between the member states of the PTA-Rule 2 (a), (b) i-v.

24.   See Article 15 and Annex III, Rule 2.

25.   Speech made by Mr. Nyanganyi, Minister of State, President's Office on the signing ceremony of the PTA Treaty by Tanzania.

26.   Report on the Third Summit of the Authority on the Implementation of the PTA Work Programme.

27.   A report of the case study was probably discussed in the April meeting of the Trade and Customs Committee.

28.   Report on the Third Summit of the Authority on the Implementation of the PTA Work Programme.

29.   Ibid.

30.   Articles 32 to 39 PTA treaty.

31.   The US dollar, the Deutsche Mark, the British pound, the French franc and the Japanese yen.   The US$ has a weight of 42%; the DM that of 19%; and the remaining a weight of 13% each.

32.   Report on the Third Summit of the Authority on the Implementation of the PTA Work Programme.

33.   Ibid.

34.   Articles 5-11 of PTA Treaty.

35.   Report on the Third Summit of the Authority on the

Implementation of the PTA Work Programme.

36.   So far payments have been in US$.

37.   Recommendations made by the Group of Experts in a Report on the Activities on the Launching of the PTA Bank.

38.   Article 23, and Annex VII of PTA treaty.   See also items on the agenda for the Transport and Communications Committee meeting for 1985, Annex V, Protocol on Transit Trade and Transit Facilities, and Annex X, Protocol on Simplification and Harmonization of Trade Documents and Procedure.

39.   The TIA (PTA) Carnet means the intra-preferential trade area transport document whose form must comply to format in Appendix II to the Protocol on Transit Trade.

40.   Article 25 and Annex IX on Protocol on Cooperation in the Field of Agricultural Development.   Also see the Agenda of the meeting of the Committee on Agricultural Cooperation in May 1985.   Among the topics considered here: food security for PTA members, improvement of production and the quality of livestock, staple food crop production, manpower training, the development of forests and forest-related industries etc.

41.   Article 24 and Annex VIII; see Protocol on Cooperation in the Field of Industrial Development.

10. SADCC in the Aftermath of the Nkomati Accord
Douglas G. Anglin

INTRODUCTION

The Nkomati Accord, launched in a blaze of publicity by President Samora Machel of Mozambique and Prime Minister (now President) Pieter Botha of South Africa on 16 March 1984, was acclaimed by both leaders as a dramatic breakthrough, heralding the dawn of a new era of "peaceful coexistence, mutual respect and relations of good neighborliness" in Southern Africa.[1] The immediate consequence of this startling development was considerable confusion and consternation among other SADCC members, especially those most closely associated with mozambique. now with the benefit of a year's experience and reflection and particularly with the evidence of Pretoria's bad faith in failing to live fully by its solemn commitments under the Accord, it is possible to assess the significance of Nkomati with somewhat greater confidence, even if with waning optimism.

The special concern of this chapter is the impact of Nkomati on the operation of and the outlook for SADCC, the Southern African Development Coordination Conference. It makes no claim to present a comprehensive critique of the multifarious implications of the Accord for the Southern African region generally or to pronounce judgement on the success of SADCC as an organization. At the same time, these wider questions inevitably provide the context within which the focus of this chapter must be set. Accordingly, it is important to make explicit certain assumptions that underlie the subsequent analysis. These are:

a) The Nkomati Accord represented a Mozambican surrender to superior South African military and economic power and pressure; the fact that Maputo had little alternative to submission does not make the Accord any less of a diktat. In the words of the Economist, "Nkomati was little more than a gun held at President Machel's head".[2]

b) Nkomati constitutes a decisive turning-point in regional relations rather than simply a temporary setback or tactical retreat.

c) Even if, in the light of all the circumstance, the terms of the Accord are judged beneficial on balance to Mozambique, its one-sided implementation clearly is not.

d) The shift in South African policy from destabilization to detente – to the extent that this has actually occurred – in no way represents a retreat from the goal of regional hegemony. On the contrary, Nkomati was specifically designed to consolidate and legitimize South Africa's position as the "dominant power" on the subcontinent. And

e) SADCC remains a major target of South African policy, with Nkomati one of the instruments of that policy. Its present and potential impact on SADCC is both profound and perturbing.

REACTION TO NKOMATI

In the aftermath of Nkomati, two broad schools of opinion emerged concerning the implications of the Accord for Southern Africa in general and for SADCC in particular. The first, widely subscribed to in Western capitals, was naively optimistic that Nkomati would open up new opportunities for SADCC initiatives. Now that its members were supposedly relieved of the constant specter of exemplary South African retribution, and had in turn renounced any active support for the liberation struggle in South Africa, they would be better able to concentrate their energies on their primary task of promoting regional coordination of national development plans. "The end of armed aggression by South Africa – if it does end," Reginald Green argued, "will facilitate implementation of many critical SADCC projects, especially in transport and energy," while "lessened RSA economic pressures – if they are lessened – will facilitate a more orderly and less costly process of dependence reduction."[3] In particular, the restoration of secure rail access to

Mozambican ports promised to constitute a major step forward in realizing SADCC's aim of reducing dependence on South African routes and ports. "The Accord of Nkomati will help to end this dependence," Carlos Cardoso of AIM, the Mozambique Information Agency, explained: "Thus we can conclude that the Accord is not a threat to SADCC. Quite the contrary, the principles of SADCC have become operative for the first time."[4]

For many of the members of SADCC, a much less sanguine scenario seemed more plausible. Despite their reluctance to break ranks publicly they remained acutely apprehensive that Nkomati could seriously undermine SADCC's mandate, and perhaps compromise it fatally. Moreover, if Pretoria failed to live up to its obligations fully and faithfully – as has clearly proven to be the case – the outlook would be even bleaker. This chapter seeks to evaluate these sharply conflicting prognoses.

What has made any conscientious attempt to assess the full significance of Nkomati so difficult and delicate is that both Pretoria and, initially, Maputo hailed it enthusiastically. If Mozambique had pleaded force majeure, its actions would have been readily understood and sympathetically supported. Instead, President Machel joined fully in turning the signing ceremony into an international propaganda extravaganza, possibly in the hope of committing Prime Minister Botha irrevocably to implementing the agreement in good faith. Moreover, he proclaimed that "Nkomati crowned our socialist policy of peace with success:"

With the signing of the Accord of Nkomati, the main (South African) project, the destruction of our state, failed. In signing the Accord of Nkomati, we guaranteed the objective of our fight – peace. Only with peace can we achieve our objective of defending our country, defeating underdevelopment and building socialism.

Thus, Nkomati was perceived not only as a major victory for Mozambique but also as a signal defeat for South Africa's destabilization policy; Mozambique had survived the "total onslaught". Pretoria had been compelled to abandon its aggressive militarist intrusions, in part because of the "very high" cost to "South African society in human lives and in resources," but more importantly because the adverse impact on the economy had caused "serious concern to the major financial groups" in the country. So persuaded was Maputo that Nkomati constituted a diplomatic triumph that anyone who questioned "the patriotic significance" of the Accord was denounced as either a defeatist right-wing

opportunist or a pseudo-revolutionary left-wing divisionist.
As late as November 1984, Mozambique criticized even
President Nyerere, who as OAU Chairman, had dared to denounce
dialogue with Pretoria as "a betrayal of the peoples of the
continent."[5]

The depth of Mozambican feelings and the universal
respect in which Machel is held by his fellow SADCC heads of
state blunted most public expressions of concern.
Nevertheless, the announcement of Nkomati left them stunned,
perplexed and initially in a state of disarray. President
Nyerere, leader of the country farthest from the Front Line
in Southern Africa, flew to Maputo in a futile last-minute
endeavor to talk Machel out of the deal. President Kaunda,
normally an incorrigible optimist, confessed that "We will be
less than honest if we did not admit that the Nkomati Accord
was a setback". He added: "We accept we are weak ... (but
if we glorify this (pact) we will be making a tactical
error." President Quett Masire of Botswana went even
further. Referring to the Front Line State (FLS), he charged
Pretoria with "bullying us all into signing accords like
this. The (Nkomati) pact was not entered into because both
states saw it to their mutual advantage. It was more out of
fear."[6]

After six weeks of agonizing, the FLS heads of state and
the Presidents of SWAPO and the African National Congress
(ANC) assembled in Arusha to assess the situation and hammer
out a common stand. In a cautiously-worded and carefully-
balanced communique, they "reaffirmed their total and
unqualified commitment to the liberation struggles" in
Namibia and South Africa. At the same time, they supported
"Mozambican actions aimed at the total elimination" of the
"vicious" Pretoria-sponsored armed "bandits", masquerading as
the Mozambique National Resistance (MNR). The meeting also
"expressed appreciation of Mozambique's commitment to
continued moral, political and diplomatic support for the
ANC."[7] Thus, while an open breach was averted in the
interests of solidarity, differences and doubts remained and
grew - especially when it became evident that South Africa
had no intention of fulfilling its side of the bargain. As
the SADCC secretariat has since pointed out sadly in its
preparatory documentation for the 1985 conference:

Economic aggression against SADCC and SADCC members has
continued throughout 1984. It may have abated somewhat
but the hope expressed in the (February 1984) Lusaka
annual conference communique that South Africa would
cease all attempts to destabilize the economies of its
neighbors has remained unfulfilled. The Nkomati and

Lusaka agreements have not yet led to the return of peace to Mozambique and Angola.[8]

By this time, Maputo too was acknowledging "the non-observance of the Nkomati Accord by South Africa." Until early December 1984, it was still "convinced that the South African government (was) fulfilling the Nkomati Accord." Then, "towards the end of December, Mozambique's attitude hardened noticeably." According to a government account,

> The belief is growing in both official and unofficial circles that South Africa has not respected the Nkomati Accord because it was the agreement as a mere tactic ... Retrospectively, even the Pretoria Declaration of October 3 is now seen as an attempt by the Pretoria regime to pull the wool over the eyes of international public opinion ... Therefore, it is not surprising that public opinion in Mozambique feels that there has been bad faith on the part of the South African government right from the start.

As a result, on the anniversary of the Accord in March, there was "very little to celebrate."[9]

Perhaps the principal victim of Nkomati was the ANC. Even before Pretoria's duplicity became apparent, the shock of the Accord left the party devastated. ANC leaders made comradely attempts to "understand" Mozambique's painful dilemma, to overlook Maputo's failure to consult them, and to dismiss the Accord publicly as merely "a temporary setback." Nevertheless, they found it difficult to hide completely their fury and sense of betrayal.[10] Admittedly, there had been a hint of things to come when the SADCC Conference in Lusaka in February 1984 withdrew the ANC's (and SWAPO's) observer status, and publicly welcomed the "signs of a less aggressive stance from South Africa."[11] Nevertheless, the ANC was ill-prepared for the rigor with which its expulsion from Mozambique was enforced and limitations imposed on even its "diplomatic" presence in Maputo.

Inside South Africa, the perception of Nkomati as a humiliating Mozambican surrender was widely shared by black and white alike. The government was particularly ecstatic as it confidently awaited the demise or decline of SADCC as a serious rival to its own pet project for a Constellation of Southern African States (CONSAS). "I have a vision", Prime Minister Botha exuded at the signing ceremony, "of the nations of Southern Africa cooperating with each other in a veritable constellation of states."[12] Similarly, the Financial Mail - the organ of big business in South Africa-predicted the "inevitable" dissipation of SADCC's "fragile economic initiative," and proposed its replacement by an enlarged South African-dominated rand monetary zone embracing all SADCC members except Angola and Tanzania. As Presidents Machel and Kaunda noted, following their meeting on 5 February, South African aggression against Mozambique was "aimed against SADCC."[1]

SADCC OBJECTIVES

The Lusaka Declaration of April 1980 identified four broad "development objectives" for SADCC. These were:

a) the reduction of economic dependence particularly, but not only, on the Republic of South Africa;
b) the forging of links to create genuine equitable regional integration;
c) the mobilization of resources to promote the implementation of national, interstate and regional policies; and
d) concerted action to secure international cooperation within the framework of our strategy of economic liberation.

In addition, implicit in the document and in much subsequent SADCC rhetoric was a fifth and final objective. This was a somewhat imprecise commitment to "complete" the struggle for "genuine political independence" in Namibia and ultimately in South Africa. "We, the majority-ruled states of Southern Africa," the SADCC members declared, "recognize our responsibilities ... to assist in achieving a successful culmination of our struggle." Even as late as July 1984, a Tanzanian minister was insisting that "SADCC is a child of the liberation movement in Southern Africa. It is the economic side of the liberation coin."[14] Each of these aims will be probed with a view to assessing the organization's prospects of realizing its proclaimed purposes in the aftermath of the "new order" Pretoria has succeeded in imposing on Southern Africa.

ECONOMIC LIBERATION

"Our urgent task now," the founding fathers of SADCC resolved, "is to include economic liberation in our programs and priorities." In practise, this meant concentrating on reducing members' dependence on South Africa - as much for

Table 10-1

SADCC Project Programmes by Sector, 1984

SECTOR	COORDINATOR	NO. OF PROJECTS	(COST US $ MILLIONS)		
			Estimated	Foreign	Secured
TRANSPORT & COMMUNICATIONS	Mozambique	127	$ 2,935	$ 2,373	$ 740
Mozambique Ports		32	1,489	1,170	314
Dar es Salaam Port		11	382	314	83
Lobito Port		4	210	205	33
Intra-regional Surface Transport		22	407	304	67
Civil Aviation		11	107	87	48
Telecommunications		25	325	278	189
Coordiation & Training		22	15	15	6
AGRICULTURE		62	312	297	63
Food security	Zimbabwe	28	177	163	16
Animal Disease Control & Research	Botswana	22	127	126	46
Fisheries, Wildlife & Forestry	Malawi	11	6	6	---
Soil, Water Conservation & Land Utilization	Lesotho	1	2	2	1
INDUSTRY	Tanzania	88	1,304	943	221
ENERGY	Angola	30	34	c.30	4
MANPOWER DEVELOPMENT	Swaziland	37	15	9	1
MINING	Zambia	9	n/a	n/a	n/a
SOUTHERN AFRICAN DEVELOPMENT FUND	Zambia	---	---	---	---
TOURISM	Lesotho	---	---	---	---
TOTAL		353	$ 4,600	$ 3,652 (79%)	$ 1,029 (22%)

sound economic reasons as for their intense antipathy to apartheid. More specifically, the "key" to disengagement was identified as a radical reorientation of the inherited regional transport and communications network away from reliance on South African routes and facilities.[15] In operational terms, this strategy involved redirecting a significant proportion of the trade of the landlocked SADCC states - other than Lesotho, for geographical reasons- through alternative ports, principally in Mozambique but also Dar es Salaam, Lobito and eventually, it was hoped, in Walvis Bay in Namibia. In view of the crucial role played by Mozambique, it was assigned administrative responsibility for the Southern African Transport and Communications Commission (SATCC) within SADCC. Since then, two other sectors with direct relevance to economic liberation have been accorded priority standing - food security (coordinated by Zimbabwe) and energy (awarded to Angola) - while the importance of a fourth, human resources development (allocated to Swaziland), is receiving increasing recognition (Table 10-1).

The status of trade remains somewhat uncertain. The "enlargement of intra-regional trade," the current SADCC handbook declares is "an essential component of SADCC strategies for reducing external dependence." Yet, it was not until July 1984 that trade was officially designated a regional area of interest.[16] Even so, "the formal articulation of the SADCC trade sector has, to date, progressed relatively slowly." According to the SADCC secretariat, two reasons account for this caution. The first is "a concern to avoid overlapping or conflicting with the basically complementary tariff reduction and clearing union programs" of the Preferential Trade Area of Eastern and Southern Africa (PTA), which has its offices in Lusaka and Harare and with which relations have not always been entirely smooth. The PTA's membership includes six SADCC states - all but Mozambique, Botswana, and Angola. The second is "the need to avoid replicating the mistakes of former regional trade promotion organizations.[17] Memories of membership in such institutions are not very happy. As the late President Seretse Khama explained at SADCC II in 1980:

> Each of our states in SADCC has experience with those models of trade creation, the Federation of Rhodesia and Nyasaland, the Portuguese colonial 'economic union,' the East African Common Market, the Southern African Customs Union - all were, or are, free trade areas or common markets. All have served to limit our development, to enrich externally-based firms and interests, and to hamper national planning.[18]

One sphere of close interaction with South Africa not on SADCC's agenda is migrant labor. Its omission is especially curious as the tradition of trekking to mines and farms in the South is one of the most conspicuous marks of the northern neighbors' continuing dependence. In 1983, the Republic recruited over 140,000 miners alone from the five principal labor-exporting SADCC states. Evidently, members see in economic development over the long term the only hope of ending this "exploitative" practise.[19]

The speed with which SADCC operations have gotten off the ground and the momentum that has been sustained have been impressive. As of mid-1984, over 250 projects had been identified and approved. Nearly half were in the process of being implemented or are under active review by potential donors, while a further quarter had received detailed study with a view to early discussion with possible partners. The estimated cumulative cost amounted to $4.6 billion, or a quarter of the combined GNPs of member states. $1.1 billion had already been committed or spent, and a further $1.25 billion was the subject of active negotiations.

Of the total, 64% was accounted for by projects in the strategic (for the West as well as for SADCC) transport and communications field. This remains the sector which has registered the greatest progress to date, including ten completed projects as well as the largest single project currently in process of implementation (the $195 reconstruction of the Nacala-Cuamba Railway). In addition, it is the sector with the strongest appeal to overseas donors, with fully a quarter of the funds requested now committed, compared with only one-sixth in other fields. Overall, the foreign aid component sought amounts to nearly 80% of the projected costs.[20]

Yet, despite all the energy, effort and ingenuity that has gone into promoting economic liberation, it is difficult to escape the conclusion that the majority of SADCC states are now not only economically weaker but also more firmly incorporated into the South African orbit than they were when the organization was launched with such high hopes in 1980.

A major explanation for this depressing trend is the widespread and prolonged drought that has decimated staple food production throughout much of the region. As a result, many of the countries, including Zimbabwe which normally records a healthy food surplus, were compelled to turn to South Africa for emergency maize supplies (though in 1984 the Republic, too, found itself a net grain importer). The global recession has also taken its toll in the form of increasingly adverse terms of trade, rapidly mounting external debts and declining industrial production. Yet, the decisive factor has been the success of South Africa's skillfully-engineered strategy of regional destabilization.

Although some uncertainly remains concerning the final fate of Pretoria envisages for its neighbors, the immediate objective of its bullying behavior appears to have been the cause the maximum dislocation to their economies. The major targets selected were Angolan and Mozambican rail routes, harbors and food supplies as well as Zimbabwe's oil pipeline from Beira. This strongly suggests a carefully coordinated campaign to frustrate SADCC efforts at disengagement. In pursuing its purposes, South Africa has indulged in sanctions, sabotage, subversion and open aggression. While it has preferred to operate through allies (UNITA in Angola and, at one stage, the Lesotho Liberation Army) or surrogates (MNR in Mozambique), it has not hesitated to deploy preponderant military force to drive home to its hapless victims the costs of non-compliance with its demands. To the extent that Pretoria has now eased up on overt destabilization, however temporarily, in favor of its self-proclaimed "peace process," it must be seen as a measure of the success of its strategy rather than any reversal of its policy or purpose; regional hegemony continues to be pursued as vigorously as ever, though in part by subtler and more economical means.

Pretoria's resort to force as an instrument of national policy has proved exceedingly rewarding – more so than for the Israelis whose example South Africa has consciously sought to emulate. The Benguela Railway has been effectively inoperative for nearly a decade, and rail traffic to Maputo, Beira and Nacala has virtually ceased following repeated dissident attacks. Similarly, despite the posting of Zimbabwean troops inside Mozambique as guards, the Beira-Feruka pipeline and port installations have regularly suffered from sabotage. What freight cannot be diverted to Dar es Salaam and TAZARA – itself severely crippled by inadequate locomotive power – has to rely on South African ports and facilities – much to the delight and profit of Pretoria, to the chagrin of SADCC members, and to the discomfort of the West (which is belatedly coming to recognize the extent to which its access to the mineral resources of Central Africa is dependent on insecure South African routes). Meanwhile, both Botswana and Swaziland have developed plans to link their networks more closely with South African Railways.

In the aftermath of Nkomati, South Africa's determination to neocolonize its neighbors seems stronger and more brazen than ever. Here, Mozambique appears to provide the pattern for future penetration. Pretoria has not only signally failed to restrain the disruptive activities of its MNR creation, it has wasted no time in exploiting its power advantage to tie the country ever more tightly into the South African economy. The extent to which it will succeed is still unclear. SADCC officials appear persuaded that there is little risk that Maputo will succumb to Pretoria's blandishments and bullying. Nevertheless, a flood of high-level missions have already been exchanged between the two capitals, leading to a growing list of new cooperative enterprises with respect to agriculture, air services, fisheries, health, labor, power, rail transport, security, telecommunications and tourism. The establishment of a Joint Security Commission and the revision (in Mozambique's favor, at least financially) of the Cabora Bassa hydroelectric power agreement (in May 1984) have attracted the closest attention, but the announcement of new labor and fisheries agreements (November 1984) and joint collaboration in promoting the tourist trade could prove equally significant.

In terms of new foreign investment, little has materialized so far, but the Nkomati Accord in conjunction with Maputo's new investment code virtually ensure that any fresh injection of capital will come from South Africa or be funnelled through South African-based multinationals. Increasing recognition of the beneficial spin-offs accruing to South Africa from Western aid and investment as well as its own inability to "foot the bill for a successful neo-colonization of Southern Africa" largely explain Pretoria's concerted diplomatic drive to enlist the financial support of the West Europeans (in the course of Botha's post-Nkomati overseas tour) and of the Americans in subsidizing the consolidation of its empire.[21]

Despite the generally depressing prospects for significant progress towards economic liberation, some success has been achieved, especially in the communications field. Every SADCC capital is now linked to every other one by national air carriers, though it is still often more convenient to transit through Johannesburg. Moreover, as a recent SADCC survey points out,

In 1980, ... a high proportion of intra-state telecommunications had to pass via Europe or South Africa or both. Today, eight SADCC members have functioning grounds at stations while the ninth has one at an advanced stage of construction and by 1985 direct communication by satellite among all SADCC member states will be a reality.[22]

This example is a reminder that, under the Lusaka Declaration, SADCC states are seeking to reduce their dependency "not only on the Republic of South Africa." While this injunction does not apply to foreign aid or investment from the West, it does find expression in attempts to conserve scarce foreign exchange by, for example, not only expanding fertilizer production but also developing regional sources of phosphates and other inputs. To the extent that such efforts at disengagement succeed, the possibilities for regional integration will improve.

REGIONAL INTEGRATION

In calling for "genuine and equitable regional integration," the authors of the 1980 Lusaka Declaration and Programme of Action envisaged an innovative departure from classical models for rationalizing regional planning. Two features of SADCC's modus operandi are distinctive: a) the emphasis on sectoral coordination and b) the primacy conceded to national decision-making. The collapse of the East African Community (EAC) left a profound impression on the minds of SADCC leaders and injected a cautionary note into their deliberations, especially at SADCC I which, significantly, met in Arusha, the ex-Community's capital. The lesson they drew from the EAC's painful experiences was that, where sharp ideological differences in development strategies existed, national priorities should, in the last analysis, be allowed to take precedence over regional economic goals. Accordingly, SADCC took a deliberate decision to retreat from earlier experiments in genuine regional integration. While members accept a political commitment to consult and cooperate, they are under no compulsion to conform.

This voluntarist approach to the regional harmonization of national development plans has proved in practice more effective than might have been anticipated. For this happy outcome, much of the credit must go to SADCC's Council of Ministers which, ably served by its modest secretariat, performs an important central coordinating function. Also helpful has been a detectable, if incomplete, convergence in the political stances of member governments. Confronted with the harsh economic and political realities, the three aspiring Marxist-Leninist regimes have been compelled to temper their ideological preferences in the interests of national (and personal) survival. Pragmatism, however, is no assurance of strengthened regional cooperation. It could equally well excuse closer collaboration with South Africa, especially in the case of hard-pressed countries courted or coerced by Pretoria. Nevertheless, the outlook for enhanced regional cooperation appears reasonably promising. Nkomati- even if implemented, and perhaps especially so - poses a continuing threat to SADCC's hopes of integrated regional development. Yet, the overall impact may well be less than in the case of economic liberation, and may indeed provide an additional incentive to press ahead with greater vigor.

In this connection, a number of SADCC projects are sufficiently advanced to provide solid grounds for restrained optimism. Of particular relevance are the development of a regional microwave network, the construction of an interconnected electricity power grid based on the present Zambia-Zimbabwe backbone, the explorations into the possibilities of achieving regional self-sufficiency in oil, the rehabilitation (when security conditions permit) of ocean port facilities and interior rail links so essential to the welfare of the landlocked states, and the establishment of regional research and training institutions.

Outside the formal structures of SADCC, the network of joint commissions that has burgeoned in recent years has served to strengthen bilateral ties between members. One result has been a "steady growth in total levels of intra- regional transactions," facilitated in part no doubt by PTA's payments clearing house located in the Reserve Bank of Zimbabwe. In addition, SADCC can claim with some justice that the organization is "increasingly becoming perceived as a meaningful regional entity" by a growing number of non- governmental institutions and individuals within as well as beyond the region.[23] As examples, a Southern African Trade Union Coordinating Council has come into existence and chambers of commerce in the SADCC region are developing cooperative arrangements.

Nevertheless, the habit of regional cooperation comes hard. Admittedly, the really tough bargaining over conflicting national interests has yet to come. To date,

> the surprise has been how much scope there is for serious regional development without major concessions. The successful search for projects that have a firm national base (and market) has clearly delayed the time when national concessions will be required, thus allowing a firm basis of cooperation and trust to be built up first.[24]

Even so, there is already evidence of fiercely-held parochial interests rearing their awkward heads. These have been more evident at the political level than among government

officials. Four SADCC states are planning to establish steel
industries and, in the meantime, are importing supplies from
South Africa or elsewhere, despite the existence of
substantial excess steel capacity in Zimbabwe. Again, Zambia
has recently acquired a DC-10 plane, thus frustrating efforts
of SADCC airlines to standardize on Boeing aircraft as a
first step to reconstituting and expanding the defunct
Central African Airways. For its part, Zimbabwe has
restricted imports on cheap Botswana textiles.[25] It has
also, in the interests of self-sufficiency and security,
preferred to exploit its own Wankie coal resources to
generate power domestically at great expense rather than rely
on surplus supplies of vastly cheaper Zambian or eventually
Mozambican electricity – with consequences that are as much
political as economic. "Whatever the merits of Zimbabwe's
choice," one observer has noted, it left Cabora Bassa "with
only one customer – South Africa – and inevitably moved
Mozambique further down the road to the Nkomati Accord."

> There is a certain sad irony in this, because the
> (Zimbabwean) argument of security of supply was based
> partly on fears that South African-backed bandits would
> cut any power line from Cabora Bassa. Thus South Africa
> has been able to use its military power to scare-off
> Zimbabwean electricity consumers and then use its
> economic power to the electricity, forging yet another
> chain making the SADCC states dependent on it.[26]

Despite the deliberate eschewing of any compensatory or
corrective mechanisms to ensure equity in the distribution of
the benefits of integration in the industrial development
sector, some effort has been made to promote a "coordinated
basic industry program" based on "regional market-oriented
production."[27] As a result, initial fears that Zimbabwe
might emerge as the dominant regional "sub-imperial" power
have not materialized. Of the industrial projects currently
up for international auction, 36% (in terms of cost) are
destined for Mozambique, 22% for Tanzania, 16% for Zambia,
11% for Malawi, and only 10% for Zimbabwe. Nevertheless, in
the final analysis, the allocation of industries and markets
will be determined primarily by the availability of domestic
resources, the vagaries of regional market forces, and the
judgments of overseas donors and investors.
It is still too early to accept Prime Minister Mugabe's
confident assertion that SADCC's "step-by-step approach to
problems of economic union ... assures that there is harmony
at every stage of development and that the gains from
integration accrue to all member states."[28] Whether this

admirable sentiment is translated into policy will depend greatly on the political will member governments manage to muster to steer clear of both the Scilla of seductive nationalism and the Charybdis of a South African embrace.

DEVELOPMENT

"SADCC's basic commitment and raison d'etre," a conference report declared in 1981, "is to development."[29] The four goals, as spelt out in the Lusaka Declaration, are in fact collectively designated "development objectives." Yet the economic performance of members in general during the first four years of the organization's existence has been characterized by stagnation and decline, with the average SADCC citizen at least 10% poorer than in 1981. In relating an account of the "present imbalance, deterioration of infrastructure and production capacity, under-utilization of existing capacity and declines in per capita output" in the region, a recent SADCC document concludes that:

> Six of SADCC's member states face very serious debt service burdens – in one case amounting to nearly 50% of export earnings and in several others at or above 25% ... Only Botswana can reasonably be described as having fully regained internal and external economic balance and avoided significant deterioration or under-utilization of capacity ... Output per capita in at least four SADCC countries – Angola, Mozambique, Tanzania and Zambia – is 30% or more below previous peak levels.[30]

In the circumstances, the energies of member governments are necessarily concentrated on the immediate tasks of stabilization, rehabilitation and recovery of their economies rather than seeking sustained economic development and structural transformation.

The underlying cause of the present economic plight of SADCC states is indisputably the extreme vulnerability of their small, frail economies to global forces. Unfortunately, the birth of the organization coincided with a sharp deterioration in the external economic environment. This, combined with the burden of drought and, above all, the consequences especially for food production of South African destabilization activities in addition to certain "less than optimal project and policy choices,"[31] has exacted a heavy toll in human misery.

Improvements in administrative efficiency and a more

careful selection of priorities could help in the medium-term, but any real possibility of renewed rapid development rests crucially on the responses of Pretoria and SADCC's overseas partners. True peace throughout Southern Africa would undoubtedly give a welcome fillip to development, but the peace that Nkomati promised has predictably proved a mirage, and will continue to be so as long as Western governments persist in tolerating South Africa's relentless drive to dominate its weaker neighbors. Development in the SADCC states, then, is doubly dependent - economically and politically - on the support the West is prepared to provide.

EXTERNAL PARTNERSHIPS

No other regional organization has made such a conscious effort to solicit the sustained cooperation and support of the world community as SADCC. The institutional expression of this concern is the consultative conference with cooperating governments and aid agencies convened each year with a view to jointly "surveying results, evaluating performance, identifying strengths and weaknesses and agreeing on future plans."[32] Although SADCC states reserve the right in the final analysis to set their own national and regional priorities, these annual dialogues with donors have not proved mere polite formalities; while open and friendly, they have also at times been frank. The current emphasis on food security owes its adoption to a US suggestion at SADCC I in Arusha in 1979 and at SADCC V at Lusaka in February 1984, the invited guests were quite outspoken in their criticisms of the agricultural pricing policies of SADCC governments, with results that have been generally positive.[33]
In addition to welcoming constructive advice, SADCC looks to its overseas partners for assistance in several other areas. First and foremost, it seeks foreign financing for its projects. Although SADCC is committed to reducing its external dependence, it sees development as a precondition for economic liberation, and foreign aid as a prerequisite. The response to date has been moderately reassuring, especially in the agricultural and transport and communications sectors. Interest, particularly from the private sector, in industrial development has also picked up considerably, but there is still no enthusiasm at all for the proposed Development Fund, particularly as PTA is preparing to launch its own regional development bank.
Of the billion dollars in commitments received so far, the great bulk has come from Western and especially EEC sources. This offends the non-aligned sensibilities of some

members, and partly accounts for the fierce reaction to US discriminatory funding. In the end, Washington was forced to abandon its attempt to specify that none of its money should contribute to projects of benefit to the three socialist-oriented regimes in SADCC-Angola, Mozambique and Tanzania.[34] The embarrassing fact is that the Soviet Union has shown scant interest in SADCC and even some suspicion, especially since Nkomati. Although routinely invited to annual meetings, it has never turned up, let alone contributed any funds; instead, the East Germans keep a watching brief on Moscow's behalf. China, on the other hand, now attends regularly, and is financing one project. The Arab capital-surplus countries have also maintained their distance, though the Kuwait Fund and BADEA have participated in recent years, and have underwritten a few projects. Arab detachment cannot be explained away entirely by the fact the Blantyre, Maseru and Mbabane - the sites of three of the last four SADCC conferences - maintain diplomatic relations with Israel (and Taiwan).

The importance SADCC attaches to Western aid and investment is not simply a reflection of the limited alternatives available. The West's preoccupation with stability in Southern Africa and its genuine enthusiasm for the organization, especially its lean bureaucratic structure and its disposition to eschew politics, have generated unrealistic expectations of further substantial financial support. SADCC members also argue that Western governments should accept two wider responsibilities: to redress the injustices of an inequitable global economic system and to take Pretoria's predatory instincts. In the case of the latter, the West's encouragement, if not actual promotion of South Africa's "peace process," it is felt, obligates it to assist neighboring states to cope with the consequences. In a recent appeal for diplomatic support, the organization reiterated that:

SADCC and its member states do not, by themselves alone, have the strength to repel South African economic aggression. SADCC's partners in cooperation do have substantial economic and political leverage on South Africa. In the interest of the welfare of the peoples of Southern Africa, SADCC again calls on them to make effective use of their influence to cause South Africa to cease its strategy of regional economic aggression.[35]

Yet, realistically, the prospects of any effective diplomatic, let alone economic pressure on Pretoria are slim. The role of the Contact Group on Namibia in this respect is hardly encouraging. Rather than discipline the South Africans, Western governments are more likely to urge SADCC states to settle with South Africa on whatever terms they can obtain in the interests of preserving their inherited economic ties with the South. Certainly, no opportunity was lost to impress on SADCC members Western disquiet with their support for the armed struggle. In the case of Mozambique, which was facing bankruptcy, President Machel was told bluntly in the course of his European tour in October 1983 that a non-aggression pact with South Africa was a precondition for a renegotiation of his country's debts.[36]

LIBERATION

The attitude of SADCC members to the liberation of South Africa has always been somewhat ambivalent, in sharp contrast to their firm commitment to the independence of Namibia. It has never been clear whether economic disengagement from dependence on the South was intended to free members to engage South Africa more effectively in battle, or whether economic disengagement implied political disengagement and the effective abandonment of the liberation struggle.[37]

Even before Nkomati, ANC leaders were beginning to question the wish and the will of SADCC governments to accept the obligations and sacrifices incumbent on Front Line States. Reiteration of the view that SADCC was "first and foremost non-political" suggested that it represented an alternative to the liberation strategy of the Front Line States rather than a complement to it. "It is not our objective," Seretse Khama assured South Africa in 1980, "to plot against anybody or any country." Samora Machel was even more explicit: "We are not declaring a war against South Africa" and, later at the Nkomati signing ceremony: "SADCC was not created against South Africa."[38] When, therefore, the ANC found itself excluded from SADCC V in February 1984 in a gesture of conciliation to Pretoria and, a few weeks later, virtually expelled from Mozambique in compliance with the Nkomati Accord, its worst fears were confirmed. At the SADCC summit in Gaborone in July 1984, President Nyerere, as the conscience of the continent, addressed an impassioned appeal to his colleagues not to lose sight of their mission. He warned them that pursuit of the "mirage of prosperity" through collaboration with Pretoria threatened to "weaken the anti-apartheid struggle as well as the real independence of our sovereign states." Yet, much as his listeners might agree, they felt helpless to take up the challenge. Moreover, the more integrated into South Africa their economies become, the greater their "vested interest in stalling sanctions."[39]

In the circumstances, active support for the armed struggle in South Africa is no longer a viable proposition for any of its neighbors, greatly to the relief of Western governments. Nevertheless, contrary to predictions in Pretoria, the realization among black South Africans that they are now essentially on their own has not moderated their militancy or deterred them from mounting the most powerful and pervasive domestic campaign of defiance of apartheid in nearly a decade.

PRETORIA'S "PEACE PROCESS"

As a result of the striking successes of South Africa's coercive diplomacy culminating in Nkomati, the initiative in policy on the subcontinent passed firmly into the hands of Pretoria. Moreover, the exuberant mood there scarcely suggested that it was ready to forego any fresh opportunities to exploit its political leverage further and fully. On the contrary, the more Pretoria managed to impose its mastery on the region, the more its appetite for power was whetted rather than appeased. Even compliant Malawi felt the lash of its displeasure.[40] Accordingly, it pressed for additional Angolan and Mozambican concessions before fulfilling its own obligations under the Lusaka Agreement (with Angola) and the Nkomati Accord. Having surrendered once, the target regimes were in a weak position to put up further effective resistance.

In many respects, SADCC states find themselves in a "no-win" situation. This can be seen in the case of the revised Southern African Customs Union agreement (SACU) negotiated in 1982, but since blocked by the South African cabinet. As a result, the BLS countries - Botswana, Lesotho and Swaziland- have been denied the substantial increases in revenue to which they are entitled. Yet the dilemma they face is that, if Pretoria were to lift its veto in return for BLS recognition of bantustan independence (which apparently is the price demanded), these three small countries would end up even more deeply dependent on South Africa than at present.[41] Harare faces a similar difficulty with respect to the renegotiation of its Preferential Trade Agreement with Pretoria. Meanwhile, Pretoria continues to profit financially as well as politically from its ongoing destabilization efforts. Disruption of Angola's and Mozambique's railways and ports not only deprives these countries of vital foreign exchange; it also forces Zambia and Zimbabwe to divert their traffic through South Africa, once again undermining SADCC efforts to promote economic independence and further enriching Pretoria's coffers.

South Africa's ultimate intentions with respect to SADCC remain unclear. For the business community, access to the regional market is its primary concern and, for this purpose, SADCC with some flexibility could well prove useful, especially in enlarging the market through development. The government, however, clearly has broader political ambitions. These need not include the actual breakup of SADCC or the toppling of any of its governments. Weakening it through bilateral deals with individual members and otherwise creating divisions within its ranks might suffice and, at the same time, minimize the risk of marring the carefully cultivated image of harmonious regional relations being purveyed abroad. In any case, at least as important as any residual threat to South African regional hegemony posed by SADCC is Pretoria's determination to press for recognition of bantustan independence and legitimacy for UNITA and MNR, for the extension of the operations of the Development Bank of Southern Africa to neighboring states and, in its more fanciful moments, for a tour of SADCC capitals by President Botha.

SADCC PROSPECTS

What, then, can be said in conclusion concerning the development prospects of SADCC in the altered regional environment consequent on Nkomati? The implications of the Accord for SADCC can best be summarized in terms of the five basic goals of the organization.

Economic Liberation

While SADCC leaders have always conceded that disengagement from dependence on South Africa was a long-term objective and could never be complete, it must now be accepted that the process will be even more protracted than earlier anticipated and will inevitably suffer periodic distressing setbacks. Moreover, since Nkomati, there seems to be a lessened sense of urgency to disengagement as well as less of a stigma attached to retaining economic links with the South and even to soliciting fresh South African capital investment.

Regional Integration

The most positive potential outcome of Nkomati could
well be the incentive it gives member states to "think
SADCC", rather than "South African", especially with respect
to regional trade and development planning. Historically, a
credible external threat has provided the principal
invitation for governments to submerge their differences in
defense of their common cause. In the case of SADCC, much
will depend on the vision its statesmen display, the external
support available from the West, and the counter-measures
Pretoria takes to browbeat or bribe its members into
acknowledging continued South African regional hegemony.

Development

The constraints on development within the SADCC area are
not simply regional: national and international factors are
equally critical. Clearly, the elusive peace that Nkomati
promised remains a prerequisite for significant progress in
development, especially in the case of states bordering South
Africa. Nevertheless, peace would not in itself be a
sufficient assurance of success. In this regard, too, the
willingness of the West to treat the concerns of the
developing world seriously will prove crucial. What are
required are radical reforms in North-South relationships,
and not merely increased injections of aid and investment,
welcome as these would be to SADCC members.

External Partnerships

Nkomati has altered overseas perceptions of SADCC in two
directions. In the case of the Soviet bloc, there has been a
further dwindling of interest in undertaking financial
commitments. In the West and especially in Washington, on
the other hand, the retreat of SADCC states from military
adventurism and their acquiescence in the new regional
dispensation have been widely applauded. There is also
growing recognition that Maputo, unlike Pretoria, has lived
up to its solemn obligations, and that apartheid in South
Africa rather than "terrorist bases" in Mozambique
constitutes the principal source of instability in the
region. Whether the warmth of sympathy evident at the
rhetorical level will find expression in the commitment of
substantial additional resources to SADCC's priority projects
is as yet unclear.

Pressing for augmented assistance to SADCC, however, is
not without its dangers. It could provide donors with a

convenient excuse for not facing up realistically to the political implications of their economic involvement in South Africa, especially as Nkomati has to some extent sanctioned the continuation of such ties. The Botswana chairman of SADCC VI evidently had this fear in mind when, in his concluding comments, he pleaded with government representatives present not to use "the currently inevitable link between some of our member states and South Africa ... as excuses for removing the international pressure on South Africa to eliminate completely the apartheid system which humiliates us all."[42]

Liberation

Mozambican acceptance of unreformed apartheid as essentially a South African domestic concern has accorded respectability to a policy that was already implicit in the action of other Front Line States, notably Zimbabwe. Similarly, Luanda's willingness to parley with Pretoria "in an atmosphere of tolerance" has further lessened the opprobrium attached to "dialoguing with the devil." The moral commitment of SADCC leaders to eradicating racism remains as fervent as ever but, confronted with the realities of power and poverty, it is hardly surprising that they have continued to opt for "pragmatic survival rather than ideological martyrdom."[43] Whether, in the event of further rapid deterioration in the security situation inside South Africa, SADCC governments will find it possible to remain safely on the sidelines without being drawn into the conflict is highly problematical. Pressure from their own people, from the OAU and from the liberation movements as well as provocation by the South African Defense Force may take this critical decision right out of their hands.

Nkomati has undoubtedly taken its toll on SADCC by laying bare the economic weakness and vulnerability to penetration of the region. Yet, despite dire predictions of its inevitable demise, the organization has survived the first period of the Accord. While the commitment to the long-term goal of economic liberation may have been weakened, in the short-run, the political resolve of member states to pr4ess ahead energetically with closer regional cooperation appears to have been strengthened. In the final analysis, however, the fate of the organization may depend more on the course of events inside South Africa than on developments within the SADCC area. No real peace or progress is possible in Southern Africa as long as racialism continues to flourish in South Africa and white privilege remains firmly entrenched.

NOTES

1. Speech by Samora Machel, Komatipoort, 16 March 1984, AIM Information Bulletin, (Maputo) (93), March 1984, Supplement, p. 8.
2. Economist, 30 March 1985, p. 25.
3. "External Cooperation and the Work of SADCC: Some Notes and Annotation," address to the Conference on Development in the SADCC Region: Progress and Problems, London, 18 July 1984, mimeo., p. 7.
4. Cited in Review of African Political Economy (29), July 1984, p. 150.
5. "Accord of Nkomati: A Victory for Peace – speech by President Samora Machel at a ceremony in Maputo praising the achievement of the agreement," 5 April 1984, Aim Information Bulletin (94), April 1984, Supplement, pp. 7, 8, 14 and (101), November 1984, p. 12.
6. Financial Times, (London), 17 April 1984, p. 1; Star Weekly, (Johannesburg), 26 March 1984, p. 14.
7. "Final Communique from the Meeting of Front Line Heads of State and Government, Arusha, 29 April 1984," AIM Information Bulletin (94), April 1984, Supplement, pp. 20–21.
8. "Southern African Development Coordination Conference, Mbabane, Kingdom of Swaziland, 21 January – 1 February 1985: Overview," p. 14. The SADCC VI communique also "regretted that these hopes remain unfulfilled" (AIM Information Bulletin (104), March 1985, p. 5).
9. AIM Information Bulletin (102), January 1985, p. 4, (104), March 1985, pp. 11–13 and (105), April 1985, pp. 7–10. See also "Mozambique: An infamous accord," Africa Confidential 25(24), 28 November 1984, pp. 4–7 and Joseph Hanlon, Mozambique: The Revolution under Fire, (London: Zed Press, 1984), pp. 255–59. Machel even threatened to take South Africa to the International Court of Justice for breach of promise (Economist, 30 March 1985, p. 25).
10. "Southern Africa: Oliver Tambo's View," AfricAsia (London), (8–9), August-September 1984, p. 35; Hanlon, Mozambique, pp. 259–62. Hanlon considers that "both Frelimo and the ANC acted badly, as the Nkomati Accord brought to the surface long simmering disagreements" (p. 260).
11. Times, (London), 12 March 1984, p. 7.
12. AIM Information Bulletin (93), March 1984, Supplement, p. 16.
13. Financial Mail, (Johannesburg), 27 April 1984, pp. 31–34; AIM Information Bulletin (104), March 1985, p. 11.
14. Amon J. Nsekela, (ed), Southern Africa: toward economic liberation, (London: Rex Collings, 1981); Joseph Hanlon, SADCC: progress, projects and prospects, Economist

Intelligence Unit Special Report No. 182 (1984), p. 95.
15. Nsekela, Southern Africa, pp. 3–4.
16. Southern African Development Coordination Conference: A Handbook, (Gaborone: SADCC, 1984), p. 17; Africa Research Bulletin: Economic, Financial and Technical (ARB: EFT), 1984, p. 7327. See also, SADCC Secretariat, "SADCC: Toward Regional Trade Development," December 1983.
17. SADCC, "Overview", p. 11.
18. Nsekela, Southern Africa, p. xiii.
19. The Employment Bureau of Africa Limited, Report and Financial Statements for the year ended 31 December 1983, p. 9; Nsekela, Southern Africa, p. 6.
20. SADCC: Annual Progress Report covering the period July 1983 –June 1984; SADCC, "Overview," pp. 2, 10, 16.
21. Heribert Adam and Stanley Uys, "Eight New Realities in Southern Africa," CSIS Africa Notes (Washington) (39), 28 February 1985, p. 4.
22. SADCC, "Overview," p. 17.
23. Ibid, pp. 11, 18.
24. Hanlon, SADCC, pp. 99–100.
25. Ibid, pp. 88–81; ARB: EFT, 1984, p. 7404.
26. Joseph Hanlon, "A Closer Look at Some of the Problems," address to the Conference on Development in the SADCC Region: progress and problems, London, 20 July 1984, pp. 2–3.
27. SADCC, "Overview," pp. 7, 24.
28. Susan Turner, (ed), "SADCC: Development in the region, progress and problems: conference report," London Commonwealth Institute, 1984, p. 4.
29. SADCC Blantyre 1981: Proceedings, (Blantyre: SADCC, 1982), p. 12.
30. ARB: EFT, 1984, p. 7364; SADCC, "Overview," pp. 6, 8, 10.
31. Ibid., p. 6.
32. Nsekela, Southern Africa, p. 6.
33. ARB: EFT, 1984, p. 7143; "Policies in Agriculture and Rural Development – A Nordic View."
34. ARB: EFT, 1983, pp. 7142, 7327.
35. SADCC, "Overview," p. 15; ARB: EFT, 1984, p. 7363.
36. Hanlon, Mozambique, pp. 255–56.
37. Douglas G. Anglin, "Economic Liberation and Regional Cooperation in Southern Africa: SADCC and PTA," International Organization 37(4), Autumn 1983, pp. 701–702.
38. SADCC Blantyre 1981, p. 60; Record of the Southern African Development Coordination Summit Conference Held at Mulungushi Conference Center, Lusaka, on 1 April 1980, pp. 20, 30; AIM Information Bulletin no. 93, March 1981, Supplement, p. 10.

39. ARB: EFT, 1984, p. 7326.
40. Hanlon, Mozambique, p. 216.
41. ARB: EFT, 1983, p. 7002.
42. Peter Mmusi, "Chairman's Closing Remarks," Mbabane, 1 February 1985.
43. Adam and Uys, "Eight New Realities," pp. 1, 3.

PART FOUR

Legal and Institutional Aspects of Nkomati

11. Marginal Notes on the Nkomati Accord: Unequal Treaties in International Law
C. M. Peter

The Nkomati Accord is a contribution to the progressive, revolutionary and democratic forces that throughout the world are struggling for peace, detente and security between nations.

    – President Samora Machel, 27 April 1984

The Nkomati non-aggression pact is a failure.

    – President Samora Machel, 12 March 1985

INTRODUCTION

This chapter is an attempt to examine the Nkomati Accord (hereinafter referred to as the accord or the agreement) in the light of international law. International covenants, whether general or particular, are taken as the main sources of international law. Article 38 of the Statute of the International Court of Justice points out this fact. Therefore, treaties are treated seriously in international interaction. The Nkomati is one of the most controversial agreements in recent times. Maybe this is because it was not expected, given the outlooks of the two signatories.

When this agreement was signed on 16 March 1984, there were mixed feelings about it. There were those who saw it in a positive light. Among them was President Kenneth Kaunda of Zambia who termed it "a genuine step towards peace." The South African Prime Minister, P.W. Botha, saw the agreement as "signalling a new course in the history of Southern Africa." Aquiono de Braganca, a close adviser to President Machel of Mozambique characterized this agreement as:

A step backward which will permit us to consolidate our
power towards the liberation of all Southern Africa in
different ways - through economic and political
struggle.[1]

Yet there were others who viewed Nkomati negatively. For
example, Alfred Nzo, the Secretary-General of the National
Executive Committee of the African National Congress (ANC),
in a statement issued in Lusaka a few hours before the
signing ceremony said the accord was one of the attempts by
the Botha regime to reduce independent countries in the
region to the level of its bantustan creations by forcing
them to join the Transkei, Bophuthatswana, Venda and Ciskei
through so-called non-aggression pacts.[2] His colleague
Johnstone Mfanafuthi Makatini, the head of the International
Department in the ANC acknowledged that the accord was a
setback in the struggle in Southern Africa and expressed
specific reservations about Mozambique's actions, especially
the denial of the ANC to have some input into the whole
exercise.[3]

The Johannesburg Star, a paper with a wide circulation
in South Africa, was rather sarcastic about the accord. In
its opinion,

the agreement was a reward for President Machel for
nine years of Marxist incompetence and an illusory
alliance with the Soviet Union.

It went on to say that:

from now on he [Machel] toes South Africa's line on
everything from trade to suppression of the African
National Congress or face the downfall of his government
at the hand of the Mozambique National Resistance
guerrillas.[4]

Other circles remained non-committal. The Organization of
African Unity (OAU) did not condemn Mozambique for breaking
the African ban on diplomatic relations with South Africa.
Instead, the Organization expressed "sympathy and deep
understanding."[5] The Front Line States were silent but
declined President Machel's invitation to attend the signing
ceremony.

In order to appreciate the varying positions taken by
the different interest groups to this agreement, we proceed
to examine the contents of the accord. (See Appendix I.)

CONTENTS OF THE ACCORD

The Preamble

The Nkomati Accord signed by Pieter Willem Botha, the Prime Minister of the Republic of South Africa on the one hand and Samora Moises Machel, Marshal of the Republic and President of the People's Republic of Mozambique, contains eleven articles only.

The main body of the agreement is proceeded by a rambling preamble. The preamble is supposed to set out the basis of the agreement. According to this preamble, the agreement is based on recognition of the principles of strict respect for sovereignty and territorial integrity, sovereign equality, political independence, inviolability of the borders of all states and the principle of non-interference in the internal affairs of other states.

The accord also takes into consideration the internationally recognized principle of the right of the people to self-determination and independence and the principle of equal rights of all peoples. Parties to the agreement recognize the obligation of all states to refrain in their international relations, from the threat or use of force against the territorial integrity or political independence of any state and the obligation of states to settle conflicts by peaceful means and thus safeguard international peace, security and justice.

Recognized also is the responsibility of states not to allow their territory to be used for acts of war, aggression or violence against other states and the need to promote relations of good neighborliness based on principles of equality of rights and mutual advantage.

Usually, as a general rule, the preamble is not part of a document. It is a policy statement indicating what is intended to be contained in a document. Even going by that rule, it is still doubtful whether the parties to the agreement gave serious consideration to what was said in the preamble. It is as if the preamble was formulated out of pieces picked from various United Nations resolutions. Most of what is said therein contradicts the practise of one of the parties. For example, it is universally known that South Africa does not recognize, let alone respect, the principle of the right of people to self-determination and independence and the principle of equal rights of all peoples. Otherwise, it fails all senses to understand why up to now it is still occupying Namibia by force and denying the blacks within South Africa equal democratic and civil rights.

Resolution of Differences and Disputes

In the accord, the two parties undertake to respect each other's sovereignty and independence. In fulfillment of this obligation they undertake to refrain from interfering in internal affairs of each other.[6] Simply examined, this article sounds quite harmless. However, a closer examination reveals that the article is loaded with deep mischief. What does non-interference with internal affairs of each other mean? Incidentally, a similar provision is contained in the OAU Charter. What are the internal affairs of the two signatories which may tempt outsiders to interfere? Mozambique has proclaimed itself a Marxist-Leninist state building socialism. Maybe this is what South Africa should not interfere with. South Africa on the other hand practices apartheid which is the worst type of racial discrimination. South Africa has been condemned year after year for its internal policies of apartheid. By signing the Nkomati Accord, Mozambique has implied it will not criticize South Africa's policy of apartheid as that is a social system that the South African regime has chosen for itself land hence is its internal affair. This completely incapacitates and ties Mozambique down.

One should not, however, overlook the fact that the legal status of apartheid has changed over time. The international community has already characterized apartheid as a crime against humanity. Thus, the practise cannot remain an internal affair. It has become international and it should therefore be regarded so.

The accord goes on to provide for modalities for resolving differences and disputes that may arise between them and that may endanger mutual peace and security in the region. Disputes are to be dealt with through negotiation, enquiry, mediation, conciliation, arbitration and other peaceful means. Parties to the agreement undertake to refrain from resorting to threat or use of force against each other's sovereignty, territorial integrity or political independence.[7]

Use of force has been defined to include attack by land, air, sea forces; sabotage; unwarranted concentration of such forces at or near international boundaries of each other; and violation of international land, air or sea boundaries of either party.[8] Parties undertake not to assist in any way armed forces of any state or group of states deployed against the territorial sovereignty or political independence of each other.[9]

Elimination of Military Bases

Article III is the backbone of the whole agreement. It is the most elaborate and thus leaves no doubt as to whom it was aimed. Given the importance of this part of the accord and for ease of reference, I reproduce the whole article:

ARTICLE III

1) The high contracting parties shall not allow their respective territories, territorial waters or air space to be used as a base, thoroughfare, or in any other way by another state, government, foreign military forces, organizations or individuals which plan or prepare to commit acts of violence, terrorism or aggression against the territorial integrity or political independence of the other or may threaten the security of its inhabitants.

2) The high contracting parties, in order to prevent or eliminate the acts or the preparation of acts mentioned in paragraph (1) of this article, undertake in particular to –

   a) forbid and prevent in their respective territories the organization of irregular forces or armed bands, including mercenaries, whose objective is to carry out the acts contemporated in paragraph (1) of this article;

   b) eliminate from their respective territories bases, training center, places of shelter, accommodation and transit for elements who intend to carry out the acts contemplated in paragraph (1) of this article;

   c) eliminate from their respective territories centres or depots containing armaments of whatever nature, destined to be used by the elements contemplated in paragraph (1) of this article;

   d) eliminate from their respective territories command posts or other places for the command, direction and coordination of elements contemplated in paragraph (1) of this article;

   e) eliminate from their respective territories

communication and telecommunication facilities between the command and elements contemplated in paragraph (1) of this article;

f)   eliminate and prohibit the installation in their respective territories of radio broadcasting stations, including unofficial or clandestine broadcasts, for the elements that carry out acts contemplated in paragraph (1) of this article;

g)   exercise strict control in the respective territories over elements which intend to carry out or plan the acts contemplated in paragraph (1) of this article;

h)   prevent the transit of elements who intend or plan to commit the acts contemplated in paragraph (1) of this article, from a place in the territory of other to a place in the territory of the other or to a place in the territory of any third state which has a common boundary with the high contracting party against which such elements intend or plan to commit the said acts;

i)   take appropriate steps in their respective territories to prevent the recruitment of elements of whatever nationality for the purpose of carrying out the acts contemplated in paragraph (1) of this article;

j)   prevent the elements contemplated in paragraph (1) of this article from carrying out from their respective territories by any means acts of abduction or other acts, aimed at taking citizens of any nationality hostage in the territory of the other High Contracting Party; and

k)   prohibit the provision on their respective territories of any logistic facilities for carrying out the acts contemplated in paragraph (1) of this article.

This article is quite clear. Though not expressed, the parties had two groups or organizations in mind. Botha was thinking of the ANC, while Machel had in mind the Mozambique National Resistance. This situation is noted in Africa Now which, while discussing the preparatory stage of the negotiations leading to the accord, commented that:

any security arrangement will inevitably contain restrictions on the ANC activity in Mozambique. Otherwise South Africa will not sign it. Equally, it will include a South African pledge to drop their support for the rebels of the Mozambique National Resistance (MNR). Otherwise the Mozambicans will not sign it.[10]

Each party thought that the other would immediately take steps to deal with the so-called subversive elements operating from its territory.

Patrolling Borders

Under Article IV parties are supposed to take steps either individually or collectively to ensure that the international boundary between their respective territories is effectively patrolled and that the border posts are efficiently administered to prevent illegal crossings from the territory of one party into the territory of the other. This article is particularly directed at elements contemplated in Article III of the accord; that is, elements which plan or prepare to commit acts of violence, terrorism or aggression against the territorial integrity or political independence of these states or those who may threaten the security of its inhabitants. These should not be allowed to cross the international borders of these states. The point is whether the two states can effectively take up the challenge set by this article. The truth of the matter is that while the Pretoria regime has the resources to enable it to patrol its section of the border, Mozambique can ill-afford the exercise even if it had the desire to do so.

Parties are required under the accord to prohibit within their territories acts of propaganda that incite a war of aggression against each other or are aimed at inciting acts of terrorism and civil war in each other's territory.[11]

The agreement contains a declaration by the parties to the effect that there is no conflict between their commitments in treaties and international obligations and the commitments undertaken in the agreement.[12] In a way this is a face-saving declaration because South Africa has been flouting not only international treaties but also various resolutions of both the Security Council and the General Assembly of the United Nations and the decisions of the International Court of Justice on Namibia. In signing Nkomati - which is compromising with apartheid - Mozambique is in conflict with various commitments it has undertaken against this undesirable practice.

The agreement is to be interpreted in good faith and there will be periodic contact between the parties to ensure effective application of what has been agreed.[13] At the same time each party retains the right of self-defense in the event of armed attack.[14] This right is also provided under Article 51 of the Charter of the United Nations. One cannot avoid the conclusion that this is a safety valve to allow violation of the agreement by invoking self-defense as a justification whenever the need arises.

Joint Security Commission

Article IX of the agreement is extremely important. It sets out the Joint Security Commission. Each party to the agreement is supposed to appoint high-ranking representatives to serve on the Commission whose aim is to supervise and monitor the application of the accord.[15] The Commission is supposed to determine its own working procedure and its meetings will be on a regular basis and may be specifically convened whenever circumstances require.

The main functions of the Commission are to consider all allegations of infringements of the provisions of the agreement; to advise the parties of its conclusions; and to make recommendations to the signatories of the accord concerning measures for the effective application of the agreement and the settlement of disputes over infringements or allegations of infringements.

Each party is supposed to determine the mandate of its representatives in order to enable interim measures to be taken in cases of duly recognized emergency. For the Commission to take off effectively, parties are urged to make available all the facilities necessary for the effective functions of the organ and jointly consider its conclusions and recommendations. The Mozambican Deputy Defense Minister Segio Vieira is the Chairman for the Mozambique side of the Joint Security Commission.

The last two articles are purely procedural. Article X gives the name of the agreement. It says that "This agreement shall also be known as "THE ACCORD OF NKOMATI". Article XI provides for the effective date of the agreement coming into force: the date the accord was signed, 16 March 1984.

Any amendment to the accord has to be agreed to by the parties and would be effected by the exchange of notes between them.

Ratification of the Accord

Having signed the agrement, Mozambique presented the
same before the People's Assembly for ratification on 24
April 1984. It is reported that the accord was ratified by
acclamation. The resolution ratifying the agreement was
presented by Foreign Minister Joaquim Chissano who spoke of
the agreement as a victory for Mozambique. In his speech he
criticized the "ultra-left myopic revolutionaries who
objected to the agreement." These he said "don't hesitate in
asking us to die so that they can applaud us as heros.
Mozambique did not mind this when the sacrifice was useful,
as it had been during the independence war, but we ought to
tell them that our people don't just die to win applause.
They don't die so that statues can be built for them."
Minister Chissano, however, warned that the agreement in
itself will not bring happiness nor will it eliminate hunger
and provide clothing for the people of Mozambique. The
accord, according to him, will create conditions for efforts
in production to give better results.[16]
There were other dignitaries who spoke at the Assembly.
These included the Information Minister Jose Luis Cabaco who
argued that Nkomati reflected:

a conjunctural balance of forces favorable to peace
[and] that Mozambique's military and diplomatic
offensives, and its regional strategy had provoked a
profound crisis in the South African regime.[17]

A more rambling speech came from Segio Vieira, the Deputy
Minister. He said that the accord was:

a defeat for those in South Africa who had staked all on
racism and expansionism, and who had made their anti-
communism into a pathological obsession.[18]

He continued to argue that Nkomati was a defeat:

against those who claimed for themselves the right to
intervene in any state south of the equator. Against
those who used to boast that they could destroy any
African state between breakfast and lunch to whom the
accord obliges coexistence with our anti-racist state.
To be a revolutionary, a democrat, a communist in the
Africa of 1984 demands the defense and consolidation of
Africa's socialist revolutions. The touchstone of
internationalism in Africa today is the concrete

attitude taken towards the first liberated zones on the continent.[19]

He declared that the accord was a basic part of the struggle for peace and socialism and an integral part of the global strategy to remove from Africa and the world the horrors of war and of nuclear catastrophe. After the speeches the agreement was ratified by acclamation before invited guests who included Moses Mabhida, a member of the Executive Committee of the ANC.

Having gone through the contents of the accord, the next point is to examine whether it was reached freely by willing agents. Were there underhand pressures or not? This makes it essential to examine the regime of unequal treaties in international law.

NKOMATI ACCORD AND UNEQUAL TREATIES

Whether or not there exist unequal treaties is a heavily contested issue in international law. According to conventional and customary international law, every state possesses the capacity to conclude treaties.[20] In fact, one of the most valuable evidences of statehood is capacity to enter into relations with other states.[21]

Therefore, traditionally, international law treats states as equal and hence inequality among them is not an issue. However, over time thinking has developed on the whole question of treaties. For example what socialist and developing states have already done with other aspects of international law is to come up in full force to challenge the equality implied in treaties.

Among the treaties strongly condemned as unequal are those which were entered into between imperialist powers and colonial and dependent nations. Similarly, treaties which give a state a right to exercise power on the territory of the other, such as agreements permitting establishment of foreign military bases, and economic assistance agreements, have been termed unequal.[22]

Writers also support the doctrine of unequal treaties. It is said that the doctrine is directly linked to the principles of the equality of sovereign states. States should not be forced to accept obligations contrary to the basic principles of international law. The Chinese writer Hungdah Chiu supports this by declaring that unequal treaties are contrary to international law and thus have no validity.[23] He then points out the main characteristic of an unequal treaty:

whether or not a treaty is equal does not depend upon
the form and the words of various treaty provisions but
depends upon the state's character, economic strength
and the substance of correlation of the contracting
parties.[24] (emphasis added)

It has thus been argued that unequal or inequitable treaties
imposed by duress are invalid ab initio. This is because
they are humiliating, injurious, unjust and, above all,
inequitable and do not conform to the principles, precepts
and norms of international morality universally accepted
today.

Western writers and politicians vehemently oppose the
doctrine of unequal treaties. They argue that it is vague
and that if accepted it would have adverse effects on the
sanctity of treaties. It is not, therefore, surprising that
the Vienna Convention on the Law of Treaties of 1969 contains
no provisions on unequal treaties. The problem of unequal
treaties was, however, raised by many states during the
Vienna Conference. This resulted in a Declaration on the
Prohibition of Military, Political or Economic Coercion in
conclusion of treaties being adopted. In this declaration
the conference said it:

Solemnly condemns the threat or use of pressure in any
form, whether military, political, or economic, by any
state in order to coerce another state to perform any
act relating to the conclusion of a treaty in violation
of principles of the sovereign equality of states and
freedom of consent.[25]

In a way this declaration is an acknowledgement of the fact
that people cannot always restrict themselves to the doctrine
of sovereignty as the only basis of checking the validity of
treaties. Nor can arm-twisting in various ways be ruled out
in the conclusion of certain treaties.

How does the Nkomati accord relate to unequal treaties?
Though there is no direct evidence for the purposes of
substantiation, circumstantial factors lead to serious doubts
as to whether this was an agreement between equals. It is
our respectful submission that Mozambique was an unwilling
party to the agreement. It had no alternative but to sign:
it was forced down its throat, because various economic and
military pressures including the creation of an artificial
resistance movement by Pretoria weighed so much on it. This
fact is underscored by the statement issued by the ANC on the
day the accord was signed. The liberation movement said it

was:

> profoundly conscious of the enormous political and
> security problems that confront many of the peoples of
> our region (including Mozambique - C.M.P.). The blame
> for many of these problems must be laid squarely on the
> Pretoria regime which has sought to define the limits of
> independence of the countries of our region through a
> policy of aggression and destabilization.[26]

The same views are echoed by Johnstone Mfanafuthi Makatini,
the head of ANC's International Department:

> Nkomati was the result of South Africa's ruthless acts
> of destabilization and aggression, whose adverse effects
> were complicated by natural calamities and inadequacy of
> international support for Mozambique.

There is ample evidence to support what is said above. South
Africa has withdrawn from using Mozambican ports for some of
its imports and also has cut back by over 60% the recruitment
of Mozambican labor for its mines.[27] This has adversely
affected the economy of Mozambique.

These factors and many others in their totality can
amount to what we call constructive coercion on the part of
Mozambique. Coercion against a state has not been expressly
referred to in the Treaty Convention on the Law of Treaties
(1969) although there is reference to coercion on
representatives of the state.[28] According to D.J. Harris,[29]
some members of the International Law Commission (ILC)
expressed the view that any other form of pressure such as
threat to strangle the economy of a state ought to be stated
in the treaty as falling within the concept of coercion.
However, the Commission decided to define coercion in terms
of threat to use force in violation of the principles of the
Charter of the United Nations and considered that the precise
scope of the acts covered by this definition should be left
to be determined in practice by interpretation of the
relevant provisions of the Charter. Such a decision to adopt
a narrow approach to coercion was due to the heavy Western
lobby to avoid condemnation for strangling the economies of
developing states through their multinational corporations.

It is, therefore, my considered opinion that Mozambique
was, for all intents and purposes, practically coerced into
the accord. It was faced with a _fait accompli_ - sign or
perish - and chose to sign and survive.

This being the case, can such an accord be said to be
valid? If the argument on coercion is accepted then the

accord falls into invalidity and hence cannot call for observance. Another factor likely to invalidate the accord is the very status of South Africa. Is South Africa an independent state? This is a highly contested issue. The predominant Black South African view is that South Africa is still a colony and that the old Union of South Africa in 1910 represented a Boer-British alliance to enforce a particular form of colonial domination over the black population which has since been consolidated under apartheid.

Then there are others who recognize South Africa as an independent state or republic to be precise. This view is held and entertained by many independent African states. They see the problem in South Africa as one of racial discrimination only. The views of this group have been aired by the Mozambican army Commander General Sebastio Mabote who is quoted as having said that:

> Mozambique had supported the campaign in Zimbabwe because that had been a fight against colonialism for national liberation. But the struggle in South Africa is merely one for civic rights against apartheid.[30] (emphasis added)

Notwithstanding this loose and haphazard support, the legitimacy of South Africa as an independent state is still questionable. It therefore goes without saying that agreements entered into with such entities whose recognition is at issue have doubtful legal validity. Nkomati cannot totally pass the test of legal validity without question marks.

HAS NKOMATI BROUGHT PEACE?

Press reports on Southern Africa after the agreement read like horror stories. There is no doubt that things were worse after than before the accord. This is because only one side to the accord has kept its word. While Mozambique fulfilled its obligations under the agreement to the letter in good faith, South Africa has not and it seems not in a hurry to undertake its responsibilities. Within days of the accord, Mozambique began a witch-hunt for ANC fighters. There are allegations that the Pretoria regime gave Maputo a list of people it wanted out of Mozambique heading which was Joe Slovo, a prominent white ANC member. Mozambique, like its neighbor Swaziland, made sure that what Pretoria wanted was done efficiently, meticulously and quickly.[31] South Africa on its part has refused to do anything and it seems as if it has no intention of respecting the accord at all. A relief worker in the area notes that a few weeks before the accord was signed, South Africa took out an "insurance policy" delivering extra support for the MNR and armed them to the teeth. This has given the MNR confidence and close sources report boasting within MNR that, despite the accord, the war in Mozambique would reach unprecedented levels within the next few months following the accord. According to this source, the MNR is confident that the non-aggression between Mozambique and South Africa will have no immediate effect on its operations and that the agreement will not save President Machel, but rather contribute to his downfall.[32]

MNR is also said to be in a process of diversifying its support. In the first half of 1984 the Lisbon-based Secretary-General of the Movement, Evo Fernandes, visited the US and the Federal Republic of Germany where he was assured support by right-wing groups.[33]

Sabotage of electricity supply lines from South Africa continues and modern technology, such as laser guns, are freely used by the MNR. Also, ambushes of trains and buses resulting in great losses of both life and limb continue, all done by the same MNR with tacit South African approval. Mozambique has been very bitter about this:

> The South African government has been deafeningly silent about their part of the [Nkomati] bargain. We don't know what action has been taken against MNR leadership and camps near Phalaborwa in the Eastern Transvaal.[34]

As usual the Pretoria regime is not bothered. It has achieved what it has been dreaming of. The accord was a diplomatic triumph. Photographs of the South African Ministers and Botha himself shaking the hand of Machel will make a major contribution to the regime's attempts to break out of the international isolation to which it has been subjected by the international community: arms embargoes; disinvestment; sports boycotts; and calls for economic sanctions. The accord is a recognition of the regime's existence as a full-fledged state. The Lesotho Ambassador to the U.S., Thabo Makeka, whose country rejected South African demands for a similar non-aggression pact in 1983, correctly and with regret noted that:

> What is unfortunate is that the pact will give the Pretoria regime a very wrong sense of support.[35]

Actually this misconceived sense of acceptance is exhibited

by the words of the South African Deputy Foreign Minister
Louis Nel, who is reported to have said:

> The talks with Mozambique meant that there was a stable
> order in South Africa and it was useless for people in
> the West to try to overturn this ... If the Marxist
> government of Mozambique is prepared to accept us as
> legitimate negotiating partners then why should anyone
> else try to boycott us?[56]

Quite a legitimate and logical question indeed. That having
been achieved, then MNR can continue hitting Mozambique with
impunity. The much desired peace is nowhere in sight.

CONCLUSION

As indicated at the beginning, the aim of this chapter
was to examine Nkomati in the light of international law and
in particular the law of treaties, to be specific that of
unequal treaties. In the process I have examined the factors
leading to the agreement and the contents of the various
provisions of the agreement. An attempt was made to give
interpretation to these provisions. The interpretations
given are open to debate.

I have also placed Nkomati among other treaties to test
its validity. There is overwhelming evidence that the
circumstances under which it was made cannot be said with
certainty to be conducive for free consent by both parties.
Hence some amount of coercion can be imputed with the effect
of making the accord fall among the unequal treaties. This
is another controversial and contested area in international
law.

There is no doubt that the Nkomati accord has not
brought peace in the Southern African region as anticipated
by its signatories. This is basically because it side-
stepped the root cause of the problem. The problem is the
very social system inside South Africa itself; in a word-
apartheid. Any solution suggested to solve the problems in
Southern Africa which ignores this fundamental issue is bound
to fail miserably or at best have very temporary "success."
Nkomati is a testimony to this.

The general view held by the majority is that there can
never be peace and stability in Southern Africa without a
concrete solution effecting fundamental change inside South
Africa itself. Various parties have aired this view. The
American weekly magazine *Time* of 26 March 1984 cautioned
that:

Even if South Africa does come to terms with its black neighbors, there is no certainty that peace will hasten the end of its internal policies of racial discrimination.

Speaking on negotiations between South Africa and Mozambique before the accord was signed, Archbishop Denis Hurley of Durban noted that:

Latest initiatives could not bring peace in South Africa because it left apartheid untouched.[37]

The same views were aired by the ANC in its statement issued the day Nkomati was signed which declared that:

The peoples of Southern Africa know from their experience that there can be no peaceful coexistence between freedom and independence on the one hand and colonialism and racism on the other.

In short, peace and apartheid are inherently mutually exclusive. This is an important point to comprehend.

Given things as they are now, what should Mozambique do? Opt out of Nkomati? How would this be interpreted? Will South Africa not take this as a declaration of war as it had already signed a peace accord? And what would this mean to Mozambique? These are serious questions which the people of Mozambique themselves should answer having assessed and reassessed their concrete situation.

There have been interesting developments on Mozambique after signing of the Nkomati agreement. For example the Mozambique News Review of 27 April 1984 reports that on 17 and 18 April, the Mozambique Council of Ministers decided to initiate negotiations with a view to Mozambique's joining the International Monetary Fund (IMF) and the International Bank of Reconstruction and Development (IBRD), popularly known as the World Bank. Finance Minister Rui Baltazar and the Governor of the Bank of Mozambique, Prakash Ratilal, were mandated to take charge of this process. The same session of the Council of Ministers analyzed a draft law on foreign investments and approved its basic principles.

Interestingly, an authoritative British paper, the Financial Times of 24 April 1984, reported that:

Maputo's elegant, white balustraded Palona Hotel on the seafront is coping with an influx of unaccustomed guests.

Seated at tables on the terrace, habitues from East
Germany, the Soviet Union and Cuba warily eye the
newcomers – delegations of South African businessmen
whose discussions with local officials range from multi-
million investments in tourism to the revival of plant
and machinery which stands idle for want of spare parts
worth a few thousand pounds.

One may wish to dismiss all this as propaganda against the
Peoples Republic of Mozambique. However, when all is said
and done, there seems to have been much more beneath the
surface than was presented to the public in the form of the
eleven articles that make the Nkomati accord. That
complicates the task of writing marginal notes on the accord.

NOTES

1. J. Frederikse, "The Nkomati Accord," _Africa News_, 26
March 1984.
2. J. Cason, "Black and White Reaction," _Africa News_,
26 March 1984.
3. _Ibid_.
4. See _The Johannesburg Star_, 26 March 1984.
5. M. Fleshman, "As Others See the Pact," _Africa News_,
26 March 1984.
6. Article I.
7. Article 2(1).
8. Article 2(2).
9. Article 2(3).
10. See _Africa Now_, 35, March 1984.
11. Article 5.
12. Article 6.
13. Article 7.
14. Article 8.
15. Article 9(1).
16. See _Mozambique News Review_ (Britain), 27 April 1984.
17. _Ibid_.
18. _Ibid_.
19. _Ibid_.
20. See Article 6 of the Vienna Convention on the Law of
Treaties, 1969.
21. See Article 1 of the Montevideo Convention on the
Rights and Duties of States.
22. S.K. Kapoor, _A Textbook of International Law_, fifth
edition, (Allahabad: Central Law Agency), pp. 407-410.
23. Hungdah Chiu, "Comparison of the Nationalist and the
Communist Chinese Views on Unequal Treaties," in Jerome Alan

218

Cohen (ed), <u>China's Practice of International Law: some case studies</u>, (Cambridge: Harvard University Press, 1972), pp. 239, 258-259.

24. <u>Ibid</u>.

25. See Treaty Conference Records, 1969, p. 168. See also <u>International Legal Materials</u>, July 1969, p. 733.

26. "Southern Africa 1984: Nkomati Accord", <u>Review of African Political Economy</u>, (29), p. 147.

27. See I. Msabaha and J. Hartmann, Chapter X in this volume.

28. Article 51 of the Vienna Convention on the Law of Treaties, 1969.

29. D.J. Harris, <u>Cases and Materials on International Law</u>, third edition, (London: Sweet and Maxwell, 1983), p. 614.

30. This was in an interview with the French journalist Pierre Haski referred to in "Accord debated in the townships," <u>Africa Now</u>, (35), March 1984.

31. See <u>Financial Mail</u>, (South Africa), 27 April 1984.

32. Joao Santa Rita, "Despite Accord, War will Escalate - MNR Sources Claim," <u>Star</u>, (South Africa), 23 April 1984.

33. <u>Ibid</u>.

34. See <u>Financial Mail</u>, 27 April 1984.

35. Quoted by M. Fleshman, "As others see the Pact," <u>Africa News</u>, 26 March 1984.

36. See "Squaring the Circle," <u>Africa Now</u> (35), March 1984, p. 37.

37. <u>Ibid</u>.

12. Peace and Security in Southern Africa: Legal Aspects
Reg H. F. Austin

INTRODUCTION

Although African lawyers have been more ready than most
to cross disciplinary boundaries and to reject strict
compartmentalization, there is still a need for a more
regular debate on the central problems confronting our
continent involving a wider range of African academics as
reflected in these conference proceedings. Only in this way
can we hope (within the material and manpower shortages we
all have to live with) to create an intellectually powerful
framework within which the commonly desired objective of
overcoming dependence and foreign domination can be achieved.
My aim in this chapter is to articulate my own perception of
a) some of the political realities dominating both national
and international relations in contemporary Southern Africa,
and b) the role of international law in these.

I take the view that law has been and will be an
important tool in the process of change. It has both created
guidelines for the historic decolonization and been the
product of that history. This duality must be understood by
the statesmen and people of Africa for in a real sense we
assist change, in one direction or another, by actively
participating in it. We must beware of the illusion that
change is self-generating, and this lesson, it seems to me,
is well-demonstrated by the law.

On the verge of total decolonization today, Africa is
also at a critical watershed between moving from mere
sovereign independence to what might be regarded as
substantial independence. At the same time the beneficiaries
of the status quo ante, acutely aware of this potential, are
anxious not only to slow down the last stage of
decolonization but, more important, to ensure that this
partial liberation cannot be used as a base from which to

move forward to more comprehensive liberation. This intention has been spelled out in many battlefields, real and symbolic, but it is in the development of contemporary international law that it is expressed most starkly. The most unequivocal statement of it at present is in the Nkomati Accord. We must read, understand, and decide how to react to the message broadcast by this law. My hope is that this chapter will contribute to this task of understanding and formulating an appropriate African as well as international response which will one day bring about true peace and security in Southern Africa.

THE HISTORIC LEGAL FRAMEWORK OF PEACE AND SECURITY

The Strength and Weakness of the United Nations Charter

Peace and security does not exist in Southern Africa. This fact stems essentially from the problems of the historic enormity which is apartheid South Africa, where the exploitation of man by man which characterizes that most brutal stage of capitalism -imperialism - is still expressed in as crude racist categories as it was until 40 years ago in Nazi Germany and other countries under fascist occupation. In Europe, the phenomenon of overt, aggressive, militaristic fascism accompanied by the mythology of super-race, the inhuman movement on a genocidal scale of populations, was identified relatively quickly (after a short attempt at appeasement) as necessitating absolute, resolute and armed confrontation. This even included liberal capitalist states which might have been tempted to continue supplying the fascist war machine had it not so inevitably and rapidly turned on them.

The war which ensued, and which was necessary to check and restrain the evil combination, was not only destructive but also instructive. It taught the lesson that peace in the modern world is indivisible. It demonstrated that exploitation, totalitarianism and racism tolerated within one state would result in their uncontrolled extension across national boundaries. It proved that the appetite of fascism could not be sated by appeasement, or "constructive engagement," but demanded the sacrifices of armed struggle. It showed that peace and security was not a passive, negative phenomenon, but rather a condition which could only be achieved and maintained by active opposition to exploitation and a positive readiness to oppose oppression.

The significance for international lawyers of this 40 year old lesson is that it was reduced to a legal code which lies the heart of contemporary international law; namely the United Nations Charter. The Charter articulated the dramatic awareness brought about by the war of the inextricable relationship between "the scourge of war": the denial of "fundamental human rights ... the dignity and worth of the human person ... the equal rights of men and women and of nations large and small", and the need to "promote social progress and better standards of life in larger freedom."[1] Consequently the primary purpose of the UN - "to maintain international peace and security"[2] - needed to be combined with a determination to "respect ... the principle of equal rights and self-determination of peoples"[3] and "to achieve international cooperation in solving international problems of an economic, social, cultural or humanitarian character, and in promoting and encouraging respect for human rights and for fundamental freedoms for all without the distinction."[4] This marked a major change from the standards of so-called classical international law, particularly when we note another of the Charter's basic prescriptions: the control of the unilateral use of force by states[5] and its replacement by a system of collective security for which the Security Council was given primary responsibility.

On this basis the Charter did, quite literally, offer the prospect of a better world. Looked at from the perspective of an African international lawyer, even today after so many disappointments, it constituted an exciting and promising new international legal order.

Europe and North America had learned quickly how horrific was the untrammelled power of fascism and exploitation tinged with a conviction of racial supremacy. It was an unpleasant experience with which the non-European would have had to live, in varying degrees of discomfort, since the final violent stages of imperialism had extended the natural resources, the markets and the "lebensraum" of the metropolitan states of Europe in the 19th century. Although there were important differences in the intensity, technical capacity and greed of the colonial powers, some techniques (including ironically the "concentration camps" first used by the British against the Boers) employed by fascism between 1935 and 1945, would not be strange to the Asian and African peoples occupied by the European states.

The UN Charter adopted in 1945 seen in an African, especially in a Southern African, context seemed to promise an end to exploitation and oppression not only to liberated Europe, but also to all peoples and obviously to colonial nations. Why then, forty years later, is there still in Southern Africa a threat to international peace and security? Why is there still gross exploitation combined with racial discrimination and oppression on a monstrous scale? For this is the reality of Southern Africa.

At its center there is still the racist state-system of South Africa, which continues its military occupation of the territory and people of Namibia; still asserts it right to assure its continued survival by deliberate and widespread aggressive acts in Mozambique and Angola; and proclaims its right to threaten similar aggression in Lesotho, Botswana, Swaziland and Zimbabwe should they dare offer concrete assistance to the people of South Africa seeking by armed struggle to end fascism there.

Why is this so? Has international law slipped back so far since the enlightened year of 1945? Or was the advance in law at that time limited, to deal with racism, exploitation and oppression only where its victims were Europeans? How otherwise could the phenomenon which was the recognized scourge of Europe for little more than a decade continue to blight the lives, liberty and property of the vast majority of the people of Southern Africa? These questions are at the heart of the legal aspects of peace and security of Southern Africa. It is of the greatest importance that international lawyers debating the issue be aware of this perspective and the very basic problems it poses. Too often lawyers allow themselves to be drawn into the minutiae and narrow technicalities of this basic problem, thus ignoring the dramatic unevenness and inequality of contemporary international law which statesmen have still to do so much to eradicate.

The growth of a more comprehensive Law of Decolonization and Liberation

This unevenness, which means that international law still tends to favor the states established under the old order, will only be removed by consistent efforts of new states to change it. The topic of this chapter demonstrates that the efforts cannot be intermittent, and that the struggle is an ongoing one. While the UN Charter was correct in linking national oppression - political, economic and social - with international peace and security, the harsh reality is that some of the major sources of such oppression, such as colonialism and imperialism, were not clearly prescribed by it. Consequently, legal mechanisms for their eradication are also lacking in the Charter.

Given the fact that in 1945 the major colonial and imperialist states were prominent members of the UN, this is no surprise. What is surprising, however, is the fact that within two decades the efforts of anti-colonial states combined with the energy of states newly-liberated from colonialism generated a remarkable body of law which not only established a right of self-determination for colonial peoples (including both economic and political self-determination), but also established norms as to the means by which this right could be asserted and achieved.

The latter norms grew partly as a result of formerly politically dependent peoples developing a higher awareness of the essence of independence. In particular, it became clear that the mere inheritance of the structures of colonial power by an indigenous political elite would not guarantee either independence or equality for all, these goals required that inherited structures themselves be eliminated by revolutionary action.

This awareness was further sharpened by the fact that 'managed' decolonization, (which was fostered by colonial powers recognizing the value of neo-colonialism as a means of achieving the objectives of imperialism) was resisted by die-hard conservative metropolitan regimes – such as fascist Portugal, and by entrenched racial minorities – such as the settler regime of Smith in Rhodesia. This gave time to some colonized peoples to observe the course of neo-colonialism and to look for a deeper explanation of the phenomenon.

This resulted in a real sense in the partial revolutionizing of international law, as a result of the concurrent of these two factors. The outcome of this level of awareness was particularly noticeable in Africa, especially in the South-Central part of the continent. It lay in the emergence of the two independent states of Angola and Mozambique, which were not only politically independent from their former occupier but also set on a course designed to end dependence upon the capitalist system which had been imposed upon them as an integral part of colonization. The shock to Western states of this capacity of a colonized people to achieve such fundamental change resulted in a concerted effort was, and still is, devoted to the legal framework within which the contemporary conflict between imperialism and the search for complete independence is being, literally, fought out.

Of course this conflict is not confined to Southern Africa. Similar tensions exist elsewhere in Africa; for example, in the Horn and Western Sahara. The cockpit of Central America and the Caribbean, where the invasion of Grenada reflected current Western determination to suppress revolutionary independence, is another clear example. The Middle East, despite myriad complicating factors, provides yet another example of the sharpening of basic ideological conflict and the role of international law therein.

However, for the African international lawyer what is happening in our midst requires particular attention. Africa has been at the center of the international legal developments mentioned above. Its peoples, both within existing and emerging stats, and in remarkably active national liberation movements, have demonstrated in a unique fashion and to their own benefit the scope for progressive change under international law.

One example of this was the development of international legal status for liberation movements and, even more specifically, the international legal status of the concept become reality, of war of national liberation.

The Challenge to Liberation

Africa is now confronted with a direct challenge to this record and its capacity to influence the law. More particularly, it is faced with a direct confrontation, aimed by the champions of imperialist interests and their closest ally on the continent - South Africa - at the existing central liberationary legal concepts which Africa has helped to evolve. Thus, self-determination is now being questioned as a right. The right to achieve it by means of armed struggle is also being contradicted by efforts being made to equate such resort to the use of force with banditry. The right of UN member states to support liberation struggles authenticated and endorsed by both the OAU, at the regional level, is now confronted, and is being characterized as intervention and aggression.

In addition, of fundamental significance to the search of every state for security, the sovereign right to seek assistance to protect the state against proven and insistent aggression - for example, by a militarist, racist power bent on preserving its system by the establishment of a regional hegemony - is also being questioned. This makes the events which are taking place daily, in this region, and which deny us any real peace and security, significant not only as bad news but as potential indices of the evolving international legal system.

It is interesting to note that the situations which articulate this legal confrontation do not directly touch the lives of the people in the Western states (US, Britain, France, West Germany and Canada, for example) whose governments' policies directly help create these situations in Southern Africa, especially in the case of Namibia. Consequently, their legal scholars pay scant attention to these developments and problems. The law relating to the use of force and the conduct of armed conflicts is regarded as largely peripheral. This makes it all the more important for African scholars to devote their efforts to these problems. In this context the decision to produce these conference proceedings deserves to be applauded, and to serve as a sign of the need for further such discussions.

The issue of the legal framework for the achievement of substantial independence following post-colonial independence should become as stridently advocated as was the initial demand for the ending of colonialism. It must be placed as firmly on the international agenda as that was. Africa cannot afford to become disinterested in this problem. It cannot afford to pay mere lip-service to the demand for a finalization of the process of eradicating colonial and racist domination, especially when it is becoming clear that domination in that guise was only the easiest to identify and confront. What, then, are the legal dimensions of the present problem?

THE LEGAL CONFRONTATION OF THE LAW OF LIBERATION

The complexity of decolonization and racism as its suggested root

The evolution of the contemporary right of self-determination in and out of the UN has been widely discussed and recognized by commentators and legislators alike, and is taken to be an established part of international law. It has profoundly influenced Africa, helping to change it from a European possession to a continent composed mostly of sovereign states. By purely peaceful political processes or by the resort to force, or by a combination of such means, the peoples of Africa have been able to achieve political independence within a framework of approval – in the form of international legal norms – laid down by the world community.

Colonialism, in spite of its tolerance in the Charter, was eventually condemned universally and independence for colonial peoples was endorsed. A phenomenon contemporary with this process was the universal condemnation of apartheid in South Africa. Indeed apartheid was seen as the essence of colonialism by some. Racism was in a strange consensus emphasized as the primary evil force behind colonialism by both friend and foe of South Africa.

This helped to unify the condemnation of apartheid to the point where it could be widely agreed that it constituted a crime against humanity. Imperialist states could continue to have strong relationships with South Africa on the basis that only in this way could the ignorance and errors of racism be brought home to white South Africans. In the process, the relationship between racial exploitation and the inevitable exploitation of capitalism was conveniently lost. The real target was amended from being imperialism, which expressed the needs of expansive capitalism, to racism, which was characterized as an aberration of a sadly misguided and isolated white minority.

The exposure of imperialism as the real problem

This superficial analysis was, however, eventually widely exposed. To people who lived under the system, it was obvious that white South Africans or Portuguese were not merely mentally deficient and depraved. Thus, the white Rhodesian settler was more often than not a recently arrived Briton. It was also obvious that the South African system was fundamentally supported and sustained by states whose common denominator was not their retarded intellects or morality, but their common membership of the capitalist camp.

A second instructive experience for some occupied African peoples was the problem of facing the need for armed struggle to remove colonial regimes. Here the test was almost too simple: which states were really willing to assist in the waging of a physical war of liberation? Of the states whose people did not share a common bond with the victims of Portugal, Rhodesia, and South Africa, because of colonization or being African, only those which had committed themselves to socialism were ready to match their condemnation of colonialism with the hardware needed to destroy it. So these people, whose position was tempered by the fire of armed struggle, evolved a deeper analysis and aimed for more fundamental and structural change.

Thus, in 1976, Angola and Mozambique emerged as independent states with a new vision of decolonization: independence from imperialism, a complete alternative to dependence, to be achieved by the pursuit of a revolutionary Marxist-Leninist policy. The same process was evolving in the Namibian and the Zimbabwean struggles. In the South African struggle, which had been ongoing and mobilized for longer than the others, there had long been a clear understanding of the enemy to be fought. Its methods included the exploitation of ignorance and emotion in the forms of racism and tribalism, but it was, at its base, modern imperialism. It is in this context that the fundamental international prescriptions of the 1970s agreed by all states - that self-determination was a legitimate claim of colonial and analogously oppressed peoples, obtainable by the use of force if necessary - began to be questioned openly by some states. By this stage the objective of armed struggle was a complete break with the capitalist colonial past and the establishment of an alternative socialist order. When this was transformed in Angola and Mozambique from the rhetorical to the real in 1975, capitalist states, especially those with a considerable financial stake in South Africa, Namibia, and Zimbabwe, realized that the process of legitimized liberation must be controlled.

Combined action against total liberation: from constitutions to compradors in camouflage

The process of reversal took some time to develop. It was, and still is, a closely run race. In 1976, Britain commenced its bid to reoccupy the high ground in the struggle for Zimbabwe at precisely the point when aggressive forces in the nationalist movement had advanced sufficiently to achieve the Patriotic Front on the political level and the parallel unity of military action, in the form of ZIPA.

The British diplomatic initiative was combined with Rhodesian and South African military escalation and threats of an "internal settlement" with a collaborating black party. The UN was manipulated out of the process, and Zimbabwe was hurried to independence and peace in a structural context deemed by Western states to be capable of taming the rhetoric of the newly-elected party committed to socialism. At the same time, a similar combination – diplomacy, free wheeling military aggression and the threat of an internal settlement – was launched on Namibia by its Western godmother, the five Contact States, led by the US and South Africa. The South African invasion and occupation of large areas of Angola (which would probably have resulted in nuclear war had it occurred in Europe) was guaranteed immunity from Security Council condemnation by the US veto, and allowed to become a "reality" and an incompletely characterized illegality. Only the assistance of Cuban forces and Soviet arms precluded a South African colonization of Angola with the aid of a puppet internal collaborator in the form of UNITA>

It saw the emergence of another technique which has now become well-established in the attempt by imperialism to reverse the new dimension of independence being asserted in Southern Africa – namely the use of neo-colonial collaborators in a military role: the comprador in camouflage. This phenomenon has now been repeated in relations with Namibia and Zimbabwe and, most dramatically, in Mozambique.

The effectiveness of counter-revolution and its legal objective

These South African activities, supported by the West have certainly born fruit. The Zimbabwean revolution was effectively forced to the delivery table of independence prematurely, and it continues to struggle for its identity in a largely hostile environment.

The Namibian demand for independence, although it has resolutely refused to capitulate, has made concessions over the years, while the South African occupant has continued to exploit Namibia's natural resources with its Western partners, while conceding nothing. Angola has continued to be occupied and harassed. But though it has not conceded to the repeated demand of the US and South Africa to surrender its sovereign right to collective self-defense, it has agreed to a cease-fire agreement in a conflict with South Africa which has been conducted entirely inside Angola itself.

But the most dramatic, comprehensive and significant of these activities is the South African confrontation with Mozambique. The entire regional confrontation between South Africa with its Western allies, and the African Front Line States acting in sympathy with the South African liberation movement, can be seen as action, not merely to chastise, militarily and politically, but more important, as a determined effort to reverse the trend of the law of liberation. Thus, they would seek to force the South African liberation struggle into the mould of a civil rights movement as if it were being conducted in a Western liberal state. Alternatively, the intention may be to limit the tolerance of African liberation under international law to the achievement of neo-colonial independence, excluding the genuine option of an openly asserted socialist state. The latter may include a retroactive aspect, which would require that existing socialist states in the region give up this model. The demand seems to be that they revert, at least, to a mixed and open economy (e.g. through membership of such development-oriented schemes as the IMF and the Lome III Convention).

It also demands an "open" governmental system allowing for multi-party participation. If the South American model found tolerable to the US and West European states is any indication to go by, the last demand might be expected to fall away once the economic openness is sufficiently established.

The above scenario might seem far-fetched, and in strictly normative terms it is unlikely that such detailed rules and limitations upon state sovereignty would be developed. On the other hand, it is suggested that the breadth, consistency and detail of the confrontation launched by the South African-Western axis against the evolving liberation norms indicate that the intention is not merely to establish a political-military defense, but also to support it by a legal bridgehead. After all, that was precisely the strategy adopted by the forces advocating liberation which achieved considerable advances up to the late-1970s.

THE SEDES MATERIAE OF IMPERIALIST LEGAL STRATEGY: THE NKOMATI ACCORD

The Material Bases of Nkomati

Speculation as to the "legislative" ambitions of the South African-Western axis in relation to African liberation, seems to be confirmed in the most concrete and articulate manner by the international agreement made between South Africa and Mozambique in March 1984: the Nkomati Accord. This is the sedes materiae of South African ambition regarding peace and security in the region - the Pax Pretoriana offered to Africa. Rather than an olive branch I would characterize it as a Wag'n bietjie Branch. Its essence is that, in almost every detail, it contradicts the legal principles of liberation law built up, mainly through the efforts of African states, on the foundations established by the UN after the defeat of fascism in Europe.

This Accord will either become a landmark in the reversal of the legal tide which has flowed behind the evolving process of liberation, or it will mark a hesitation in the flow of that tide, which is often predicted to lead to a certain victory and total liberation. Being either impatient or perhaps unsympathetic to a fatalistic outlook on the world, my own observation is that whether in the immediate future the Accord marks one trend or the other will depend very much upon the strength, energy and clarity of the African response to it.

The Accord, like any other law, is a growth out of the material reality of the time and place in which it was made. That reality consisted of weakness on one side - Mozambique- and strength on the other - South Africa.

That balance must be changed if the law it purports to lay down is not to flourish. The realities of contemporary superpower confrontation in 1984 and the technique of destabilization meant that the fraternal, maternal support which Cuba and the USSR gave Angola in 1976 when South Africa sought by deliberate invasion to extend the Pax Pretoriana at the expense of Angolan sovereignty, could not be repeated in relation to Mozambique.

But Africa has in the past evolved means of confronting the apparently overwhelming force of its oppressors, and it should be capable of discovering an appropriate response to this new challenge.

What must not be allowed is to acquiesce in this deliberate attempt to roll-back liberation. Protest, properly used, is a beginning but a material response is also called for. Nkomati took place in 1984, almost a century after the start of the nefarious Berlin Conference which created a legal instrument which totally ignored African interests. It is to be hoped that in a century from now our descendants will not look back in shame at a generation which tolerated the formulae set out in the Accord.

The burden of my point here is that colonialism was assisted by African disunity but was found to be vulnerable to the concerted pressures of African unity. So today the state, especially one which has been prepared to suffer and sacrifice so long and deeply for the cause of liberation as has Mozambique - which finds itself so isolated and so threatened that it must make such an agreement with the champion of continued oppression - can only be rescued from its plight by unity of effort and clarity of purpose in Africa. Recrimination and blame are largely unconstructive in such a situation, and this is apparently realized by other African states.

But to refrain from recrimination is not enough: positive and concerted assistance must be added. The urgency of this might be more readily appreciated when one realizes two things. First, that the compromise with apartheid and the withdrawal from direct involvement in the vanguard of total liberation which Nkomati represents is merely the most recent, most dramatic and most overt agreement. Other Front Line States which have not been required, yet, to sign a formal agreement are obviously immune from South African-sponsored destabilization on a Mozambique-scale only while the modus vivendi which each of them has found it necessary to reach is deemed satisfactory to South Africa.

And second, that a more detailed examination of the Accord will show exactly how fundamentally it challenges the legal framework of liberation so painfully established by Africa and the international community. It is to this second task that I will now turn with some comments and suggestions as to how the legal provisions of Nkomati might be understood and their consequences dealt with.

The Regional and International Background to Nkomati

There is a fundamental fascination for an African international lawyer in the contemplation of the Nkomati Accord. On the one hand, it must be applauded that an agreement could be made which enable Mozambique to preserve its integrity and recover from the brink of destruction. On the other hand, there is the awful quid pro quo, which an African state which has been in every sense at the forefront of the struggle for the total liberation of the continent has had to give to the apartheid regime by way of denying the legal status of the war of national liberation and the movements fighting it.

Similar feelings must have been experienced by lawyers in other contexts, from the Munich Agreement of 1938, through the German-Soviet Treaty of Non-Aggression of August 1939 to the Camp David Accords involving Egypt and Israel in 1978.

Classical international law is, of course, filled with such bittersweet legal arrangements. They were the essence of the character of international law as a system without central authority or rules of public policy. But the advent of the UN Charter, and the evolution of international law since then, has lent credibility to the idea that a fundamental change has taken place.

It is suggested that since World War II there has developed a centralized system of common values expressed at one level by the authority of the Security Council, and the prescriptions on the use of force of Article 2(4), and at a higher level by the discovery of a common international public policy giving rise to rules of international Jus Cogens in the law which would invalidate all purported legal arrangements inconsistent within. Of course, there is room for argument as to what are such rules of Jus Cogens. But a major candidate for qualification as one of them, in a world where the majority of existing states were until recently colonies, is the rule that colonialism, apartheid and racial oppression are illegal. Another is the legal cobweb which supports the idea of the legitimacy of properly, regionally authenticated wars of national liberation against such illegal systems. Thus, the question of the impact of legal status of the Nkomati Accord goes well beyond the immediate bilateral relationship with which it is concerned.

If it is accepted as an unquestionably binding document one conclusion which could be drawn is that much of the vaunted development of international law over the past four decades is mere rhetoric.

This makes it all the more interesting that not only South Africa but also Mozambique is at great pains to prove

232

its unquestioned legality and binding quality. Given the
harsh alternatives and realities facing Mozambique that is no
surprise, but the fact is that Mozambique insists on its
legal, and not merely its political, validity.

SELECTED PROVISIONS OF THE NKOMATI ACCORD

A new definition of self-determination?

The agreement opens with a somewhat ironic invocation of
the "internationally recognized principle of the right of
peoples to self-determination and independence and the ...
the equal rights of all people". The South African President
(as he now is) was understandably anxious at the signing
ceremony to apply this to the Afrikaner people and their
search for freedom from the British imperial yoke. Given the
actual content of the Accord, the phrase merely seems to
remind one of the warning of some critics of the concept that
one people's self-determination is another's Balkanization.
As a legal document expressing self-determination, the Accord
must rank with the proclamations of the Bantustans for its
contradictory character. It has little in common with the
concept that was being gradually clarified in African and
universal practice. This, of course, must have been one
intention in the use of the term, at least on the part of
South Africa. But the fact is that the document stands now
as a common expression of the two parties. And even if one
seeks to reduce its significance for the meaning of self-
determination - on the ground of its place in the Preamble
and the rhetorical nature of such paragraphs - it does create
a problem.

More interesting is the description of the Accord as
being an agreement not only of "Non-Aggression" but also of
"Good Neighborliness". The latter is a phrase not often
employed in treaties since its appearance in Article 74 of
the UN Charter, and its meaning may be vague.

It has, however, been suggested that it seeks to import
a higher level of good faith into relations between states.
Its reiteration here may have a significance in the current
context of the apparent failure of South Africa to end the
destructive activities of the MNR, its agent of
destabilization in Mozambique, for the continued existence of
the Accord.

Like many of the other provisions of the Accord, the two
principles invoked here are already operative between
Mozambique and South Africa by virtue of their common
membership in the UN. In that sense the Accord is redundant.

By expressing these concepts in a specific bilateral context, however, what the parties appear to be agreeing to is an interpretation of them which is very different to that which exists in the Charter and the UN context of decolonization where they originated and have evolved. In that sense the Accord contains clearly legal as well as political motives.

Returning apartheid to the sphere of "domestic jurisdiction"?

Article 1 reemphasizes the parties' "fundamental obligation" of mutual respect for their "sovereignty and independence", including abstaining from interference in one another's "internal affairs". Taken on its face, this may suggest an attempt to return to the debate of the late-1940s regarding the exclusion of international concern with matters within the "domestic jurisdiction" of South Africa, especially its policies of racial discrimination.

However, read in the broader context of contemporary international law, within which it has long been clear that such terms as "internal affairs" and "domestic jurisdiction" have in law, a purely relative meaning depending upon the "development of international (legal) relations", the fact is that most of the issues South Africa would wish to be regarded as "internal" and not to be "interfered in" are and have for decades been high on the agenda of international legal concern. The question posed now is: has Mozambique as a UN member bound itself to being mute and inactive on these issues?

Apart from the more general argument that apartheid, because it has been internationally condemned and recognized as a crime against humanity, makes any agreement not to "interfere" with it invalid under existing rules of international Jus Cogens, there is the more immediate point. It has become preeminently an obligation of UN members to be concerned with and to oppose racial discrimination. This exposes such new "obligation" to the argument that it must be regarded as invalid by virtue of Article 103 which creates a rule of consensual Jus Cogens under which Charter obligations "shall prevail".

Excluding the United Nations collective security system from Southern Africa?

Peace and security in this region is, of course, a part of the concern of Nkomati, and an important obligation in this regard is laid down in Article 2. This creates the extraordinary undertaking (as seen against the background of the history of international law and liberation in the region), that Mozambique will not resort "individually or collectively to the use of force" against South Africa. Thus, if (though it is unlikely given the vetoes of the US, Britain and France) the Security Council were to impose military sanctions (or arguably even economic sanctions, because a wide definition of "the use of force" to include economic coercion is conceivable under the article) against South Africa under Chapter VII of the Charter, Mozambique is bound in terms of Nkomati to refuse to participate. All the more so, it is bound to refrain from such collective action taken by the Front Line States, the OAU or other collective groupings. This gives real meaning to the preamble's reference to Good Neighbourliness. Again the provision of Article 103 and the argument based on Jus Cogens can be raised to question the validity of this undertaking.

A Real Sacrifice?

Given the fact that prior to Nkomati there was little evidence of any such collective action (or for that matter even of sufficient collective support for Mozambique) it might be argued that what has been surrendered in law was nothing in reality. This point underlines an important general question arising from Nkomati: was the law of liberation merely a fantasy? Would the acts of resistance to apartheid, to Namibian occupation and to the Rhodesian regime have happened in any event without the legal framework? Did it really make any difference?

On an even more concrete level the questions might be asked: How much compensation have the Front Line States been given for the injuries received at the hands of the international derelicts committed by South Africa and the Smith regime? How many freedom fighters benefitted during the wars of liberation from combatant states and were treated as prisoners of war? Or, with regard to giving reality and respect to the law ex post facto, how many war criminals, and officials who committed "crimes against humanity" during the liberation wars in the Portuguese colonies and Rhodesia have been prosecuted or even investigated? Have the states whose nationals and companies violated economic sanctions against Rhodesia felt the disadvantages of their illegality either in the newly liberated state, within liberated Africa, or in the world at large? Or has the reward of illegality been an advantaged position in the economy which was avoided by more law-abiding states and businesses during the period of UN sanctions?

If the answer to all these questions is largely

negative, is it not pertinent (and more honest) to suggest that if Mozambique's undertakings, such as this one under Nkomati, undermine the law then it is only a hollow structure which is being undermined? Faced with the necessity of survival is it reasonable to expect that Mozambique should have risked destruction for the sake of loyalty to empty, rhetorical rules?

The answer to this general question is by no means easy. There is a real sense in which the symbolism of the law even at its most hollow is important; and it must be remembered that the law is normative and not descriptive. The law asserts the opinio juris of states, not the reality. Violation does not easily abrogate the law, particularly international law, where the tempo is very different to that of municipal law. That view, however, may be characterized as a typical (and unrealistic) lawyer's view of the matter.

The abolition of the concept of the war of national liberation?

The most overt incorporation of South Africa's fundamental desire to stem the tide of war of national liberation and the prospects of revolutionary as opposed to reformatory change at its borders is to be found in Article 3. It is reminiscent of the schemes for the emasculation of a future independent Namibia, floated in 1982 in the so called Non-Paper. Apart from effectively neutralizing Mozambique in relation to almost every aspect, physical and psychological, of the liberation struggle, it seems, in addition, to seek to extend considerably the duties of international responsibility which oblige every state not to allow its territory to be used to as to cause harm to another state. This clearly has advantages for Mozambique, given the origins and the continued dependence of the MNR on South Africa. But, on the other hand, it suggests that the presence and the activity in Mozambique of the South Africa liberation movement, in the form of the ANC is legally indistinguishable from the MNR. This implies the abandonment of a platform which is an important and central part of contemporary international law; namely the legitimacy of support by UN member states for national liberation movements.

The undertaking is combined with an obligation for joint supervision and enforcement of the new international regime, under 4 and 9, by Mozambican and South African officials. Again, the Good Neighbourliness theme is given substance and meaning. The combined effect is dramatic, not only in its consequences for the liberation movement concerned, but for other such organizations which have fought long and hard to achieve and maintain a distinction between national liberation movements and "terrorists", especially in relation to legal instruments dealing with international terrorism. From the point of view of general policy in today's world where unconventional warfare is the predominant means of waging armed conflict, this is a particularly dangerous and negative development. It reduces the incentive on the part of national liberation movement to abjure indiscriminate and terroristic tactics if they are nevertheless to be characterized as "terrorists".

This point applies with much greater force in the case of the South African conflict where <u>Umkhonto We Sizwe</u>, the military wing of the ANC, has obviously made great efforts and sacrifices to avoid the temptations of terrorism. Hijacking and sabotage of South African Airways flights is only one example of the kind of action which has been avoided. Of course, it might well be that one intended side-effect of the new situation is to force the liberation movement into precisely such terrorism in the belief that it would be discredited as a result. Again, if such a provision is allowed to spread by similar agreements made with other Front Line States, it would have serious consequences within Africa itself.

Caveat Refugee?

Another area of international law which appears in jeopardy is the law relating to refugees. Regional developments in this field have put Africa ahead of other continents, and no doubt the scale of the refugee problem in Africa has contributed to that fact. However in Article 4, the undertakings include one "to prevent ... illegal crossings ... particularly by the elements referred to in Article 3". These "elements" include "organizations or individuals planning or preparing to carry out acts of violence ... against ... the political independence of the other, (party) or which could threaten the security of its inhabitants". This could cover almost all acts of opposition to the regime in South Africa and is obviously not limited to persons who have actually committed acts of physical violence. It means that almost anyone who opposes apartheid and finds it necessary to flee the police state and to seek asylum is to be denied the rights which should be guaranteed to such a person under contemporary refugee law, if the flight is attempted into Mozambique.

Of course, South Africa might not insist on the letter of the law if it is sure that the individual is to be sent out of Mozambique and neutralized. But if the Accord is valid and enforceable it might in some cases be more convenient for South Africa to insist that the would-be refugee is actually prevented from making an "illegal crossing". Joint enforcement measures would make the possibility of this more realistic. Given the contemporary fact of increasing resistance to apartheid inside South Africa and the official response of increasing repression, it is conceivable that another massive wave of refugees- especially of young people – might be generated. It is thus an urgent question as to whether this provision is really going to be allowed to operate so as to force such people back into South Africa and into the arms of its security forces?

The restoration of an unlimited right of self-defense to South Africa?

One final indication of how the Nkomati Accord may be seen as a particular example of the general intention of South Africa to reshape the norms guaranteeing self-determination and the means (armed struggle) necessary to achieve it, is to be found in Article 8. This provides a superficially bland restatement of the right of self-defense under Article 51 of the UN Charter. That Article allows the use of force "if an armed attack occurs". A fundamental part of the debate from which has developed the legal status of wars of national liberation, is the question whether any government is entitled to be challenged by armed force if necessary, because it denies self-determination to those entitled to it, can use force in purported self-defense? The claim to this right, under the misleading title of the "Right of Hot Pursuit", was made by the illegal Smith regime when its forces attacked targets in Zambia and Mozambique during the national liberation war for Zimbabwe.

A long series of resolutions by both General Assembly and Security Council has denied the existence of such a right, or its description as "self-defense" as that term is understood in Article 51 of the Charter. To the extent that Article 8 of the Accord seeks to modify that it is contrary to Article 103 of the Charter or possibly Jus Cogens rules denying the right of self-defense to the apartheid regime when facing armed resistance to the system. It is precisely to try to change this rule that South Africa has gone to so much trouble, military and diplomatic, to obtain a legal agreement with an African state. Article 8, one might note in passing, also changes the basis on which the right is established in the Charter: from "an armed attack" to "armed attacks". It has been suggested that this is a deliberately inaccurate reference to or intended modification of the Charter provision, designed to allow South Africa greater scope for "self-defense" against lesser dangers than an armed attack by another state.

The Nkomati as the new security code for Southern Africa?

Finally, it must be noted that the parties to the Accord must have been acutely aware of potential arguments about the invalidity of the agreement by the virtue of its contradiction of existing obligations in the Charter or of rules of Jus Cogens. Article 6 thus contains a safeguard against this, in the form of a mutual assertion that "there is no conflict between undertakings entered into by them in treaties and international obligations and the undertakings stemming from the present agreement". If the provisions of Article 103 are infringed by the Nkomati Accord, then, although the parties are entitled to auto-interpret their rights and obligations in the first instance, the organs of the UN are also entitled to their interpretation. Thus, if the General Assembly or Security Council decide authoritatively that this agreement does conflict then, as UN members, South Africa and Mozambique are bound by that decision. Likewise, if a rule of Jus Cogens is involved, the mere assertion of "no conflict" does not enable them to avoid the consequences. It is unlikely, of course, that this issue will arise, unless and until one or other of the parties finds itself in a position where it is in its interests to challenge the validity of the Accord. In the case of Mozambique that is unlikely to arise as long as it is vulnerable, as it is at present.

Conclusion:
Total Strategy in Southern Africa—
An Analysis of South African
Regional Policy Since 1978
Robert Davies
Dan O'Meara

On 16 March 1984 the Republic of South Africa and the
Peoples' Republic of Mozambique signed an "Agreement on Non-
Aggression and Good Neighbourliness", known as the Nkomati
Accord. This event dramatically focussed attention on South
Africa's regional policy objectives and strategy. It is now
generally recognised by all but its apologists that the
apartheid state has in recent years engaged in an intense
struggle both to assert its hegemony over the states of the
region and to become the internationally recognized "regional
power" in Southern Africa. This can now also be seen as
having implications in the wider international as well as the
regional arena. Prime Minister P.W. Botha's controversial
June 1984 visit to Western Europe made it clear that the
regime sees the consolidation of its regional domination
formalized linkages with neighboring states as the via media
through which to break out of South Africa's longstanding
international isolation.

The post-Nkomati period has now also finally brought to
public attention the fact that the South African state has
long had at its disposal a wide range of regional policy
instruments or tactics. These go beyond the mere crude
"destabilization" measures widely discussed in much recent
writing on the region. At least since the accession to the
premiership of P.W. Botha in September 1979, under the rubric
of the "Total National Strategy" these tactics have included
a sophisticated matrix of economic and other "incentives"
applied together with military and other "disincentives".
Moreover, the Botha regime has also developed a more defined
understanding than its predecessors of the specific socio-
political conditions of each of the states in the region, and
employed a different combination of "incentive/disincentive"
tactics towards each of them.

This chapter analyses the regional strategy of the South

African state under the Botha regime and its effects in its different phases since 1978. It attempts to asses the results and prospects, as well as the limits and possibilities of this strategy. It does so from a perspective different from much of the existing literature. The highly active regional policy stance of the apartheid regime in the past five years, and particularly its more blatant efforts to undermine the stability of neighboring states, give rise to much written comment. Through the heavy focus of this literature on the more dramatic elements of, and moments in, what came to be called South Africa's "destabilization policy", the role of the apartheid regime as an aggressor in Southern Africa has been firmly established. Nevertheless, within such writings a number of erroneous conceptions became crystallized.

The first and most prevalent approach reduced the totality of South African regional policy to "destabilization strategy" on the part of Pretoria. The entire South African regional policy effort becomes collapsed into an attempt by Pretoria to inflict maximum material damage on the economies and social structures of regional states – as a prelude to undermining their political systems and/or overthrowing their governments.[1] A second and sometimes linked approach tried to grapple with conflicts within the South African political "establishment" over regional policy. Basing itself on the clear militarization of the South African state since 1978, and in particular on the decisive policy formulating role of the militarily-dominated State Security Council, this approach discusses Pretoria's regional policy in terms of the conflicts between the allegedly "hawkish" military establishment on the one hand, and the allegedly more subtle "diplomatic" tactics favored by the Ministry of Foreign Affairs.[2] Growing out of, and collapsing these two views is the argument which the Nkomati Accord as on the one hand as a defeat for the "militarists" in the South African state, and on the other as a defeat for South Africa's destabilization strategy –in the sense that the Pretoria regime has been forced to abandon the "military option."[3]

There are number of problems with such approaches. The apartheid regime has clearly acted as the aggressor since 1975 and has inflicted great material damage on particular South African states in specific periods. However the view which reduces Pretoria's entire regional strategy to destabilization, fails to recognize that since at least 1978 this strategy has also envisaged what might be called "formative action" – the attempt to create a new network of regional economic and social relationships which would persuade Southern African states that it is in their interests to collaborate with Pretoria. Thus the various twists and turns of South African regional policy have been consistently geared around the clear and articulated strategic objective of restructuring the pattern of relations between the states of Southern Africa - repeatedly expressed by policy makers as the establishment of a "constellation of states". In the context of this strategic vision therefore, the various military, economic and other disincentives commonly labeled "destabilization" can in no sense be elevated to the status of either objectives or a strategy. It cannot be too strongly stressed that, together with other more "formative measures", these are specific tactical options within a broader strategy. The adoption of any particular tactical mix by Pretoria towards specific states has depended on various factors. The most important of these include the rhythm of struggles at the regional level and the pattern of internal relations within the target state(s). Moreover, "destabilization" has never been a first option of Pretoria. As will be argued below, particular emphasis on such "disincentive" tactics has specifically emerged in periods of defeat/crisis for the broader strategy of the apartheid regime.

The associated view that "destabilization" is the result of military predominance in the apartheid state is likewise seriously misleading on a number of grounds. Following the assumption of the Premiership by P.W. Botha in 1978, the South African state was thoroughly reorganized. New decision-making structures appeared, in which the military now plays a key institutionalized role. This reorganization of the state was itself a response to a profound crisis confronting South African capitalism. It represented both the consolidation of a new dominant alliance between monopoly capital and the military within the state, and the reorganization of the ruling capitalist class to deal with this crisis.[4] This new consolidation of a crucial role for the military in the basic decision-making structures of the South African state can thus in no sense be reduced to a simple rule by trigger-happy generals through the "inner cabinet" of the State Security Council. This new monopoly/military alliance organized in the Botha government produced a new strategic response to the crisis of the mid-1970s, articulated in the Total National Strategy. Though first developed by military strategists, this now represents the strategy of the South African ruling class as a whole- and is accepted as such by all institutions of the South African state, including the Foreign Ministry. There clearly have been disagreements between decision makers over the tactics to deploy in some specific situations. However such disagreements can also not be reduced to an ongoing conflict and divergence of vision within the state between the interests of different institutional structures, ie. military "hawks" versus Foreign Ministry "doves". Such disagreements as have occurred have been located within the framework of a shared and unquestioned vision of strategic objectives.[5] There is another aspect to this. The Total Strategy has never been a simple militarist strategy. The generals themselves have repeatedly stressed that the survival of South African apartheid capitalism depends primarily on the development of an adequate _political_ response - both internally and in the region - and not mere mindless mobilization of military might.

This chapter presents an analysis which attempts to overcome some of these problems in other approaches. It deals firstly with the historical context within which the Botha regime's regional policy was formulated; secondly, with the institutional processes of policy formulation; thirdly, it periodizes the application of that strategy in practice; and finally assesses the current balance of forces in the Southern African region.

THE HISTORICAL ROOTS OF CURRENT SOUTH AFRICAN STRATEGY

Historically the development of capitalism in Southern Africa led to the formation of a regional sub-system in which the principal poles of capital accumulation were located in South Africa. The other territories of the region became subordinated to serve the needs of capital accumulation in South Africa in various ways - as labor reserves (supplying 300,000 migrant workers for the mining industry alone in 1973); as suppliers of cheap raw materials and/or specific services such as transport; and as markets for South African-produced commodities. One longstanding objective of South Africa's regional policy has thus been to ensure that neighboring territories continue to serve South African capitalism in these ways. Moreover, with the emergence of anti-colonial struggles in Africa, hand in hand with the development of a mass nationalist movement inside South Africa itself in the 1950s, Pretoria's regional policy also increasingly concerned itself with attempts both to thwart struggles against colonial regimes in the region and to isolate the national liberation struggle inside South Africa from potential support from surrounding territories.[6]

Until the mid-1970s the fundamental bedrock on which the apartheid state based its attempts to achieve these objectives was the existence of a number of so-called "buffer" states which surrounded it. To the west was the Portuguese colony of Angola and the South African-occupied territory of Namibia; in the center the settler-ruled British colony of Southern Rhodesia; and to the east, the Portuguese colony of Mozambique. Regional policy was principally directed towards reinforcing these buffer states to serve as a protective barrier for South Africa itself. This involved the formation of alliances with the colonial regimes of these territories and the rendering to them of various forms of support, including direct military assistance.

With respect to the other countries of the region, until the mid-1960s South Africa sought to direct incorporation of Botswana, Lesotho and Swaziland. These three so-called High Commission territories were administered from South Africa by the same British High Commissioner (who also served as British ambassador to South Africa). The absorption of these territories by South Africa would have had the advantage from the point of view of the apartheid state of placing them under its own direct control and reducing them to the status of South Africa's bantustans. The three territories would then have been led to Pretoria's version of bantustan "independence." This would also have had the additional ideological advantage of providing a semblance of legitimacy to the entire bantustan project by enabling the racial division of land in a "greater South Africa" to be presented as a "fair" 50:50, instead of the existing 87% white, 13% black division introduced by apartheid.

When it became clear that in the era of decolonization Britain would not accede to these demands, but was on the contrary "preparing" these territories for eventual independence, the Verwoerd regime proposed in 1963 the establishment of a "common market/commonwealth" in Southern Africa. This envisaged as a first step the establishment of a free trade zone in the region. Once this was established it was considered that the economic links between territories would be so strong that the basis would be laid for the establishment of a regional political institution - a commonwealth, described by apartheid ideologues at the time as an "association of black and white states", with South Africa as the "mother country".

This commonwealth project failed to materialize. However increasingly close links were forged throughout the 1960s and early 1970s with the colonial regimes in the buffer states. Moreover as the High Commission territories approached independence, Pretoria's interventions in their internal policies escalated. The most glaring example of this was in the case of Lesotho. Operating through the secret Afrikaner Broederbond, the Verwoerd government

provided crucial financial and organization support to the
Basutholand National Party of Chief Leabua Jonathan.[7] This
enabled the BNP to emerge with a one seat parliamentary
majority over the then more "radical" Basutholand Congress
Party, and so form Lesotho's first government. Less
grandiose Broederbond interventions in Swaziland led to the
formation of a "King's party" - the Imbokodvo National
Movement -which likewise defeated a more radical party to
emerge as Swaziland's first post-colonial government.[8] Such
measures helped to ensure that these territories came to
independence under governments unlikely to challenge
Pretoria's interests. Moreover the independent BLS States
(Botswana, Lesotho and Swaziland) were all incorporated into
the South African dominated Southern African Customs Union
(SACU) as well as the Rand Monetary Area. These formal
economic linkages gave Pretoria enormous leverage over these
states - deployed with effect on a number of occasions,
particularly through the 1969 renegotiation of the SACU
agreement.[9]

With its base in the region thus apparently secure, an
offensive was launched by the Vorster regime in the late
1960s in direct response to the process of rapid
decolonization and increasing international condemnation of
apartheid. This offensive, known as the "outward looking"
policy or "dialogue initiative", had as it objective a search
for allies with the Organization of African Unity (OAU). As
such, it scored some initial successes. The most spectacular
was the establishment of formal diplomatic relations with
Malawi in 1968, followed by an exchange of state visits by
Prime Minister Vorster and President Banda in 1970 and 1971
respectively. Malawi henceforth became one of South Africa's
most consistent defenders in the international arena. This
initiative was finally blocked by an OAU resolution in 1971
condemning Pretoria's dialogue proposals as a "manoeuvre"
designed to "divide African states and confuse public opinion
in order to end the isolation of South Africa, and thus to
maintain the status quo in South Africa."[10] However, an
index of Pretoria's success was the fact that six OAU members
(Malawi, Gabon, Ivory Coast, Mauritania, Madagascar and
Lesotho) voted against the motion while five other states
(Dahomey, Niger, Swaziland, Upper Volta and Togo) abstained.

Despite the limited achievements of the dialogue
initiative, in reality the balance of forces in Southern
Africa was being slowly but fundamentally shifted by the
advancing liberation struggles in territories still under
colonial rule. This finally became evident in April 1974
when the Portuguese fascist regime was overthrown as a direct
result of the heightening of contradictions in Portugal

through the impact of the colonial wars. The overthrow of the Caetano regime in Portugal was followed by the independence of Mozambique and Angola in 1975, under governments formed by the liberation movements - FRELIMO and MPLA. This dramatically changed the regional balance of forces and undermined the basis on which South African policy had hitherto been built. With the independence of Mozambique and Angola two of South Africa's key buffers collapsed. By mid-1976 it had also become clear that the Smith regime in Zimbabwe had been forced onto the defensive in large measure due to the facilities made available to the Zimbabwean liberation struggle by FRELIMO. Moreover, South Africa's own forces in Namibia were being placed under increased pressure from SWAPO guerrillas now able to operate along the entire 1,000 km. northern border. The situation in the region, in short, had changed dramatically. The bedrock on which South Africa's regional policy had hitherto been built - the buffer states - finally proved to be sandstone rather than granite.

The collapse of Portuguese colonialism gave rise to a hasty reformulation of regional strategy by the Vorster regime in 1974. This initially proceeded in a somewhat ad hoc fashion. South Africa's military capacity had to be expanded. The military budget for 1974-75 was one-and-a-half times that of the previous year, and by 1977-78 it had risen to a level three-and-a-half times that of 1973-74. In October 1974, Vorster launched a new diplomatic/political initiative known as "detente". Its objective was somewhat vaguely defined as drawing the states of Southern Africa in a "constellation of completely independent states" which would form a "strong bloc" and "present a united front against common enemies."[11] Orchestrated and conceived by the Bureau of State Security, detente involved a desperate search for influential allies within the OAU, and particularly in the Southern African region. Bribery, secret diplomatic contacts (often arranged through BOSS's connections with western intelligence services) and eventually a visit by Vorster to a number of countries in West Africa as well as a meeting with President Kaunda of Zambia, were all means used in the attempt to achieve this end. At the same time, some minor internal changes were made, such as the scrapping of some forms of "petty apartheid". This had the clear objective of giving credence to the notion that "negotiation" could be a viable alternative to "confrontation".

Despite some important initial successes, however, the detente initiative began to crumble in the debacle of the South African invasion of Angola in 1975, and the eventual expulsion of South African forces by MPLA and Cuban troops in March 1976. While there still remained some impetus from

Zambia and some other Southern African states to maintain dialogue with South Africa, this was finally destroyed by the brutal repression of the Soweto uprising. Not even the most conservative African regime could now afford to be seen to be collaborating with a regime which slaughtered unarmed black school children in the streets.

By the end of 1976 then, in addition to its gathering internal crisis, the apartheid regime faced a collapse of its regional policies. At the same time, top military strategists, in growing collaboration with monopoly capital, had become more stridently critical of the bases on which regional, as well as the other dimensions of state security policy, had hitherto been conducted. This critique covered, inter alia, important aspects of the organization of military interventions in the region as well as the approach towards winning allies which relied on influencing individual decision makers rather than the objective environment in which decisions were made. In the 1977 Defence White Paper-the document in which top military commanders first publicly laid out and called for the adoption of their "Total Strategy" - it was argued that the mobilization of economic, political and psycho-social as well as military resources was necessary to defend and advance the interests of the apartheid state both at the internal and regional levels. More specifically, the White Paper identified the need "to maintain a solid military balance relative to neighboring states and other states in Southern Africa." At the same time it called for "economic action" and "action in relation to transport services, distribution and telecommunications" to promote "political and economic collaboration among the states of Southern Africa."[12]

TOTAL STRATEGY AT THE REGIONAL LEVEL

Objectives

Following the assumption of power by P.W. Botha in September 1978 the apartheid state was substantially reorganized and the Total Strategy adopted as official state policy. This led to a restructuring of regional policy in a number of important aspects. The objectives of this policy have been somewhat reformulated. The vague notion of a constellation of states first put forward by Vorster in 1974 was substantially developed and was now defined as the ultimate objective of regional strategy.[13] The need to bring about such a constellation was seen as being partly derived from the worsening situation for the apartheid regime in

Southern Africa, and partly from South Africa's then deteriorating relations with the major Western powers. In this new regional situation, the "moderate states of Southern Africa" were seen as facing a common "Marxist onslaught" but could not depend on support from the Western powers. This led to a need to construct a regional alliance in which South Africa would play the pivotal role. However, it was recognized that aspects of apartheid policies were a barrier to formalized alliances with surrounding states. Therefore it was seen to be necessary to generate a "counter-ideology" to Marxism in the region.[14] This would be partly consolidated by the promotion of a number of joint economic projects between South Africa and other regional states. These were to demonstrate the superiority of South African capitalism over "socialist" alternatives, and would thus depend on a high level of involvement by the "private sector".

The other crucial element in the consolidation of such a counter ideology was seen from the outset as the luring of regional states into "Non-Aggression Pacts" with Pretoria as a first step towards promoting "the concept of mutual defense against a common enemy."[15] Such action on both the economic and security fronts would significantly deepen the ties between South Africa and its neighbours and slowly bring into being the objective basis for what Foreign Minister Pik Botha described as "a common approach in the security field, the economic field and even the political field."[16]

From the outset of its adoption by the Botha regime, the promotion of a constellation was seen as an attempt to seek regional solutions to regional problems. This would lead to South Africa becoming internationally recognized as the de facto regional power with whom the major powers would have to deal, and Southern Africa would now effectively be acknowledged as a sphere of South African influence.

Finally, the constellation was to be linked to domestic apartheid politics. Its component states would include the so-called "independent" bantustans. This would perform two functions for Pretoria. First, it would finally create the institutional mechanism to regulate relations between the now fragmented parts of South Africa and the central apartheid state – for which the regime had long been searching. Second, by drawing the bantustans into an association with independent black states, it was seen to be the means of finally providing them with a measure of international recognition.

In addition to the ultimate objective of the bringing into being of a "constellation of states", the Total Strategy also defined a number of more immediate limited regional

objectives. These have been clearly summarized by Deon
Geldenhuys - one of the Botha regime's leading academic
consultants on foreign policy issues. In a commissioned
paper published by the Institute of Strategic Studies of the
University of Pretoria in early 1981,[17] Geldenhuys defined
the first of these objectives as being to ensure that:

> neighboring states are not used as springboards for
> guerrilla or terrorist attacks on South Africa. South
> Africa clearly not only wants neighboring governments to
> give an undertaking to the effect but also wants them to
> implement it effectively, thus ensuring that
> unauthorized incursions do not take place. Furthermore,
> South Africa would wish that black states in the region
> (not merely neighboring countries) would not provide
> training facilities for anti-South African liberation
> movements and, ideally, would not allow the movements to
> establish offices in their countries.

This clearly demanded not only that independent states in the
region refrain from actively supporting the armed liberation
struggles in South Africa and Namibia, but also that they act
as police agents for Pretoria and prohibit political activity
by refugees resident in their territories.

The second objective reflects the Botha regime's
definition of the crisis confronting it as a product of a
Soviet-orchestrated "total onslaught". It seeks to ensure
that "Soviet bloc powers do not gain a political and least of
all a military foothold in Southern African states." The
third and fourth objectives are directly aimed at thwarting
any attempts by independent states to reduce their economic
dependence on South Africa. As Geldenhuys puts it, South
Africa wants to see that:

> Existing economic ties with states in the region are
> maintained and indeed strengthened. An obvious pre-
> condition for the strategic application of economic
> relations is that these links have to exist in a
> meaningful way.

Linked to this is the demand that:

> Black states in the region [do] not ... support calls
> for mandatory trade sanctions against South Africa. For
> some of them, implementation of sanctions would have
> devastating results; others may perhaps be prepared to
> run the risks, as in the case of sanctions against
> Rhodesia. The stronger the economic ties with South

Africa, perhaps the lesser the chances of their supporting sanctions. Black states could, in other words, shield South Africa from mandatory economic sanctions.

Finally, the apartheid regime wants:

> Black states in Southern Africa [to] display some moderation in expressing their customary criticism of the republic's policy and in suggesting solutions. To try to induce some moderation in the heady anti-South African rhetoric is however a secondary objective and its limits are obvious: it simply cannot be expected of OAU member states to refrain from denouncing apartheid: at issue is the manner in which it is done.

The Institutions of Policy Formulation

In the last years of the Vorster government, particularly after 1974, a great deal of bureaucratic infighting developed between the various state apparatuses which had responsibility for aspects of regional and foreign policy. Thus, conflicts between the ministries of Foreign Affairs and Information over the strategy, conduct and control of foreign policy both in Southern Africa and abroad were widely discussed in the South African press at the time. Less widely known, though ultimately at least as important, were wide-ranging conflicts between NOSS and Military Intelligence over the entire thrust of security policies. Indeed the elaboration of the Total Strategy doctrine by the military in 1977 grew out of these conflicts, which eventually culminated in the so-called "Muldergate" crisis, and led to the fall of Vorster.

When P.W. Botha acceded to the Premiership in September 1978 he attempted to end these institutional conflicts through reorganizing the structure of decision-making in the state. The new policy initiatives of the Botha regime, both internal and regional, have been accompanied by, and indeed achieved through, this reorganization of the state. The most notable features of this have been: a) a decisive centralization of power in the hands of the Prime Minister and a corresponding diminution in the role of the Cabinet and Parliament; and b) a striking militarization of the decision-making and administrative structures of the state.

The Total Strategy programme called for a "comprehensive plan to utilize all the means available to the state according to an integrated pattern in order to achieve the national aims within the framework of specific policies."[18]

The so-called 12 point plan enunciated by Botha in August 1979 spelled out these specific policies. The planned utilization of the means available to the state was referred to by one of the key architects of the Total Strategy as "the management of South Africa's four power bases (the political, economic, social/psychological and security bases) as an integrated whole."[19] As Minister of Defence, Botha had already declared that the Westminster model on which South Africa's government was based was inappropriate to the needs of the moment.[20] Thus in order to achieve such an "integrated management" of the resources of the state, the very structures of the state themselves had to be overhauled and the political and administrative structures appropriate to the implementation of the Total Strategy erected.

A three-phase "rationalization programme" was begun in March 1979.[21] Phase one led to a progressive and profound reorganization of the structures of decision-making. As a first step, a cabinet secretariat was set up in the Office of the Prime Minister. The twenty Cabinet Committees which had existed on an ad hoc basis in the Vorster regime gave way first to six, then five and finally four permanent Cabinet Committees - for National Security, and Constitutional, Economic and Social Affairs. These revamped Cabinet Committees were not the advisory bodies to the Cabinet they had been under Vorster but became integral components of the highest level of the decision-making machinery. They were given the right to make decisions, and Ministers could now refer particular matters directly to a Cabinet Committee without first going through the Cabinet. Each of the four Committees is headed by a Minister nominated by the Prime Minister, but whose identity is not public knowledge.

By far, the most important of the Cabinet Committees and the one which deals with foreign policy issues, is the Committee for National Security, known as the State Security Council (hereafter SSC). Set up by an Act of Parliament in 1972, it functioned under Vorster as a purely advisory body and met but sporadically. However according to General Magnus Malan, the debacle of the first South African invasion of Angola 1975-76 "focussed attention on the urgent necessity for the State Security Council to play a much fuller role in the national security of the Republic than hitherto." An interdepartmental committee on which the South African Defence Force (SADF) was strongly represented met to devise the organizational structure for "the formulation of strategy at a national level". Out of this emerged the components of what is now termed the "national security management system" at whose pinnacle stands the revamped SSC.[22]

The Prime Minister himself presides over the SSC. Its

other statutory members include four Ministers - Defence, Foreign Affairs, Law and Order, and the Senior Cabinet Minister, if not already included in the above portfolios- and the following senior state officials: the head of the National Intelligence Service (NIS), the Chief of the SADF, the Director-General of Foreign Affairs, the Director-General of Law and Order, and the Commissioner of Police. Apart from these statutory or "primary" members, other Ministers and officials may be coopted at the Prime Minister's discretion. There are currently eight Ministers in addition to the Prime Minister serving on the SSC in an apparently permanent capacity, together with other senior SADF personnel and other officials. The State Security Council has its own secretariat, headed by Ltd. General A.J. van Deventer - the man who commanded the first South African invasion force into Angola in August 1975. This secretariat is responsible directly to the Prime Minister and its staff is drawn from various government departments, probably with a very high military component.[23]

In effect, the SSC is now the primary decision-making body in the South African state. Its statutory responsibility is to advise the government on the formulation and implementation of "national policy and strategy in relation to the security of the Republic."[24] This is wide enough to embrace virtually every area of government internal and external activity. In practice, the SSC concerns itself with and manages the total range of policy strategies of the state. Under the Total Strategy, everything deemed to be connected with the security of the state falls under its purview - from foreign policy to the price of bread. It is the SSC which coordinates and plans the utilization of all the means available to the state to achieve specific objectives as spelled out in the formulation of the Total Strategy. While the fiction of superiority of the Cabinet is maintained, the SSC meets the day before the fortnightly Cabinet meetings and is thought to prepare its agenda. Ministers may only attend SSC meetings if they are statutory or coopted members, or are specifically invited by the Prime Minister. Moreover the SSC alone is specifically exempt from the rule that the decisions of Cabinet Commissions be circulated to the Cabinet and be subject to its ratification. The Cabinet is only informed of SSC decisions after the fact, and at the discretion of the Prime Minister.

Apart from reorganizing the process of strategic and tactical decision-making in the SSC, the Council itself also presides over new structures created to implement such decisions. Thus, the SSC directly supervises the 15 Interdepartmental Committees which now coordinate public

sector activities in what Magnus Malan has described as the
"fifteen areas of common interest in the national security
field which would affect more than one government
department."[25]   These commissions range from Political
Action, Manpower, Transport, to "Cultural Action".   The
activities of each of these committees have a direct bearing
on aspects of regional policy.[26]

The SSC further supervises a network of 15 internal and
external Joint Management Centres.   The ten internal Centres
serve different geographical areas of South Africa, whose
demarcation coincides with the ten Area Commands of the
Defence Force.   The eleventh Centre deals with the Namibian
port of Walvis Bay claimed by South Africa, while the four
external Centres cover Namibia and unspecified Southern
African countries.   thus spread over the whole of South
Africa and involved in at least four other countries of the
region, these Joint Management Centres are designed to
implement the Total Strategy in a coordinated fashion in all
areas of South and Southern Africa.

Within the context of these reorganized decision-making
and implementation structures, new instruments have been
developed to achieve the reformulated regional policy
objectives.   These include a wide range of military, economic
and other resources.

Following the debacle of South Africa's first invasion
of Angola in 1975-76, the strategic role of the South African
Defence Force was reconceived, and its structures reorganized
to turn it into a highly mobile conventional force to be used
against neighboring countries, whilst raising its capacity to
fight a "counter-insurgency war".   Deficiencies in armaments
revealed in the Angola intervention were corrected in a crash
armaments development programme through the state-owned
armaments company, ARMSCOR.   The SADF now claims to be
equipped with the most advanced weapons of their type in the
world.   In the large scale invasion of Angola known as
"Operation Protea" in late 1981, the SADF claimed that 95% of
the equipment used was locally produced.   Military
expenditure more than doubled between 1977-78 and 1984-85 to
reach almost R3,755 million (an amount greater than the Gross
Domestic Product of Zimbabwe).

Particular capabilities were developed for aggression
against neighboring states, most of which have now been
tested in practice.   These include: reconnaissance commandos
(Recces), specialist units containing a high proportion of
mercenaries, for use in hit and run operations.   The first of
these was established in 1975, and the SADF is now thought to
have six such units.   Of these, it is known that No. 1
Reconnaissance Commando is based in Durban and is responsible

for training. It also carried out the 1981 Matola raid
against ANC residences near Maputo. Recce No. 4 specializes
in sea borne operations, such as the attack on the Luanda oil
refinery in November 1981. Based at Dudkunduku in Natal, No.
5 Recce is responsible for training members of dissident
groups such as the MNR and UNITA. It is also known to have
operated in Namibia as a "phoney SWAPO unit". Recce No. 6,
based in the north eastern Transvaal, has specialized in
operations against Zimbabwe and Mozambique.[27] The
Reconnaissance Commandos, along with other "special forces"
now constitute a separate command within the SADF. They
operate their own intelligence section and also have access
to the Directorate of Military Intelligence, but do not
report to it.

Ethnic Battalions, units stationed near the borders of
neighboring states, are composed of black soldiers and of the
same language/cultural group as the people of the neighboring
states. These are ready for raids into those territories and
to support puppet groups. The most notorious is Battalion 32
which operated in Namibia and Angola and has been named for
being responsible for a number of atrocities.[28]

Dissident groups, such as UNITA, the MNR, the LLA, and
the so-called "super-ZAPU", purport to be indigenous
"resistance movements" and indeed draw recruits from the
country concerned, but have been supplied, led and directed
by the South African Defence Force.

However, since the Total Strategy envisages the
mobilization of economic, political and psycho-socio as well
as military resources, considerable effort has been devoted
to examining ways in which economic links in particular can
be used either as "incentive levers" or "techniques of
persuasion", on the one hand, or as "disincentive levers" or
"techniques of coercion" on the other. Among such possible
incentive levers are the offer of aid and cooperation in
joint infrastructural projects to those states willing to
collaborate with Pretoria. There are a number of different
mechanisms through which this can be channeled. The
presentation of the constellation of states proposals at the
1979 "Carlton Conference" between the government and 200
leading South African capitalists first envisaged that such
"incentives" would be funnelled through a "Southern African
Development Bank". This was, however, very slow in getting
off the ground and other institutions, such as the Southern
African Customs Union and straight and bilateral channels,
have been used to pass on such 'aid'.

At the level of economic "techniques of coercion" the
1981 paper of Geldenhuys is again revealing. Published
before the extensive application of such tactics in practice,

this paper had as its objective to recommend ways in which "South Africa [could] use its economic links for strategic purposes."[29]   Various measures were recommended for consideration.   As will become apparent in subsequent sections, a number of these have been applied or threatened.

1) Limiting or prohibiting the use of South Africa's railway and harbour facilities for the export of goods from black states. There are, needless to say, numerous ways of limiting the use of these facilities, for example, by manipulating the availability of railway trucks or berthing facilities in harbors, or harsher measures such as imposing surcharges on goods transported, or officially announcing restrictions on the amount of goods that may be exported via South Africa.

2) Limiting or banning the importation of labor from states.

[While the reasons for the reduction in the numbers and proportion of 'foreign' migrant workers in the South African mining industry are complex, it is no accident that the country most affected has been Mozambique. Moreover, the threat of a reduction in the numbers recruited from, for example, Lesotho, has been made on a number of occasions.]

3) Regulating the access to and movement through South Africa of nationals from black states. Without going to the extreme of prohibiting entry into the Republic, the authorities have various means open to them to make access more difficult, e.g. by deliberate delays at border posts.

4) Placing curbs on the imports of goods from black states ... [or] regulating the export of goods to black states. The two most crucial items are undoubtedly food and oil, but machinery, spares and various other goods could also be added.

[Zambia was subject to precisely such action in respect to maize imports immediately prior to the Lancaster House negotiations in 1979, as was Zimbabwe in respect of oil imports in a crude attempt to force into negotiations at ministerial level following the sabotage of the Beira-Mutare pipeline in 1982.]

5) Curtailing or terminating the provision of technical expertise to these states, e.g. in the operation of Maputo harbour.[30]

One important point stressed by Geldenhuys is that if South Africa were to be seen to be openly applying economic coercion against other states, it would at least in principle be more vulnerable to calls for sanctions against it. For this reason some "explanation" or "justification" for such actions in terms other than attempts to exert pressure is suggested and indeed, in practice, some such explanation has been proffered on each occasion that these techniques have been applied.

THE APPLICATION OF THE TOTAL STRATEGY

The Constellation of States Initiative

The first phase in the application of Total Strategy ran from the end of 1978 until mid-1980. It saw the launching and promotion of the Constellation of States proposal. In November 1979, at the first of several meetings between officials of the Botha regime and leading capitalists, Botha called for support from the private sector for a proposed Southern African Development Bank to finance the infrastructural projects which would be the key to the establishment of the constellation.

According to press reports at the time,[31] apartheid strategists had drawn up a schedule for incorporating independent states in the region into the proposed constellation. The key to the whole project was to have been Zimbabwe. If Zimbabwe could be brought to an internationally recognized independence under a government led by Muzorewa, it was calculated that it would be a ready adherent to the Constellation. With Zimbabwe secured it was felt that the two most conservative states with already existing strong economic links with South Africa - Malawi and Swaziland- would easily be attracted. This would virtually compel the other two members of the Southern African Customs Union- Lesotho and Botswana - to join. Zaire could then be persuaded to affiliate, which would then place strong pressure on Zambia to associate. Apart from Namibia, which apartheid strategists were then hoping to bring to a Muzorewa-type independence under the Democratic Turnhalle Alliance, this left three states - Angola, Mozambique and

Tanzania. According to these sources, these three countries
were not then seriously considered as likely adherents to the
constellation under their existing governments. In the event
the implementation of the constellation project as originally
conceived was blocked. There were two main factors
responsible for this. First was the defeat of Muzorewa in
the Zimbabwean independence elections. ZANU(PF)s victory put
to rest any hopes that Zimbabwe would become the key to the
early establishment of a South African-dominated
constellation in the region. Instead independent Zimbabwe
became a member of the Front Line States alliance.

The other factor which thwarted early constellation
initiatives, was the formation of the Southern African
Development Coordination Conference (SADCC). SADCC was
officially established in April 1980, although the proposal
had been discussed at a meeting of the Front Line States in
Arusha in July 1979. SADCC defined its principal strategic
objective as "a reduction of external dependence and in
particular dependence on the Republic of South Africa."[32]
Its documents identified three levels of transformation that
would be necessary in order to achieve this: a) a
transformation at the level of the economies of each of the
individual member states; b) a transformation in the
relationships between SADCC member states; and c) a
transformation in the relationship between the member states
as a group and the outside world. In its attempt to bring
about such transformations, SADCC formulated a multilateral
development programme, concentrating on infrastructural
development, particularly transport (seen to be indispensable
for a restructuring of relations between member states) and
food security. Other areas of SADCC activity were to include
semi-arid agricultural development, energy policy, industrial
cooperation and training.

SADCC clearly was not established merely to frustrate
South African regional policy. A reduction in external
dependence and a radical change in the historical patterns of
accumulation in the Southern African region are the sine qua
non for the implementation of any development programme
capable of satisfying the needs of the region. However, it
is important to note that the SADCC project represented a
challenge not only to the constellation, but also to one of
the more immediate objectives of South Africa's regional
policy - the maintenance and even deepening of economic ties
with independent states. Moreover, SADCC succeeded in
incorporating all the nine independent states in the region,
including the more conservative. The establishment of SADCC
and the accession to it of all the key target states of the
Constellation project, thus represented an important defeat

for South African strategy.

One immediate effect of this was that when the apartheid regime eventually established the various constellation related apparatuses, these were confined to their operations, at least initially, to the "inner constellation" – white South Africa and the "independent" bantustans. Their extension to the "wider constellation" was a project deferred to the future, pending the softening up of key target states.

The Turn to Destabilization Tactics

The above developments blocked Pretoria's efforts to remold the pattern of regional relations. They thus precipitated a second phase of South African action in the region. This lasted roughly from mid-1980 until the end of 1981. It involved the application of destabilization tactics in a fairly generalized and indiscriminate manner. The period saw, firstly, increased military action against neighboring states. There were a number of large-scale invasions of Angolan territory; a raid against ANC residences in Matola near Maputo; a substantial increase in the level of activity by South African-sponsored dissident groups, in particular the MNR and LLA; threats to turn Swaziland into a "second front", backed up by a number of operations by South African agents against refugees; and assassination of ANC personnel in a number of countries.

In addition, the period saw the first major attempts to apply economic "techniques of coercion". In mid-1981, South African Transport Services withdrew over 20 locomotives on hire to the National Railway of Zimbabwe at just the time of record demand in Zimbabwe – created by a bumper harvest and the reopening of export routes following the removal of sanctions. At the same time, bottlenecks were artificially created for Zimbabwe exports passing through the South African ports and railway system. Pretoria also threatened to cancel a longstanding trade preference agreement under which Zimbabwean manufactured goods were admitted to the South African market on favorable terms. Following the advice of their consultants, apartheid spokesmen offered various "justifications" for these actions such as having to give preference to the movement of South African produced maize. However, as a Zimbabwean minister has noted, such circumstances "were never experienced during UDI"[33] and there is no doubt that such measures were in fact a "strategic application of economic links." More precisely, such steps were a response to a number of limited measures taken by Zimbabwe to eliminate various privileges previously given to South African – as distinct from other foreign – investors, as well as a general warning to Zimbabwe that attempts to reduce its ties with South African capitalism could lead to costly retaliation.

Mozambique also found itself subjected to this type of action. Shortly after the January 1981 Matola raid, South African officials were withdrawn from Maputo harbour, and for some time South African Transport Services refused to send railway wagons into Mozambique. Once again, various "justifications" were offered in a thinly disguised attempt to conceal the fact that these actions were in reality a means of putting futher pressure on Mozambique.

Intensified and Selective Destabilization

This policy of generalized destabilization up to the end of 1981 remained relatively mild by comparison with what followed. The regime appeared still to be in the process of determining precisely what it wished to achieve through such tactics. However, in early 1982 a new phase of intensified destabilization measures was initiated in which Pretoria nevertheless attempted to act more selectively in the region. The regime now appeared to have a clearer perspective of what such destabilization was intended to achieve, and what measures would be most effective against particular states.

Two immediate objectives were singled out. The first was its demand that states in the region cooperate with Pretoria to limit both the numbers and activities of ANC members in their territories. The regime's Foreign Minister declared in 1983 that South Africa was determined to force the African National Congress out of all neighboring countries: "Out – they must get out. There is no compromise on this one."[34]

The intensified action in pursuit of this demand flowed directly from the deepening internal crisis in South Africa and particularly the advances made in the armed struggle since 1977. In response, the apartheid regime attempted to internationalize its own crisis in a number of ways. It had long tried to present what is in reality a conflict arising from the internal contradictions of South African society as one derived from external aggression. By presenting such conflict as "externally" (and more precisely, Soviet) orchestrated, Pretoria hoped to draw in the major Western powers into a more open defence of apartheid. By the beginning of 1982, the regime appeared to seek to internationalize this conflict in a further sense. Action against the neighboring states now seemed to be designed to force these states to withdraw support from the ANC and perhaps even become forces pressurizing the ANC to dampen down its armed struggle.

The second immediate objective singled out by apartheid strategists during this period was to ensure the maintenance of existing economic links and frustrate efforts by states in the region to reduce their economic dependence on South Africa. This has involved both the offer of greater economic "incentives" and various actions, including direct economic sabotage, to impede attempts by SADCC countries to forge alternatives (see below).

In addition to greater selectivity at the level of objectives, after 1982 it also appears that some attempt was made to distinguish between states in the region in the application of particular tactics. Apartheid strategists appeared to have divided these states into three broad categories. The first consisted of the more conservative states, seen as vulnerable to pressure, whilst the third embraced states whose political systems and development strategies were seen to constitute the most fundamental challenge to apartheid capitalism.

The states in the first category were offered greater concessions designed either to encourage them to deepen their economic links with South African capitalism or to reward them for "good behavior." The most striking example was that of Swaziland. Among the incentives offered and accepted by the Swazi regime were assistance in building a railway line through Swazi territory linking the Eastern Transvaal with the port of Richards Bay, with a supplementary R50 million payment in 1982 under the Customs Union Agreement. The latter was described by a well informed US diplomat as "a R5-million bribe by South Africa to its friends."[35] Moreover, a controversial offer was made by South Africa to cede the KaNgwane bantustan and part of the KwaZulu bantustan to Swaziland, an offer enthusiastically embraced by the dominant political faction in the Kingdom.[36] In return, on 17 February 1982 the Swazi regime signed a secret "Non-Aggression Pact" with Pretoria whose terms were only made public more than two years later. In terms of this Agreement, both governments undertook "individually and jointly" to combat and eliminate from their territories "terrorism and subversion."[37] This was followed by a severe clamp down on ANC members in Swaziland. Swaziland also indicated that a considerable part of its sugar and other exports would be diverted from the existing link connecting the country to the port of Maputo to the planned new route linking the Kingdom to Richards Bay. These measures had a severe political impact within Swaziland itself. The conservative Swazi ruling class has been split into violently squabbling factions. The most reactionary of these now appears to have established its dominance through drastic measures which may have undermined the very ideological framework of Swazi "traditionalism" on which its rule has hitherto rested.[38]

States in the second and third categories were singled out for intensified destabilization measures. Throughout 1982 and 1983 this was the principle and most visible form of South African action in the region. The brunt of these assaults fell on Lesotho, Angola and Mozambique.

In the case of Lesotho, South African aggression was in large part directed at trying to force the government to crack down on South African refugees and expel ANC members. Pretoria appeared also to be trying to compel Lesotho to negotiate with the administrators of the Transkei bantustan. Moreover, there were some suggestions that the South African regime believed that by destabilizing the Jonathan government a pro-South African faction might be brought to power.[39]

In this period Lesotho was subjected to a wide range of destabilization measures. There was a dramatic escalation in the level of armed action by the South African sponsored LLA, with the tourist industry and government officials being singled out as the main targets. The most spectacular actions were an explosion in the luxury Hilton Hotel in which several people were killed and an attempt to assassinate Prime Minister Leabua Jonathan in a car bomb attack in August 1983. In December 1982, a South African Reconnaissance Commando made a brutal night time attack against ANC members and Lesotho nationals living in the capital, Maseru. Forty-two people were murdered, including a large number of women and children. During the same period, Lesotho was also subjected to economic coercion. In May 1983, South Africa imposed restrictions on the movement of goods and people across the border of Lesotho. These were temporarily lifted in June, following a meeting between the Foreign Ministers of the two countries, but restrictions on the movement of people were again imposed in July – the movement of goods across the border was apparently now exempted from these new restrictions following complaints about the loss of business from South African capitalists in the city of Bloemfontein, close to the Lesotho border. Threats were also made to repatriate Basotho migrant workers in South Africa. Lesotho is the most dependent of all the SADCC states on migrant labor. In 1981, there were over 140,000 Lesotho nationals working on the South African mines alone, and their remitted earnings comprised by far the largest single source of foreign exchange for the tiny Kingdom.[40]

The measures eventually took their toll. In mid-August 1983, the Lesotho government advised the United Nations that it would soon begin evacuating South African refugees. Shortly thereafter, sixty ANC members were withdrawn from the country on Lesotho's request. Announcing these measures, the Lesotho Foreign Minister, Evaristus Sekhonyana, said they were being taken because his country "could no longer withstand South African military and economic pressures."[41]

Pretoria's tactics against Angola and Mozambique in this period appeared to involve additional considerations. Apart from the considerable political and other support which these states rendered to the ANC and SWAPO, Angola and Mozambique are the only states in the region ruled by Marxist-Leninist parties, and committed to a process of socialist transformation. As such, they posed a direct ideological challenge and potential alternative to apartheid capitalism. Indeed, one of the major rationalizations of Pretoria's first constellation of states proposals had been to half "the advance of communism" - the major Southern African bases of which were seen to be Angola and Mozambique. Moreover, apart from being one of the prime movers of SADCC, Mozambique was always also of strategic importance to the realization of the SADCC project. The country's ports and harbors offer the only realistic alternative to continued dependence on South African transport facilities for many of the SADCC states. Angola, as a country of considerable mineral wealth and economic potential, was the state in the region whose economy was least dependent on South Africa. Undermining its economic viability thus became a prime South African objective.

Angola and Mozambique thus became particular victims of South African destabilization. The southern provinces of Angola were repeatedly invaded by large concentrations of SADF conventional forces, and from the end of 1982 the South of the country was under virtual full time South African occupation. At the same time support for the dissident UNITA group was greatly increased, with the likely ultimate objective of compelling the MPLA government to form a coalition with Savimbi.[42] These attacks on Angola were also clearly linked to South African policy towards its colony of Namibia. Whilst the apartheid regime had long claimed to have accepted the principle of an early internationally acceptable independence for Namibia, since 1978 at least its tactics had been those of delay and provocation as it sought to build up an "acceptable" internal alternative to SWAPO through the DTA. However the fragile political support for the DTA withered fairly rapidly and the Alliance was dealt a fatal blow in early 1982 when its President, Rev. Peter Kalangula, withdrew his Ovambo National Democratic Party claiming that the DTA had failed to tackle the dismantling of apartheid in the colony. As the Pretoria administration desperately cast around for a successor to the DTA, SADF generals appeared to shift to the view that they could win the war against SWAPO through predominantly military means. This involved intensified attacks on SWAPO inside Angola whilst simultaneously raising the costs to Angola of support for the Namibian struggle through a sustained programme of regular invasions of its territory and destruction of infrastructure and installations. The Angolan government has estimated the costs of South African-inflicted destruction at over US$10 billion.[43]

In the case of Mozambique the major instrument of destabilization was the Pretoria-sponsored MNR. From the end of 1981, there was a notable escalation of MNR attacks. Over the following two years enormous damage was caused. Official Mozambican sources estimated that 140 villages were destroyed, together with 840 schools, 900 rural shops, and over 200 public health installation. The total cost of MNR destruction has been put at US$3.8 billion.[44] Moreover, Mozambique was directly attacked on a number of occasions by units of the South African Defence Force. These included acts of sabotage against strategic transport installations-in one attack on a railway line an SADF lieutenant, Alan Gingles, was killed by his own bomb - as well as on the May 1983 air force attack on Matola/Liberdade. The office of the ANC Representative to Maputo was attacked by an SADF "special unit" and a number of bomb attacks were made against ANC members - one of which killed Ruth First. At the same time a number of "economic disincentives" were applied against Mozambique. A partial economic boycott was imposed against the port of Maputo. South African traffic in 1983 fell to half that of 1982 and only 16 per cent of the level of 1973.[45]

At the beginning of this phase there were indications that the apartheid regime was unclear over what it sought to achieve by destabilizing Mozambique. Indeed, basing itself on sources in the SADF, the Financial Mail suggested in July 1982 that there had been some internal debate over this.[46] "Hardliners" appeared to believe that it would be possible to overthrow the FRELIMO government in the near future, whilst others believed that this would be difficult and would in any case have disruptive effects on South Africa itself. Destabilization tactics should, according to this school of thought, be directed at weakening the economy so as to reinforce the propaganda offensive alleging that socialism equals economic chaos and deprivation, and also at disrupting SADCC projects. This lack of clarity over objectives seems to have been resolved in favor of the second position by the

end of 1982. An academic with close connections to the
regime's foreign policy makers characterized Pretoria's
objectives in destabilizing Mozambique as follows:

> Assuming that South Africa is either engaged in
> destabilizing Mozambique or contemplating it, several
> objectives are readily discernable. First and foremost,
> South Africa would want FRELIMO to abandon its active
> support for the ANC, which means denying it sanctuary.
> A more ambitious objective would be to influence
> Mozambique to loosen, if not cut, its close ties-
> particularly in the military field - with communist
> powers. South Africa would also welcome Mozambique
> toning down its revolutionary fervour and moderating its
> condemnation of the republic. What Pretoria essentially
> desires is a friendly cooperative neighbor instead of a
> Marxist state threatening its security. To achieve
> these objectives, support for the MNR and severe
> manipulation of economic ties are two obvious means to
> apply. To talk of the MNR overthrowing FRELIMO, or even
> forcing it into a compromise, seems highly premature and
> indeed highly unrealistic. South Africa would therefore
> have to confine its objectives to changing political
> behavior, not political structures.[47]

In a later article, Geldenhuys elaborated this point,
indicating that policy makers had recognized that it would be
infinitely more costly and troublesome to have to sustain an
MNR regime in Mozambique than simply to maintain the country
at a level of instability which would make it virtually
impossible for a FRELIMO government to govern - thereby
compelling it to "change its political behavior."[48]

Whilst the intense destabilization of Angola, Mozambique
and Lesotho remained the dominant feature of South African
regional policy during 1982 and 1983, other states in the
region were also subjected to lower levels of
destabilization. In the case of Zimbabwe the earlier
disruption of trade links partially gave way to a concerted
attempt by the South African Transport Services (SATS) to
wean traffic away from routes through Mozambique by offering
attractive competitive facilities to Zimbabwean exporters and
importers. Control over freight handling services in
Zimbabwe remained in the hands of a small number of firms
with links to the South African capital. These companies had
made investments in South African ports during the UDI period
and were now reluctant to ship goods via Maputo and Beira.
In this context, and given the ongoing sabotage of the
Mozambican railway network, SATS was able to secure the bulk

of Zimbabwean traffic.[49]   At the same time, however,
particular destabilization tactics were applied to Zimbabwe.
These seized upon and sought to exacerbate real existing
contradictions and conflicts in Zimbabwean society, and in
particular the sharp political tension between the ruling
ZANU(PF) party and the minority Patriotic Front (ZAPU).   A
radio station ("Radio Truth") was established inside South
Africa to broadcast anti-ZANU propaganda to the Matabeleland
province where ZANU support was weakest.   Military support
was given to various dissidents who were then purported to
have some connection with ZAPU and who have been styled
"super-ZAPU." The activities of these elements also had the
effect of generating border tensions between Zimbabwe and
fellow Front Line State and SADCC member, Botswana.
Moreover, in early 1983, following the sabotage of the Beira-
Mutare oil pipeline, a number of measures were taken by
Pretoria to block oil imports to landlocked Zimbabwe.   These
caused a temporary fuel shortage, and were linked to demands
for a meeting at ministerial level.   Pretoria's overall
objectives towards Zimbabwe were summed up by Geldenhuys as
follows:

> The possible objectives of destabilizing Zimbabwe are
> not so easy to discern [as in other cases].   Zimbabwe
> does not support "terrorists" in the same way as Angola
> and Mozambique; it does not fall in the communist sphere
> of influence like Angola and Mozambique, and Zimbabwe
> openly maintains close economic ties with South Africa.
> True, Zimbabwe is avowedly hostile to apartheid and has
> declared its solidarity with the ANC and also SWAPO.
> The only conceivable objective of destabilising Zimbabwe
> could be to prevent it from becoming economically strong
> enough to reduce its economic ties with South Africa to
> an insignificant level, and militarily strong enough not
> to be deterred by the Republic ... A Zimbabwe
> economically vulnerable and closely tied to South Africa
> and domestically faced with political disaffection,
> unrest and violence, may be an appealing scenario to
> those South African decision-makers favoring
> destabilization.[50]

By late 1983, it was clear that Pretoria had made a
number of overt gains in the Southern African region.   Most
obviously, Swaziland had signed a secret "Non-Aggression
Pact" with South Africa and Lesotho had been coerced into
denying sanctuary to a number of ANC members.   Enormous
material and political damage had been inflicted on Angola
and Mozambique.   However, all of this had been achieved

through what The Economist described as the "flexible and
amoral application" of "military and economic power."
Pretoria had succeeded in "throwing its weight" around the
region but "not yet in ruling it."[51] Moreover, the costs of
this policy had begun to rise. The continued colonization of
Namibia was draining R1,000 million a year from the South
African treasury and casualty levels were rising steadily.

The apparent absence of "formative action" at the
regional level- as envisaged in the original formulation of
the Total Strategy - began to be recognised by a number of
leading academics with close links to the Botha regime.
Several of these began to criticize what they saw as an
overemphasis on destabilization tactics. Such critics now
began to argue publicly that the "sophisticated" approach
envisaged in the original Total Strategy had given way to a
tendency to resort to "military quick fix solutions" not
located within a broader strategy. The broader strategic
vision had become blurred while the application of diplomatic
techniques and economic and other incentives had, by and
large, been a failure. A continuation of this trend, they
argued, would lead to an escalation of the conflict in the
region and an even more widespread resort to destabilization
tactics. Whilst this would be costly for the "target
states", these academics foresaw that this would carry
"formidable risks" for the apartheid state. "Outside forces"
might be drawn in and "a wider conflict would severely affect
foreign investment and destroy South Africa's vision of a
Constellation of Southern African States." To avoid such an
outcome, these academics advocated a more effective use of
diplomacy and economic action as called for in the original
formulations of the Total Strategy.[52]

Equally significantly, the sheer scale of South African
destabilization in Southern Africa was beginning to embarrass
its international allies by mid-1983. The accession to power
of the Thatcher government in Britain in May 1979 and
particularly the Reagan administration in the US in early
1981 created greater breathing space for the apartheid regime
internationally. The Reagan administration, in particular,
clearly had as a major foreign policy objective the ending of
South Africa's international isolation - or status as a
"pariah state" as Chester Crocker put it - and the
"reintegration" of the apartheid regime into the "network of
Western Security interests."[53] The adventurist and
militarist South African policy towards Angola was possible
only because of the overt backing of the US administration
which pointedly refused to condemn such action on a number of
occasions. Moreover, in contradistinction to its initial
position, the Reagan administration had by the end of 1981

adopted Pretoria's view that the resolution of the Namibian question was conditional on the prior removal of Cuban troops from Angola. However, by mid-1983, the Reagan administration was becoming worried that this US-backed destabilization was generating greater dangers for its interests in Southern Africa than it was delivering results. The Under Secretary of State for Political Affairs, Lawrence Eagleburger, argued in a keynote policy address in June 1983 that "a cycle of violence has begun: unless it is reversed the interests of the West will be severely damaged."[54] The US administration accordingly modified its position, and now advocated what it termed a "regional security doctrine." In Eagleburger's formulation, this doctrine rested on several premises:

> First, [the need] to recognize the rights and obligations of statehood [and] respect for international boundaries and the renunciation of the use of violence across them. Second, the cessation of organized activities within their territory by guerrillas or dissidents planning acts of violence in the territory of another another state ... Third ... our task is not to impose a structure of security. The structure must rest on regional realities, mutual interests, and direct channels of communication ... Fourthly, peaceful change in Southern Africa and regional security are both urgently needed if the risks of growing international strife are to be avoided ... A structure of regional stability in Southern Africa is unlikely to take root in the absence of a basic movement away from a system of legally entrenched rule by the white minority in South Africa.[55]

Thus, by mid-1983, the United States was actively pushing for rapprochement between the states of Southern Africa. The "softening-up" impact of South Africa's prolonged destabilization measures, particularly against Angola and Mozambique, now rendered these states more disposed to negotiate within the framework of the "regional security doctrine." At the end of 1982, the FRELIMO Central Committee adopted a three-pronged strategy to counteract South African aggression. One element of this was the decision to attempt to isolate Pretoria through improving Mozambique's relations with the West. A number of overtures were made in which it appears that the Mozambican government was urged to seek some accommodation with Pretoria. Two ministerial level meetings were held in the border town of Komatipoort in December 1982 and May 1983. According to Eagleburger, these meetings were the result of US "efforts."[56] These early negotiations broke down on a number of issues - among them, according to the South African Foreign Minister, was the ANC car bomb attack on the South African Air Force Headquarters in Pretoria in May 1983.[57]

By the end of 1983, both the regional and international environment was changing. The US had increased its pressure on all states for some form of settlement within the framework of its "regional security" doctrine. In December 1983, the Soviet Union officially warned South Africa that it would not tolerate the fall of the MPLA government in Angola.[58] Moreover, South Africa's December invasion of Angola in "Operation Askari" met with a level of resistance and casualties which shocked both the regime and the white South African public. For the first time, the pro-regime Afrikaans press now hesitantly began to call for South African withdrawal from Namibia, arguing that the costs were becoming prohibitive.[59] On the eastern coast of the sub-continent, the Mozambican economy was in tatters - ravaged by drought and then a flood, on top of the effects of sustained destabilization. At the beginning of 1984, the government was forced to petition its creditors for a renegotiation of the country's US$4.5 billion debt to the Western countries alone. All of these factors congealed to separately dispose the governments of South Africa, Angola and Mozambique to negotiate an accommodation with each other. The result was the Lusaka Agreement between South Africa an angola, by which South Africa undertook to disengage its forces from Angola, and the Nkomati Accord between Pretoria and Mozambique, signed on 16 March 1984.

The Post-Nkomati Period: Pax Pretoriana?

The Nkomati Accord marked the inauguration of the fourth phase of South African regional policy since 1978. The Accord committed both states to prohibit the use of their respective territories by any "state, government, foreign military forces, organizations or individuals which plan or prepare to commit acts of violence, terrorism or aggression against the territorial integrity or political independence of the other or may threaten the security of its inhabitant."[60] This agreement clearly committed South Africa to end its support for the MNR. In return, Mozambique would restrict the activities of ANC members on its territory.

The Accord was signed with great flourish in a public ceremony by Prime Minister Botha and President Machel. There is no doubt that Pretoria regards it as a fundamental breakthrough in regional and foreign policy. The apartheid regime had long striven to conclude "Non-Aggression Pacts" with regional states. As indicated above, these had been seen as a key step in Pretoria's plan to bring into being a Constellation of States in Southern Africa. Not surprisingly then, the signing of the Nkomati Accord was seen by South Africa as finally creating the conditions for a relaunching, albeit with a modified timetable, of its stalled constellation initiative. Indeed, in his address at the signing ceremony, P.W. Botha pointedly referred to his "vision" of a "veritable constellation of states in Southern Africa."[61] Moreover, it was seen as giving Pretoria its greatest opportunity in a quarter of a century to break out of its isolation on the wider international level. Returning to one of the themes of the original constellation formula, Foreign Minister R.F. Botha declared that "the way to the world" was "through Africa."[62]

Various steps have now been taken to implement the security provisions of the Nkomati Accord. A joint security commission has been set up to monitor the application of the agreement. Mozambique has vigorously implemented its side of the Accord by restricting the ANC presence to a small diplomatic mission. For its part, Pretoria has taken more limited measures against the MNR in South Africa – and it is known that shortly before the signing of the accord, several hundred armed MNR members were infiltrated into Mozambique from South Africa.[63] On the other side of the sub-continent, the South African military withdrawal under the joint supervision of the SADF and the Angolan armed forces was undertaken, and in May 1984, negotiations were held in Lusaka between the South African government and SWAPO over Namibian independence. Although these broke down there were some indications that Pretoria was perhaps now more willing to reach a settlement on Namibia than it had been in the past few years.

While all these developments to some extent represent a suspension of Pretoria's use of "the military option" in the region, the more than 20% increase in the military budget for 1983-85 clearly shows that this option remains in reverse. However, for the moment, other tactics apparently dominate Pretoria's current efforts to assert its role as the internationally recognized "regional power." In this phase, the apartheid regime clearly views its relations with Mozambique as the key to the success of its whole strategy. Following the Nkomati Accord, the South African ruling class has seen a number of opportunities for "formative action" on the economic front in accordance with the original constellation conception. The apartheid regime is now patently engaged in an attempt to demonstrate in the case of Mozambique that "economic cooperation" with Pretoria holds out greater advantages than "socialism."

There are a number of dimensions to this. At the level of direct state action, a new tri-partite agreement was reached on the supply of power from the Cabora Bassa hydro-electric scheme. The agreement can be seen in part, as a concession to Mozambique in that tariffs have been considerably increased and are now calculated on the basis of the amount of power leaving the turbines, rather than that received in South Africa. It also provides that South Africa and Mozambique will have joint responsibility for the security of the power lines. Other formal agreements on the use of Maputo port and possibly the recruitment of additional Mozambican labor for the South African mines are also expected and a South African government "economics committee" has been set up to deal with Mozambique.

In accordance with a basic premise of the constellation approach, the regime has also made a concerted effort to persuade the "private sector" to involve itself in Mozambique. A large number of leading South African capitalists were invited to the Nkomati ceremony, and there have been numerous appeals for businessmen to make the new relationship work. This appeal has found a resonance amongst South African capitalists, who have shown real interest in investigating the possibilities for profitable investment in Mozambique. In the words of the Chief Executive of the South African Associate Chambers of Commerce (Assocom):

> Most businessmen today – in the aftermath of the Nkomati Accord with Mozambique, new arrangements with Swaziland, conciliatory remarks by President Kaunda of Zambia, and peace moves in South West Africa (Namibia) – stand closer to the Prime Minister's goal (of a constellation of states) than ever before. Businessmen have an enormous stake in the success or otherwise of recent developments in Southern Africa, especially in Mozambique.[64]

Assocom itself has given "top priority" to the preparation of a "radical new master plan aimed at boosting two way trade with black Africa." Triggered by the Nkomati Accord, this exercise by Assocom aims at producing a blueprint intended to prove to neighboring states "as far as the equator" that "free trade flows hold the key to mutual economic growth." The organization expects a wave of "business safaris" to explore new trade routes. The Assocom strategists working on this new trade plan are concentrating initially on an economic pact with Mozambique. According to the Johannesburg Star:

Talks are likely to be sought with both the SA Department of Foreign Affairs and the Department of Commerce on the necessity of recruiting the private sector to the economics committee being set up in the wake of the Nkomati Accord. The aim will be to persuade Mozambique and other black neighbours – already showing disillusionment with loan-packages from both the East and West – that "Trade and Aid" should be the new slogan behind economic planning.[65]

Other capitalist organizations and individual companies have also actively explored the prospects for greater economic links with Mozambique. A delegation from the South African Foreign Trade Organisation[66] and another representing the South African Federated Chambers of Industries, as well as Assocom, the South African Agricultural Union and the Afrikaner Handelsinstitut visited maputo in May and June 1984. There have also been a number of exploratory visits by individual South African businessmen.

Although most of the details of such discussions are not yet public knowledge, the broad outlines of a pattern can already be discerned. Such South African investment as is likely to be forthcoming will clearly be largely confined to certain defined sectors of the Mozambique economy which will tend to reproduce the relationship of subordination to South African capital. These areas are primarily transport and tourism, with possibly a small involvement in agribusiness, fishing and mineral exploitation. Some of the more rabid free enterprise ideologists of South African capital see these new links as creating a basis to undermine fundamentally the SADCC project. Thus the influential Financial Mail editorialized that the closer trade links between South Africa and Mozambique

the dissipation of the Southern African Coordination Conference's fragile economic initiative is inevitable ... For instance, Mozambique was to have played a key role in the coordination of transport in the SADCC region. It is a role that South Africa is much better placed to fulfil more efficiently. Close trade ties between SA and Mozambique must lead to recognition of that fact.

While this editorial thus implicitly advocated that Maputo becomes a South African rather than SADCC-oriented port, it also explicitly urged the creation of "an enlarged Rand currency area," incorporating neighboring states so as to "give these countries the access to capital markets that their poverty denies them."[67]

A further feature of the post-Nkomati phase has been Pretoria's attempt to use the Accord as a springboard to break out of its international isolation. Firstly, there has been a clear attempt to draw Western governments, international financial institutions and foreign capital into the proposals for "economic cooperation" in the region. In April 1984 Foreign Minister Botha urged diplomats from the United States, West Germany, France, Canada, Britain, Japan and Italy to "involve themselves in greater development efforts in Mozambique." It was necessary, he added, to "match political expectations with economic progress."[68] Negotiations over tri-partite investment packages would involve American or Western European finance and Portuguese technical assistance in joint ventures with South African undertakings. Secondly, Pretoria has sought to capitalise on its increased prestige in Western countries generated by the Nkomati Accord to become internationally accepted as "the regional power" and "key to peace" in Southern Africa. This was evidently one of the principal objectives of P.W. Botha's visit to Western Europe in June 1984 - an event inconceivable before Nkomati.

This apparent success of South Africa's latest regional offensive has led it into a concerted attempt to pressurize other states in the region to conclude "Non-Aggression Pacts" similar to those signed with Swaziland and Mozambique. Lesotho particularly has been threatened with "economic havoc" - and more specifically with the repatriation of its migrant workers in South Africa and Pretoria's withdrawal from the Highlands Hydro-electric scheme - unless it entered into an agreement obliging it to "notify SA of every refugee escaping from Lesotho and provide for deportations or repatriation if Pretoria insists."[69] Botswana has likewise been threatened with the disruption of the flow of goods and people across the common border unless it entered into a formal security agreement with Pretoria. This South African pressure on Botswana was condemned by a number of European Heads of Government during P.W. Botha's European tour.[70]

CONCLUSION: LIMITS AND POSSIBILITIES

It is clear that since the beginning of 1984 Pretoria has achieved an important breakthrough in the Southern African region. It now has "Non-Aggression Pacts" with two countries, and a ceasefire agreement with Angola. A degree of international recognition unprecedented in the past 25 years has flown from these agreements and Pretoria's foreign policy makers have acquired something of an aura of "statesmen." Moreover, the other states in Southern Africa have clearly been forced onto the defensive in their attempts to resist Pretoria's pressure to conclude similar "Non-Aggression Pacts." In the case of Swaziland, the current ruling group has taken action against the ANC with an intensity previously unknown outside of apartheid South Africa itself.

However, it is by no means certain that the momentum of Pretoria's latest regional offensive can be sustained. Clear contradictions exist at the level of South Africa's current policy objectives. On the one hand, Pretoria evidently desires to maintain regional states in a position of weakness as a basis on which to exercise its dominance over them. It certainly does not wish to see economically strong independent states arising in the region, and much of its activities over the past six years have been explicitly designed to undermine the economic viability of other Southern African countries. On the other hand, in the wake of the Nkomati Accord, the apartheid regime is now obliged to be seen to be able to deliver economic benefits to demonstrate that "cooperation with Pretoria works."

However, the apartheid regime's capacity to mobilize economic "incentive levers" is clearly limited. South Africa's own economy remains in the grips of its worst recession since the 1930s. The continued deficit in its balance of payments places clear limits on its potential to act as the regional banker. The 1984–85 South Africa budget introduced extremely unpopular new taxes simply to sustain the expanding SADF and spending on apartheid's "new constitutional dispensation" and even these taxes had to be increased barely weeks after the budget was announced. Moreover, the now resurrected constellation initiative assigns a central role in establishing such economic links to South Africa's private sector. The experience of the bantustans, where the state for years placed great political pressure and offered extraordinarily attractive incentives to businessmen to invest in Pretoria's political projects, suggests that hard-headed South African capitalists are not now likely to furnish large amounts of capital in Pretoria's new political schemes unless it is clearly profitable for them to do so. Some indications have emerged that a number of South African businessmen have already concluded that the prospective profits and the bureaucratic administrative processes in neighboring countries do not make large investments worth their while.[71]

Furthermore, the response of the target states to

Pretoria's latest offensive is a decisive factor. The level of resistance from Botswana and Lesotho to attempts to bully them into formal security agreements with South Africa has surprised Pretoria's foreign policy makers. In the case of Mozambique, a debate over how to respond to South African initiatives is clearly under way. FRELIMO did not enter into the Nkomati Accord because it accepted South African objectives, and has its own agenda to follow in the new arrangements. The Mozambican government evidently intends to use South African offers of economic cooperation for purposes different from those intended by Pretoria. To what extent this can succeed remains to be seen. But such attempts must clearly have an impact on the effectiveness of South Africa's economic "strategic levers." Moreover, a number of press reports have indicated that the Mozambican government is clearly unhappy with Pretoria's lukewarm action in controlling MNR activity, and this could lead to a strain in relations in the medium term.[72]

Finally, the fact remains that the root cause of the crisis confronting the apartheid state - and also the fundamental cause of Pretoria's isolation at both the regional and wider international levels - derives from the nature of the internal apartheid system. Despite numerous weird and wonderful schemes and "new dispensations"- reminiscent of the twists and turns of Kenyan settlers in the late 1950s - the Botha regime is far from a resolution to this internal crisis as its Verwoerdian predecessor. It is fundamentally incapable of resolving this crisis without destroying itself. Attempts to export or internationalize the internal crisis of the apartheid capitalist state may gain for it a measure of time, wreaking havoc on the states and peoples of Southern Africa, but cannot solve the fundamental issue of South Africa - apartheid. As the April 1984 meeting of the Front Line States in Arusha concluded, real peace in Southern Africa is impossible while the apartheid system continues to exist.

NOTES

1.   For example, Simon Jenkins, "Destabilization in Southern Africa", The Economist, 16 September 1983.
2.   Such a position is argued in, inter alia: K.W. Grundy, The Rise of the South African Security Establishment: an essay on the changing locus of state power, (Bradlow Paper no. 1, Johannesburg, South African Institute of International Affairs, 1983); and D. Geldenhuys, "The Destabilization Controversy: an analysis of high risk foreign policy option for South Africa", Politikon 9(2), December 1982.

274

3.   This position was expressed by the Director of AIM, (Mozambican Information Agency), Carlos Cardoso, in an interview on Mozambican television (TVE), 16 March 1984.
4.   See R. Davies and D. O'Meara, "The State of the Southern African Region: issues raised by the total strategy", Review of African Political Economy (29), 1984.
5.   See the discussion of the timing of the South African Air Force attack in June 1983 on Matola in J. Seiler, "The South African State Security System: rationalization to what ends", mimeo, Yale University, 1983.
6.   For background see S. Nolutshungu, South Africa in Africa, (Manchester, 1975); D. Geldenhuys and D. Venter, "Regional Cooperation in Southern Africa: a constellation of states?", South African Institute of International Affairs Bulletin, December 1979.
7.   B. Schoeman, Van Malan tot Verwoerd (Cape Town, 1973).   This has now been admitted by the South African Foreign Minister when he responded to Lesotho's protest over Pretoria's pivotal role in the formation of the opposition United Democratic Alliance in January 1984 (see note 39), to the effect that the Basotho National Party could not complain as South Africa had played a similar role in its formation.
8.   M. Fransman, "Labour, Capital and the State in Swaziland, 1962–1977", South African Labour Bulletin 7(6), April 1982.
9.   S. Ettinger, The Economics of the Customs Union Between Botswana, Lesotho, Swaziland and South Africa, Ph.D., University of Michigan, 1974.
10.   Nolutshungu, p. 276.
11.   Geldenhuys and Venter, p. 149.
12.   Department of Defense, White Paper on Defense, (Cape Town, 1977).
13.   The following two paragraphs draw on the history of the constellation idea in Geldenhuys and Venter.
14.   It must be stressed that this definition of 'marxism' was extremely broad and embraced the ideologies of the non-marxist ruling parties of Zambia and Tanzania.
15.   Geldenhuys and Venter, p. 52.
16.   Ibid., p. 54.
17.   D. Geldenhuys, "Some Strategic Implications of Regional Economic Relationships for the Republic of South Africa", ISSUP Strategic Review, January 1981, p. 20.
18.   Defense White Paper, p. 5.
19.   Gen. Magnus Malan, "Die Aanslag Teen Suid Afrika", ISSUP Strategic Review, November 1980, p. 14.
20.   South African Institute of Race Relations, Survey of Race Relations in South Africa 1977, (Johannesburg, 1978), pp. 7–9.

21. D. Geldenhuys and H. Kotze, "Aspects of Politics Decision Making in South Africa", South African Journal of Political Science 10(1), June 1983.

22. Malan, pp. 14-5.

23. Thus apart from the Prime Minister and the other 'primary' Ministerial members of the SSC - currently Gen. Magnus Malan, Pik Botha, Louis le Grange and Piet Koornhof respectively - the other four Ministers are probably now Chris Heunis and Owen Horwood, and the leaders of the Transvaal and OFS Nationalist Parties, F.W. de Klerk and P.T. du Plessis. In the order of positions named, the senior bureaucrats are: Lukas Neil Barnard, Gen Constandt Viljoen, J. van Dalsen, J.P.J. Coetzer and Gen. Johan Coetzee. Other nominated members of the SSC include at least the secretary of its secretariat, Lt. Gen. A.J. van Deventer, the Head of Military Intelligence, Lt. Gen. P.W. van der Westhuizen, and two 'observers', the Deputy Minister of Foreign Affairs, Louis Nel, and one other unknown senior official. There may well be others as the full composition of the SSC has never been divulged.

24. Geldenhuys and Kotze, p. 40.

25. Malan, p. 15.

26. In September 1979, the General Manager of South African Railways, Dr. J. Loubser, wrote a paper entitled "Transport Diplomacy with Special Reference to Southern Africa", Sandton, Southern African Editorial Services. Here he considered the role "transport can play towards the furtherance of such a diplomatic strategy ... A country's infrastructure can be regarded as one of its most important assets, giving it a bargaining power", p. 5.

27. This information is based on a memorandum entitled "South African Special Forces and the Seychelles Coup", mimeo 1982, whose author wishes to remain anonymous.

28. See Resister (Bulletin of the Committee on South African War Resistance), (17), Dec. 1981 - Jan. 1982.

29. Geldenhuys, "Strategic Implications", p. 17.

30. Ibid.

31. The Star, 20 November 1979.

32. SADCC, Southern Africa: towards economic liberation - a strategy paper, (Maputo, 1980), p. 1.

33. Interview with the former Zimbabwean Minister of Industry and Energy, Simba Makoni, by Gottfried Wellmer, Harare, February 1984.

34. Rand Daily Mail, 13 October 1983.

35. Personal communication.

36. South African Research Services/Development Studies Group, Information Publication No. 7, "The Swaziland-South Africa Land Deal", Johannesburg, 1982.

37. The Citizen, 2 April 1984.

38. Centro de Estudos Africanos, The Kingdom of Swaziland: a political, economic and social profile, (Maputo, 1984).

39. Pretoria's initial choice seemed to be Charles Mofeli's United Democratic Party. Mofeli was expelled from the Lesotho parliament in July 1983 after giving an interview to the South African Broadcasting Corporation advocating Lesotho's virtual capitulation to Pretoria – Rand Daily Mail 13 July 1983. More recently, attention seems to have been focused on the United Democratic Alliance. In April 1984 two of its members revealed that the Alliance had been formed in January of that year at the suggestion of Pretoria's Foreign Minister who had promised financial backing for its electoral campaign – The Observer, (London), 8 April 1984.

40. "Destabilization: a brief to the Lesotho parliament by the Prime Minister, the Right Honorable Dr. Leabua Jonathan, on South Africa's activities against Lesotho", Maseru, 1983. The Star Weekly, 15 August 1983 carries a chronology of acts of destabilization against Lesotho.

41. Ibid.

42. Portuguese archival sources subsequently published in Angola provide conclusive proof of the collaboration of Savimbi and UNITA with the Portuguese colonial state in its war against the MPLA. See Savimbi's letters to Lt. Col. Armenio Nuno Ramires de Oliveira, Portuguese Chief of Staff in the then colony's eastern military region cited in Jornal de Angola 21 April 1984, republished in English in Angola Information Bulletin, London, (73), 2 May 1984, pp. 10–12.

43. See People's Republic of Angola, White Paper on Acts of Aggression by the Racist South African Regime Against the People's Republic of Angola, 1975-1982, (Luanda, 1983).

44. People's Republic of Mozambique, Economic Report, (Maputo, National Planning Commission, January 1984), p. 41.

45. Ibid., p. 30.

46. Financial Mail, 16 July 1982.

47. Geldenhuys, 1982, p. 29 (our emphasis).

48. The Cape Times, 8 March 1984 quotes Geldenhuys as follows: "SA's hawkish strategy towards its neighbors had the intended effect of producing or aggravating domestic instability in target states. But SA does not possess a master plan for removing regimes in power in neighboring state, nor has it the resources to dislodge several governments and sustain perhaps unpopular puppet successor regimes in the face of determined resistance."

49. See "Research re Shifting Trade From South Africa to Mozambique", Economics Department, University of Zimbabwe, mimeo, 1981.

50. Geldenhuys, "Destabilization Controversy".

51. Jenkins, "Destabilization".

52. See Geldenhuys, "Destabilization Controversy" and a three part series of articles in The Star, 22-25 March 1983. On the other hand, another pro-apartheid academic argued in the official journal of the SADF that: "All terrorist concentrations threatening peace and security in SWA/Namibia or South Africa, regardless of where they are located, must be attacked and destroyed. So-called diplomatic considerations must not be allowed to interfere - that is the road to defeat ... Standing on the defensive is not enough. The ANC must be attacked abroad. Attacks like that on ANC Headquarters in Maputo [sic] and Maseru must be repeated-again and again ... Containment is not the aim. Destruction is." R.K. Campbell, Parantus, April 1983.

53. "Scope paper", Chester Crocker to Secretary of State Alexander Haig, January 1981, published by the Trans Africa Forum, 1981 ("leaked" internal State Department Document).

54. Lawrence S. Eagleburger, "America's Responsibility for Peace and Change", Washington, United States Department of State, 23 June 1983.

55. Ibid.

56. Ibid.

57. See Sunday Times, 15 January 1984.

58. Financial Times, 5 January 1984.

59. Rapport, 15 January 1984.

60. "Accord of Nkomati signed by the Honorable Pieter Willem Botha and his Excellency Samora Moises Machel at the Common Border on the banks of the Nkomati River on 16 March 1984 on behalf of the Republic of South Africa oand the People's Republic of Mozambique.

61. "Remarks by the Honorable P.W. Botha, DMS MP, Prime Minister of the Republic of South Africa, on the Occasion of the Signing of the Accord of Nkomati: Friday 16 March 1984", p. 4.

62. The Citizen, 22 February 1984.

63. Rand Daily Mail, 22 May 1984.

64. The Star, 23 April 1984.

65. Ibid., 24 April 1984.

66. The SAFTO delegation was led by its Chief Executive, W.B. Holtes, who had previously published an article in ISSUP Strategic Review, August 1983 on ways in which South African trade could undermine SADCC.

67. 27 April 1984.

68. Sunday Times, 8 April 1984.

69. Africa Times (UK), 3 May 1984 and The Guardian, 26 May 1984.

70. See response by Deputy Minister of Foreign Affairs

and Information, Louis Nel, in <u>Rand Daily Mail</u>, 14 June 1984.

71.   <u>The Citizen</u> reported that "one of the first South
African businessmen to enter Mozambique after the Accord of
Nkomati, returned this week disillusioned and with conviction
that any trade between the two countries will be impossible"
(5 June 1984).

72.   <u>The Guardian</u>, 18 May 1984.

Appendix I
Nkomati Accord,
Signed Between Mozambique and
South Africa, March 1984

Agreement on non-aggression and good neighbourliness between the Government of the People's Republic of Mozambique and the Government of the Republic of South Africa.

The Government of the People's Republic of Mozambique and the Government of the Republic of South Africa, hereinafter referred to as the High Contracting Parties:

RECOGNISING the principles of strict respect for sovereignty and territorial integrity, sovereign equality, political independence and the inviolability of the borders of all states;

REAFFIRMING the principle of non-interference in the internal affairs of other states;

CONSIDERING the internationally recognised principle of the right of peoples to self-determination and independence and the principle of equal rights of all peoples;

CONSIDERING the obligation of states to refrain, in their international relations, from the threat or use of force against the territorial integrity or political independence of any state;

CONSIDERING the obligation of states to settle conflicts by peaceful means, and thus safeguard international peace and security and justice;

RECOGNISING the responsibility of states not to allow their territory to be used for acts of war, aggression or violence against other states;

CONSCIOUS of the need to promote relations of good neighbourliness based on the principles of equality of rights and mutual advantage;

CONVINCED that relations of good neighbourliness between the High Contracting Parties will contribute to peace, security, stability and progress in Southern Africa, the

Continent and the World;

Have solemnly agreed to the following:

ARTICLE ONE

The High Contracting Parties undertake to respect each other's sovereignty and independence and, in fulfillment of this fundamental obligation, to refrain from interfering in the internal affairs of the other.

ARTICLE TWO

1) The High Contracting Parties shall resolve differences and disputes that may arise between them and that may or are likely to endanger mutual peace and security or peace and security in the region, by means of negotiation, enquiry, mediation, conciliation, arbitration or other peaceful means, and undertake not to resort, individually or collectively, to the threat or use of force against each other's sovereignty, territorial integrity or political independence.

2) For the purposes of this article, the use of force shall include _inter alia_ –

    a) attacks by land, air or sea forces;

    b) sabotage;

    c) unwarranted concentration of such forces at or near the international boundaries of the High Contracting Parties;

    d) violation of the international land, air or sea boundaries of either of the High Contracting Parties.

3) The High Contracting Parties shall not in any way assist the armed forces of any state or group of states deployed against the territorial sovereignty or political independence of the other.

ARTICLE THREE

1) The High Contracting parties shall not allow their respective territories, territorial waters or air space to be used as a base, thoroughfare, or in any other way by another state, government, foreign military forces, organizations or individuals which plan or prepare to commit acts of violence, terrorism or aggression against the territorial integrity or political independence of the other or may threaten the security of its inhabitants.

2) The High Contracting Parties, in order to prevent or eliminate the acts or the preparation of acts mentioned in paragraph (1) of this article, undertake in particular to –

    a) forbid and prevent in their respective territories the organization of irregular forces or armed bands, including mercenaries, whose objective is to carry out the acts contemplated in paragraph (1) of this article;

    b) eliminate from their respective territories bases,

training centres, places of shelter, accommodation and transit for elements who intend to carry out acts contemplated in paragraph (1) of this article;

c) eliminate from their respective territories centres or depots containing armaments of whatever nature, destined to be used by the elements contemplated in paragraph (1) of this article;

d) eliminate from their respective territories command posts or other places for the command, direction and co-ordination of the elements contemplated in paragraph (1) of this article;

e) eliminate from their respective territories communication and telecommunication facilities between the command and the elements contemplated in paragraph (1) of this article;

f) eliminate and prohibit the installation in their respective territories of radio broadcasting stations, including unofficial or clandestine broadcasts, for the elements that carry out the acts contemplated in paragraph (1) of this article;

g) exercise strict control, in their respective territories, over elements which intend to carry out or plan the acts contemplated in paragraph (1) of this article;

h) prevent the transit of elements who intend to commit the acts contemplated in paragraph (1) of this article, from a place in the territory of either to a place in the territory of the other or to a place in the territory of any third state which has a common boundary with the High Contracting Party against which such elements intend or plan to commit the said acts;

i) take appropriate steps in their respective territories to prevent the recruitment of elements of whatever nationality for the purpose of carrying out the acts contemplated in paragraph (1) of this article;

j) prevent the elements contemplated in paragraph (1) of this article from carrying out from their respective territories by any means acts of abduction or other acts, aimed at taking citizens of any nationality hostage in the territory of the other High Contracting Party; and

k) prohibit the provision on their respective territories of any logistic facilities for carrying out the acts contemplated in paragraph (1) and (2) of this article.

3) The High Contracting Parties will not use the territory

of third states to carry out or support the acts contemplated
in paragraphs (1) and (2) of this article.
ARTICLE FOUR
The High Contracting Parties shall take steps, individually
or collectively, to ensure that the international boundary
between their respective territories is effectively patrolled
and that the border posts are efficiently administered to
prevent illegal crossings from the territory of a High
Contracting Party to the territory of the other, and in
particular, by elements contemplated in Article Three of this
Agreement.
ARTICLE FIVE
The High Contracting Parties shall prohibit within their
territory acts of propaganda that incite a war of aggression
against the other High Contracting Party and shall also
prohibit acts of propaganda aimed at inciting acts of
terrorism and civil war in the territory of the other High
Contracting Party.
ARTICLE SIX
The High Contracting Parties declare that there is no
conflict between their commitments in treaties and
international obligations and the commitment undertaken in
this Agreement.
ARTICLE SEVEN
The High Contracting Parties are committed to interpreting
this Agreement in good faith and will maintain periodic
contact to ensure the effective application of what has been
agreed.
ARTICLE EIGHT
Nothing in this Agreement shall be construed as detracting
from the High Contracting Parties' right to self-defence in
the armed attacks, as provided for in the Charter of the
United Nations.
ARTICLE NINE
1) Each of the High Contracting Parties shall appoint high-
ranking representatives to serve on a Joint Security
Commission with the aim of supervising and monitoring the
application of this Agreement.
2) The Commission shall determine its own working
procedure.
3) The Commission shall meet on a regular basis and may be
specially convened whenever circumstances so require.
4) The Commission shall –
   a) Consider all allegations of infringements of the
      provisions of the Agreement;
   b) advise the High Contracting Parties of its
      conclusions; and
   c) make recommendations to the High Contracting

Parties concerning measures for the effective application of this Agreement and the settlement of disputes over infringements or alleged infringements.

5) The High Contracting Parties shall determine the mandate of their respective representatives in order to enable interim measures to be taken in cases of duly recognised emergency.

6) The High Contracting Parties shall make available all the facilities necessary for the effective functioning of the Commission and will jointly consider its conclusions and recommendations.

ARTICLE TEN

This Agreement will also be known as "The Accord of Nkomati".

ARTICLE ELEVEN

1) This agreement shall enter into force on the date of the signature thereof.

2) Any amendment to this Agreement agreed to by the High Contracting Parties shall be affected by the Exchange of Notes between them.

IN WITNESS WHEREOF, the signatories, in the name of their respective governments, have signed and sealed this Agreement, in quadruplicate in the Portuguese and English languages, both texts being equally authentic.

THUS DONE AND SIGNED AT the common border on the banks of the Nkomati River, on this the sixteenth day of March 1984.

SAMORA MOSES MACHEL
MARSHALL OF THE REPUBLIC
PRESIDENT OF THE PEOPLE'S
REPUBLIC OF MOZAMBIQUE
PRESIDENT OF THE COUNCIL OF MINISTERS
FOR THE GOVERNMENT OF THE
PEOPLE'S REPUBLIC OF
MOZAMBIQUE

PIETER WILLEM BOTHA
PRIME MINISTER OF THE
REPUBLIC OF SOUTH AFRICA
FOR THE GOVERNMENT OF THE
REPUBLIC OF SOUTH AFRICA

INTRODUCTION

The African liberation struggle is conducted on two major fronts: through armed combat and in the diplomatic field. In the pre-OAU period, the then colonial territories and peoples achieved their independence through political struggle and constitutional negotiations.

Weakened by the strain and destruction of the Second World War, the colonial powers found themselves unable effectively to withstand or contain the upsurge of the anti-colonial uprising. In other words, the colonialists became powerless in the face of the wind of change blowing across the African continent in the wake of the great and destructive war. The obvious consequence was that many colonies achieved their national independence without having to resort to armed struggle. Nevertheless, countries such as Algeria and Kenya (to mention but two) had to do it the hard way: that is, through bloody and bitter armed liberation war.

After the creation of the OAU in 1963, armed struggle became the priority option for the decolonization process. But it had to be supplemented by political and diplomatic activities. In fact, the original view of the OAU founder members was that where the decolonization process could be achieved through peaceful means, that option should be pursued. But where independence could not be achieved through peaceful means, then, other alternatives had to prevail.

The Role of the OAU Liberation Committee

Immediately after signing the OAU Charter, the founder members of the Organization decided to create a special committee to coordinate the activities of national liberation movements fighting for the independence of their territories. The establishment of this organ (with the official title of the OAU Coordinating Committee for the Liberation of Africa) at the very inaugural session of the OAU summit, was a clear testimony of the importance and urgency African leaders attached to the problem of decolonization. Their desire and aspiration, which was a reflection of the feeling of the masses of African Peoples, was for immediate and total liberation of the entire African continent. But before the child could run, it had to walk. So the initial stage of the liberation struggle was on the diplomatic and political fronts.

In the resolution by which the OAU Liberation Committee was created, the African leaders considered all aspects of the decolonization problem and were unanimously convinced of the imperious and urgent necessity of coordinating and intensifying efforts to accelerate the unconditional attainment of national independence by all African territories still under foreign domination. They reaffirmed that it was the duty of all African independent states to support colonized peoples of Africa in their struggle for freedom and independence. To this end, the founder members agreed unanimously to concert and coordinate their efforts and actions in the decolonization process; an area in which, so far, the OAU has made some achievements.

At its creation, the OAU Liberation Committee consisted of nine members: namely, Algeria, Ethiopia, Guinea (Conakry), Congo Leopoldville (now Zaire), Nigeria, Senegal, Tanganyika (now United Republic of Tanzania), United Arab Republic (now the Republic of Egypt), and Uganda. Since its foundation, the membership of the Liberation Committee has steadily increased and now stands at twenty-three, nearly one half of the entire membership of the OAU.

In brief, the Committee's responsibility is to harmonize assistance, from African states and friendly countries and organizations as well as individuals, and to manage the Special fund set up for that purpose.

In the operative paragraphs of the resolution by which the Liberation Committee was created, the following stressed the need for diplomatic approaches:

The Assembly of Head of States and Governments:

a) INVITES the colonial powers to take the necessary measures on the immediate application of the Declaration of the Granting of Independence to Colonial Countries and Peoples; and INSISTS that their determination to maintain colonies or semi-colonies in Africa constitutes a menace to the peace of the continent;

b) INVITES, further, the colonial powers, particularly the United Kingdom with regards to Southern Rhodesia, not to transfer the powers and attributes of sovereignty to foreign minority governments imposed on African peoples by the use of force and under cover of transfer of power to the settler minorities would amount to violation of the provision of United Nations Resolution 1514(XV).

c) INTERVENES expressly with the Great Powers so that they cease, without exception, to lend direct or indirect support or assistance to all those colonialist governments which ought to use such assistance to suppress National Liberation Movements, particularly the Portuguese government which is conducting a real war of genocide in Africa; INFORMS the allies of colonial powers for the African peoples and their support of the powers that oppress African peoples.

d) DECIDES to send a delegation of Ministers of Foreign Affairs to speak on behalf of all African States in the meeting of the U.N. Security Council to be called to examine the Report of the Committee of 24 on the situation in African territories under Portuguese domination (Liberia, Tunisia, Madagascar and Sierra Leone were selected to constitute the delegation).

The above operative paragraphs illustrate vividly the diplomatic but firm and uncompromising position of the OAU on the issue of decolonization.

Apart from the official position of the OAU, many other attempts were made by the colonizing powers to free the oppressed peoples from their bondage. Some of the approaches were made by independent African states on a bilateral basis. Others were made as joint ventures on a regional basis. Here we have in mind the diplomatic efforts of the Front Line States.

Lusaka Manifesto

The Lusaka Manifesto is another example of the diplomatic efforts exerted to complement the armed liberation struggle in Africa. Initially, the document was prepared and adopted by the Conference of Heads of State and Government of East and Central Africa in Lusaka, Zambia, on 16 April 1969.

It laid emphasis on the liberation struggle through peaceful means or negotiation where possible.

There are several schools of thought on the contents of the Lusaka Manifesto. But the document was another attempt at the diplomatic approach to decolonization. By adopting the Lusaka Manifesto, the desire of the leaders of independent African countries was to dispel any misunderstanding by the international community of Africa's options.

The Lusaka Manifesto was presented to the 24th session of the UN General Assembly by the then President of the Republic of Cameroon, Hamadou Ahidjo, in his capacity as Chairman of the OAU. After its consideration and adoption, the Manifesto became a document of the UN. The voting for the adoption of this Document was overwhelming. Only apartheid South Africa and Portugal voted against. In other words, out of the 126 UN members present, only two countries opposed the contents of the Lusaka Manifesto.

Dialogue

The diplomacy of decolonization has had its positive and negative sides. After the adoption of the Lusaka Manifesto by the international community, the apartheid South African regime started its so-called outward looking policy, bluffing even some OAU member states into believing that the racists had changed and time had come for dialogue. Some leaders of independent Africa brought pressure to bear on the national liberation movements the "need for dialogue" with the Pretoria regime. This was a negative application of diplomacy in the decolonization process.

After years of hard discussion the question of dialogue has been dropped, mainly for the simple reason that any dialogue between the apartheid regime and the national liberation movements, would not be a dialogue of equals.

Step by Step Diplomacy

After the failure of the so-called dialogue, Henry Kissinger, in his capacity as US Secretary of State, came up with another idea: the so-called step-by-step or "shuttle diplomacy." Here again, there was another attempt by cheating world opinion into believing that the Pretoria fascist regime had "changed its ways" and, therefore, was worthy of the diplomatic approach of negotiation.

The result of Kissinger's cunning diplomacy was the prolongation of bitter struggle in Zimbabwe for several more years before the people of that country finally achieved their true independence. His shuttle diplomacy was, therefore, another negative approach to the diplomacy of decolonization.

The So-called Contact Group

As if no lesson could be learned from the failure of Kissinger's "Shuttle Diplomacy", a group of five Western countries, the so-called Western Contact Group of Five, appeared on the stage. They followed, more or less, the footsteps of Henry Kissinger, shuttling around Southern Africa.

This group also felt that they knew how to liberate Namibia by peaceful means. But, like Kissinger, the interest of the people and their national liberation movements was never their concern.

To avoid misunderstanding, the OAU, once again, lent listening ears to the so-called Western Contact Group. It is to be noted that it was this Group that put up the draft of the document now popularly known as UN Security Council Resolution 435(1978).

From the outset, however, the OAU was skeptical about the mission and intention of the so-called Contact Group. Nevertheless, everything was done to facilitate its activities.

Bankrupt of objectives and unable to persuade the apartheid clique to wake up to political realities, the Contact Group suffered the same fate as Kissinger's "step-by-step" approach to decolonization.

The So-called Constructive Engagement

The so-called "constructive engagement" policy of the Reagan administration is the latest "diplomatic offensive" aimed at persuading the international community to adopt a policy of appeasement towards apartheid South Africa. By this policy, the Reagan administration hoped to put a human face on the brutal Pretoria regime. Yet, repeated massacres by the fascist police of innocent people show clearly the true face of the racist regime.

One of the greatest contributors to the policy of the constructive engagement is Chester Crocker, the so-called expert on African affairs.

Crocker is on record having once stated that apartheid would not be ended by ostracism, and certainly not by the "policy of oscillations" of successive American administrations. America, he said, had to understand the Afrikaners before deciding what pressure might move them.

Besides, Crocker pointed out, America had remarkably little leverage in the region. Too much had been promised; too little delivered. In his opinion, effective coercive influence was a rare commodity in foreign policy.

Nonetheless, Crocker went on to suggest that America should whatever weapons it possessed - largely commercial and economic -to promote change. To make them effective, America had to "engage constructively" in the region: diplomatic channels should be used to press for political freedom. Southern Africa, Crocker maintained, demanded "sustained and nimble diplomacy."

This approach, however, had to confront a more straight-forward ideology within Reagan's immediate entourage. This stipulated that apartheid South Africa was a good "anti-communist" country which should be brought within America's "strategic embrace." A South African solution to the Namibian independence should be supported. Right-wing dissident movements in neighboring states should be backed. Apartheid should be treated as a matter internal to South Africa.

This school, which included William Clark (who became Deputy Secretary of State and later National Security Advisor), had close links with right-wing senators such as Jesse Helms. Elements within the South African military establishment also had a direct line to Mr. Helms, a fact which later caused Mr. Crocker and some racist South African considerable embarrassment.

In the final analysis, Chester Crocker was driven into precisely the bind he had warned against in his Foreign Affairs article; that is overpromising and undelivering.

The OAU has maintained a constant position over the issue of constructive engagement. Despite sustained efforts to sow seeds of discord within the Organization, it has maintained that the Reagan administration's Southern Africa policy is negative and unconstructive. This case has been proved clearly by recent events within racist South Africa.

Advantages, Drawbacks and Constraints of the Diplomacy of Decolonization

One advantage of the diplomatic approach to decolonization is that it could be done at the highest decision-making level. An example of this is the pressure exerted on British Prime Minister Margaret Thatcher by the Commonwealth leaders during their meeting in Lusaka before the independence of Zimbabwe. Such pressures acted as a catalyst, supplementing the armed struggle, thus, expediting the independence of Zimbabwe.

An obvious advantage of liberation struggle through peaceful means is that loss of lives, property and unnecessary suffering are avoided. But this rests on the assumption that there is sincerity, commitment and political will on the part of all involved in the negotiation.

On the diplomatic front, the effort of the Front Line States is worthy of mention. Where bureaucratic necessities would allow for the convening of an urgent meeting of the OAU, the Front Line States always met at short notice to review new developments particularly in Southern Africa. Where budgetary or financial constraints did not allow for the convening of an OAU meeting, the Front Line States have always sacrificed and convened meetings at their own expense. This sustained sacrifice and commitment has won for the Front Line States considerable respect and admiration.

One of the major drawbacks of the diplomatic approach to decolonization is that it is fraught with numerous intricacies. It is usually misconstrued by the stronger party as a sign of weakness on the part of the "weaker party". To illustrate this, one only need take note of the continuous intransigence of apartheid South Africa.

In May 1981, the apartheid Foreign Minister Pik Botha visited Washington and saw the then-US Secretary of State, Alexander Haig, together with senior figures in the Reagan team. The chief item on the agenda was the Namibian issue. During this contact the apartheid regime appeared to be willing to accept Namibian independence on the basis of UN Resolution 435(1978). But it has to be recalled that while the fascist regime was projecting this image, the Pretoria-clique was actively pursuing its destabilization policy. Increasingly influential soldiers in the apartheid army were arguing for an end to South Africa's "defensive and apologetic foreign policy." It should go back on the attack, undermining those neighbors who sought the overthrow of apartheid and bullying them into treating South Africa with more respect. It would never charm them to the negotiating table; it should "whip them there."

Still vivid in my mind is the arrogance displayed by the racist South African delegation at Geneva during the Pre-Implementation Meeting (PIM) in January 1981. That meeting was meant to pave the way for the implementation of UN Security Resolution 435. But the apartheid delegation simply used it as a forum or platform for their political show.

A similarly arrogant attitude was recently displayed by the so-called internal group in Namibia during their meeting with SWAPO in Lusaka.

During the struggle for the liberation of Zimbabwe, many attempts were made at the diplomatic level to get the illegal

Smith rebel regime to come to terms with national liberation movements. But such forums were utilized by the Smith regime to bluff international opinion.

With the above points in mind, I have no alternative but to conclude that the diplomatic approach can only be effective as a supplement to armed combat. Only when a breakthrough has been made in the military field, can any noteworthy progress be made diplomatically.

Even where armed struggle is not applicable, pure diplomacy, it has been proven, rarely produces the right result at the right time. Even where peaceful means are being used to achieve national independence, the diplomatic approach should go side-by-side with activities like civil disobedience, strikes, demonstrations, etc. Only when the enemy has learned the language it understands can the diplomacy of decolonization make any sense. This has been and remains the position of the OAU.

Appendix III
Speech by Hon. V. M. Makhele,
Minister for Foreign Affairs,
Kingdom of Lesotho

Unlike most people at this conference who are presenting researched papers I am, on the contrary, supposed to deliver a speech. As a politician this is my favorite pastime. As Minister of Foreign Affairs of my country, I am only too pleased to share with you our perceptions of the unfolding scenario in the sub-continent. You will bear with me in that, for practical reasons, I shall venture to use my own country – Lesotho – as a case study for many of the maneuvers and shuttle-diplomacies under way to influence a certain definitive process in the region. You are aware that my official assignment belongs to the diplomatic plane. This imposes heavy restrictions upon me to assess critically certain dimensions and thrusts of policy, which, if I had the academic license, we would explore together without fear of reprisals from certain unnamed quarters. In case you are not aware, this region of the continent is under heavy surveillance with the idea, I am afraid, to eliminate recalcitrants. I could be the target, but I dread to be the victim.

The theme of this conference is as intricate as it is interesting. This is the reason why I flew all the way to Arusha to spend my limited time with you: to try and explore the avenues that lead to peace and security because this is what my small and indeed most vulnerable country in the region yearns for. I am sure I talk for all countries of this region for they all have similar goals and objectives. The Southern African sub-region, to the surprise of everyone, has attracted and caught the attention of the international community because of the turbulent passage it is passing through. The young Republic of Mozambique, a victim of one of the longest and most brutal forms of colonial occupation, has since independence never been able to focus on social and economic reconstruction. Angola has had a traumatic experience of a foreign occupying army stationed permanently on her territory. Botswana, Lesotho, Zambia and Zimbabwe are targets of a campaign that seeks to place them on a constant warpath. The current unfolding scenario now shows that the war is being pushed up north, which places the Republic of Tanzania as an imminent target of destabilization on a level never before experienced.

The theme of the conference, as I understand it, is premised on two cardinal observations. First, it gives cognisance to the fact that the Southern African region has been ushered into a conflagration, a war situation. And second, it further recognizes that peace and security are not sterile concepts: the war that embroils the region is a process of liberation on the one hand and of counter-revolution on the other. Peace, as an objective we desire, cannot be conceptualized in an economic or socio-political vacuum. Hence the recurring question that comes to mind is peace for whom? Security from what? It is this prism of conceptualization that brings into proper perspective the social and political forces that are at play in the region. It also helps to determine which of the forces locked in battle are participating in a process of liberation war or in counter-revolution.

A brief and cursory reference to some scholarship on the political economy of Africa - to refresh our memories and as an attempt to situate in some perspective the predicament in which the region finds itself - helps us to recall that the region's demise is a result of a colonialist grand design policy in which the Southern African region, because of its resourcefulness in mineral deposits, came to be designated as "Africa of the Labor Reserves." This policy, as you know, was geared to provide cheap African labor power for mining capital. We are aware that mining activity was mostly concentrated in the political entity that now constitutes the Republic of South Africa, which turned out to be the regional headquarters for this kind of economic activity. Academics and intellectuals are conversant with the nature and extent to which this new economic venture was promoted at the expense of all other indigenous African economic activities which were mainly agrobased. There are catalogued accounts of how traditional African leadership was used to raise various taxes from their subjects. This, as you know, was a sustained capitalist effort to dislocate and finally erode the self-sufficiency of the African peasantry through a method of depeasantization.

The former British colonies and now independent states of Zambia and Zimbabwe, although they supplied some labor power to South African mines, were themselves endowed with mining economic activities inside their national borders. Malawi and the former Protectorates of Botswana, Lesotho and Swaziland provided the major labor force for the South African mining industry. Portugal, with a harsher and cruder variant of colonial practice, provided labor to the South African mining houses through its colonies of Mozambique and Angola for which it got paid in gold.

The foregoing background was the result of an economic activity that led to migration of a European settler community which came to provide skilled and/or semi-skilled manpower for mining capital and for whom an economic and socio-political infrastructure different from that of the indigenous African peoples was created.

The present policy of apartheid in South Africa found its roots in British colonial administration which laid the foundations for capitalist relations in agriculture arising from the increased needs of mine labor within mining capital. The competitiveness of Africans within capitalist agriculture was undermined by a deliberate policy that restricted them within a barren portion of South Africa constituting 13% of the total area of the lands, thus ensuring that they continued to be suppliers of labor for the mining industry.

With a scenario now painted for the systemic oppression of the African nation inside South Africa and the other colonies, we find that the liberation movements came onto the scene first as protest political organizations whose objective was limited to equal participation within the status quo. This was the experience of the African National Congress when it was founded in 1912. Elsewhere in the region the process of independence was speeded up after World War II, especially in the 1960s when many countries acceded to political independence. In South Africa, this period coincided with the political takeover by the current apartheid regime, champions of the doctrine of the superiority of the white man. The regime's conceptual design of the road to self-determination was bent on the balkanization of South Africa into Bantustans, for which there is supposed to be "independence". The most interesting and crucial phenomenon about the Bantustans is that they are designed to "denationalize" black South Africans. But, what is important for my theme, they share borders and are adjacent to most member states in the region. I want to recall that all of them have a "defense pact" with their mentor, South Africa.

The intransigence of South Africa not to come to political accommodation with its black nationals led to a change of strategy whereby civil struggle to liberation gave way to armed struggle. We experienced a sudden shift in the configuration of forces in the sub-continent with the downfall of the Caetano regime in Portugal in 1974. This led to the independence of Mozambique and Angola, in both of which the armed struggle had assumed a better analytic shape in that it was launched with support mostly of the peasantry and some elements of the working class. For South Africa, the writing on the wall was that whereas its buffer zone was formerly along the Limpopo River, where its soldiers had once participated to guarantee "peace and security", it was now faced with the struggle along its national borders. Indeed, since then the tempo of the struggle has heightened to even a higher intensity.

South Africa, economically the richest country in Africa and militarily, the most powerful – with military, political and diplomatic support from one of the most powerful countries in the world – has been able to utilize its resources and channel them in a manner to realize short-term benefits. The past five years have been very bad for African economies as a result of recession and compounded by the worst drought in living memory. It is a result of these sad developments that South Africa took the lead to export internal contradictions to its neighboring states through the conduit of its Bantustans. Gangs of thugs and bandits are based, organized and equipped by South Africa. You have heard of the so-called Lesotho Liberation Army, MNR in Mozambique, UNITA in Angola, commando units that cross common borders and wreak havoc in Zimbabwe, Zambia and Botswana. This in my view is the armed struggle with the sole purpose to erode the gains of liberation.

Now the question that arises daily is the role and duty of individual countries in the sub-region. Here I turn to my own country which, I want to repeat, for emphasis, is the most vulnerable in the sub-continent. It exists in the belly of the enemy. We are behind the enemy line and therefore need rescue. Liberation for us impinges on our capability and capacity to continue to exist as a sovereign state. In our view the tensions in South Africa are becoming more acute virtually every day in response to the increasing tempo of the liberation struggle. It seems that we are faced with three elements in a South African "final solution."

First is the brutal repression and isolation of the vast majority of South Africans. The tri-cameral parliament belongs to this element.

The second element is based on the policy of creating a cordon sanitaire on the Limpopo – a wall cutting off Southern Africa from the rest of the world; a wall behind which the countries of the region will be intimidated at will.

And a third element is the subjugation of the countries

of the region through a determined policy of destabilization which is still continuing.

Our experience of this "final solution" has been felt in Lesotho in the following ways:

a) open aggression against Lesotho culminating in the December 1982 raid on our capital;

b) creation of a dissident military group based, organized, equipped and directed by South Africa;

c) interference with Lesotho's transit corridors and editorial claims by state-controlled Radio South Africa that Lesotho was turning itself into the Cuba of Southern Africa; and

d) imposition of an arms embargo on security equipment because it was alleged such equipment was being handed over to South African refugees to attack targets inside South Africa.

Assistance by major powers to Pretoria have led to its intransigence. It is for individual OAU member states in the region to exercise maximum vigilance.

Appendix IV
Speech by Hon. Dr. Naomi P. Nhiwatiwa, Deputy Minister of Information, Posts and Telecommunications, Republic of Zimbabwe

The primary features of Southern Africa are characterized by tension, conflict and instability stemming from the dispute between the Pretoria regime on the one hand and, on the other hand, the Southern African liberation movements, the masses within South Africa itself and the black states of the region. Broadly speaking, the dispute centers on the issue of the nature of the political, social and economic system that these two sides desire for the region. This is, however, an overview of the situation. What is taking place in Southern Africa is much more complex than what I have indicated.

As an indication of the complexity of the situation, it is better, first of all, to identify the areas of conflict and the role of South Africa with regard to these areas. There are seven areas of conflict in the region, namely:

a)   the MNR in Mozambique;
b)   the armed dissidents in Zimbabwe;
c)   the so-called Lesotho Liberation Army in Lesotho;
d)   UNITA in Angola;
e)   cross-border incursions by South Africa itself into neighboring states;
f)   the liberation struggle in South Africa; and
g)   the liberation struggle in Namibia.

The Pretoria regime is directly responsible for the existence of these areas of conflict and so, indirectly, are its imperial allies. The apartheid regime is supported and sustained by billions of dollars in loans, financial investments and technical cooperation from its Western allies. Without this support it would not have been as strong as it now is economically and militarily. Western support inevitably makes imperialism part of the Southern

African problem and this complicates the situation.

For its part, the West claims that it has vital military, economic and political interests, in particular in South Africa and, in general, in Southern Africa. These interests arise from the East-West conflict but generally what is happening is the exploitation of the people of the region.

It is true that the bulk of the strategic raw materials considered essential for American industrial and military survival are located within Southern Africa. South Africa itself is the largest world producer of chrome, manganese, vanadium and the platinum group of metals upon which the West as a whole depends in steel-making, aerospace, electronics, energy and defense industries. For this reason, it is in the interests of the West actively to maintain and strengthen ties with the racist Pretoria regime.

Notwithstanding the validity of this perspective, there is another view which says that the relative importance to the West of South Africa's minerals is declining for the following reasons:

a) there are other countries, notably Zimbabwe, the Soviet Union, Gabon, Brazil, Turkey, Albania, Malagasy, the Philippines, New Caledonia and Australia, whose production of these strategic minerals is increasing; and

b) the West itself is building national stockpiles of the same minerals and it is also researching into and developing alternative materials.

While there is some validity in this alternative view, it must be pointed out:

a) that with the exception of Australia, the countries which are increasing their mineral production are regarded by the West, especially America, as being politically unreliable and unstable and thus prone to disruption of supplies;

b) that stockpiles do not last forever; and

c) that research into and development of substitutes for strategic raw materials have not yet resulted in any immediate and significant reduction in the West's dependence on the minerals themselves.

Therefore, South African production of such minerals remains of strategic importance to the West which shapes its policies towards it accordingly. As long as this state of affairs continues, Western diplomacy in Southern Africa will remain unproductive. It also must be stressed that both the West and South Africa share similar goals with regard to the region; ie. imperialist exploitation. What is being suggested here is that the enemy to peace and stability in Southern Africa is not South Africa only but it is also its allies.

The policy of the apartheid regime towards independent Southern African states is to turn them into dependent client states which it can dominate politically and economically. To meet this objective, South Africa announced in March 1979 that it wanted to create an anti-Marxist "Constellation of Southern African States", for four main reasons.

First, South Africa desperately wants markets for its products which have failed and continue to fail to compete in overseas markets.

Second, inflation and the consequent serious economic crisis it is facing at the moment force it to look across its borders into neighboring black states.

Third, it wants to stem the growing tide of the African revolution being spearheaded by the South African liberation movements and independent Africa as a whole. A constellation of states, Pretoria hoped, would lead to the end of the liberation struggle within its borders and in Namibia.

And last, fourth, the Pretoria regime's survival depends on a gradual but effective diplomatic, political and economic penetration and domination of Africa as a whole. The constellation of states would be an effective starting point. There are indication at the moment that such penetration is underway and this has implications for the peace and security of not only Southern Africa but Africa as a whole.

South Africa is a military and economic giant within the region but politically, morally and ideologically it is a dwarf. This is because the policy of apartheid which guarantees its survival does not have the support of the majority of South Africans neither does it enjoy the support of independent Africa or other progressive forces. Politically, South Africa feels vulnerable because the central edifice of its existence is opposed from within and from without. Isolated and shunned by the world, the South Africans interpret opposition to their evil system as the entrenchment of Communism and Marxism which they equate with what P.W. Botha describes as the "powers of darkness."

Given this kind of mentality, it is no wonder that the question of who rules each independent Southern African state has become of paramount importance to the Pretoria regime. Socialist or Marxist governments especially are feared by the regime as they do seem to threaten the survival of Afrikanerdom. Consequently, security has become the first

priority in South Africa. It determines and will continue to
determine that country's future course of actions as long as
it pursues apartheid. It will continue to dictate the kind
of policies the regime should follow to protect itself.

Externally, South Africa has to establish favorable or
safe frontiers or borders. The methods it uses to achieve
this objective are well-known. It wants to secure for itself
some form of accommodation with the neighboring black states.
Denial of accommodation means that strife in the region will
continue.

Obsession with survival and security has resulted in the
military expansion of South Africa's defense forces and the
reinforcement of the army's capacity and capability. There
are now 197,400 regular South African troops who are on a
perpetual war-footing. In addition to the expansion of the
army, the military chiefs are becoming increasingly dominant
in decision-making while the importance of the politicians is
waning. There are signs that South Africa is moving towards
a "warfare" state. The current thinking among the army
chiefs is: we have got the manpower and the firepower, let
us use it. This, however, stems from desperation. The
growing militarization within South Africa could have serious
consequences for the region and for the world. Besides
beefing up its defense forces, South Africa now possesses the
technical know-how and capability to manufacture nuclear
weapons. There are indications that the apartheid regime has
developed nuclear weapons and intends to use them if
necessary.

On their part, the independent Southern African states
have responded to the idea of a "constellation" by forming
SADCC with a view to initiating economic cooperation and
development and to lessening dependence on South Africa. The
growth and development of SADCC stand in the way of South
Africa's ambitions. However, at the moment a form of
interdependence between the countries of SADCC and South
Africa still exists. The independent states to a degree
still depend on South Africa's ports, transport services and
industries. 75% of the railway network within the region is
controlled by the South African Transport Services. At the
same time, South Africa uses the markets, transport systems
and ports of its black neighbors. What we have here is a
vicious relationship of interdependence, a relationship which
the African states are determined to break while South Africa
is determined to maintain and even strengthen it.

The formation of SADCC has witnessed success especially
in the field of communications. Inter-regional cooperation
has demonstrated that the African states can lessen
dependence on the apartheid regime and gradually achieve

economic independence. These successes have exposed South Africa's vulnerability and further thrown it into isolation. South Africa is alarmed by SADCC's successes and has begun to use economic sabotage, blackmail and bullying tactics to force the black states to use its ports and transport networks and to trade with it.

With the emergence of SADCC and the existence of South Africa's limited version of a constellation of states which includes its bantustans, there exists in the region two economic and political groupings standing in deadly opposition to each other. Both groups are determined to succeed and to gain ascendancy in the region. The competing interests of these groups are largely responsible for the current atmosphere of unease and tension in the region.

South Africa wants to achieve its aim of regional domination by creating political and economic instability in the region. With the support of the Reagan administration, it is using dissident groups and destabilizing activities to destroy the political and economic structures of the independent states of Southern Africa. It would seem as if it wants a regional settlement in Southern Africa only after the establishment of puppet or submissive government in the neighboring states. Such governments would not support SWAPO, ANC or the PAC.

Faced with South Africa's military aggression and open threats of military attacks for non-cooperation, the independent states have begun to assess their individual and regional security situations. The idea of a regional joint military force has been mooted and should be pursued further. But before this idea can be fulfilled, certain problems have to be solved, namely:

a) lack of standardized military ideology, training and weaponry, all of which are vital in any joint defense and combined operations;

b) absence of unified command structure for training and organizing of the joint defense forces;

c) economic problems facing the region as a result of the drought and world economic recession;

d) Zimbabwe, Mozambique and Angola are too involved in internal security operations against bandits and dissidents to become effective participants in joint defense activities; and

e) joint military exercises may provide South Africa with a pretext for openly invading its neighbors.

These problems are not insurmountable, particularly the second one. Nigeria's forces have international experience and could provide the relevant command structure. The international community sympathetic to the region could be approached to provides logistics supplies and weaponry. This is by no means a simple exercise, but it can be done for the peace and security of the region: a joint force could act as a deterrent to South Africa.

The strength of the defense forces of the combined African states (excluding Malawi, Lesotho and Swaziland) and of South Africa is 143,000 and 197,000 troops, respectively. This shows a serious imbalance of power in the region, especially when South Africa's total military manpower compared to each individual states's strength which is as follows:

Zimbabwe	41,300
Tanzania	40,350
Angola	37,500
Mozambique	15,650
Zambia	14,300
Botswana	3,000

Individually each state is very weak numerically compared to South Africa. Besides, it is difficult to assess the capacity, capability or military performance of each country's forces. Some of them, for example those of Angola, Mozambique, Zimbabwe and Botswana, have been formed recently. What is certain is that the imbalance in military strength limits the black states' capacity to maintain peace and security in the face of a total South African onslaught.

However, it is not being suggested here that South Africa's defense forces are invincible. In the rainy season of 1983-84 they were repulsed by the FAPLA forces of Angola during one offensive and they retreated carrying a high number of casualties. They could not withstand the modern heavy weaponry of the Angolan forces. During our own war of liberation, South African forces fighting along the Zambezi suffered heavy losses at the hands of our guerrillas. However, while the South African military machine is vulnerable, given that country's economic and military strength vis-a-vis our struggling economies and small armies, we are at a disadvantage in the event of full-scale aggression from South Africa.

The independent Southern African states are currently at a disadvantage also because of the divisive tactics used by South Africa to drive a wedge between them. The policy of open threats coupled with promises of economic aid – the stick and the carrot – in the event of cooperation, pursued by the Pretoria regime, has encouraged countries in Southern

African to make individual diplomatic initiatives and contacts with the apartheid regime based on each particular country's own interests. This policy has weakened the region economically and politically. It has led to cracks in the edifice of unity and South Africa is penetrating these cracks. South Africa and its imperialist allies want to exploit the region as a whole, not just a few countries. Thus no individual accommodation with the apartheid regime can yield peace. There is need for a coordinated and synchronized approach to the threat of South Africa and its allies.

A longstanding malaise in Southern Africa has involved sympathy and covert support by some independent states for reactionary forces seeking to overthrow other black governments. Because of this support, and each individual state's even-handed policies towards the Pretoria regime, relations between the African states themselves are generally delicate and sensitive. This creates regional instability and uncertainty. Understandably, even-handed or ambivalent policies towards South Africa are the inevitable result of geo-politics and colonial history. But they are not helping any regional state.

Whilst South Africa forces each of its neighbors into some form of cooperation or other, it can still attack or destabilize them with impunity. The sooner it is realized that South Africa wants to weaken or destroy socialist of Marxist governments in the region first the better for the sub-continent. After that it will concentrate on the others. The time for fence-sitting is no longer on our side: either the Southern African states throw their full weight behind the regional liberation movements regardless of short-term consequences or they accommodate apartheid. The long-term results of the second choice seem more disastrous than those of the first option. But, whatever decisions are taken now, the ultimate future of the sub-continent lies with the internal and external responses of black South Africans themselves.

Current developments within South Africa indicate that a revolution is in the making. The South African liberation struggle and the radicalization of black South Africans are already destabilizing South Africa. The apartheid regime's response to revolutionary violence is two-fold. Internally, it engages in iniquitous acts of murdering black South Africans. And externally, it attacks its neighbors in order to discourage them from supporting the liberation movements. Thus internal violence in South Africa is spilling over into neighboring independent states. As black South African nationalist unrest continues to grow, so relations between

South Africa and the independent African states will be
marked by violence and the security atmosphere will remain
extremely volatile.

Some people maintain that apartheid is unsustainable in
the long-run. This is, of course, true. The cost of
apartheid is enormous. It is imposing a tremendous burden on
South Africa's economy. 15% of the entire white workforce,
or over 400,000 whites, administer the system. Added to
this, maintaining the bantustans costs more than US$1.8
billion last year and administering Namibia costs several
billions of dollars. Apartheid has further weakened the
South African economy by provoking international trade and
investment embargoes. In the United States, nationwide
demonstrations against the system have led to both Democrats
and Republicans joining hands in drafting legislation on
sanctions against South Africa. The Botha regime itself
knows that sanctions work; the South Africa Foundation, an
arm of the government with wide international connections,
has admitted this in its recent bulletins.

The situation inside the country is deteriorating as is
shown by the deployment of the army to assist the police to
quell the rebellions. White society sees itself as being
besieged both internally and externally, and it is becoming
desperate.

It is turning to the use of force as a last resort.
This year alone more than 150 people have been killed by
South African forces but this has not deterred black South
Africans; instead it has increased their appetite for
freedom. No force, however mighty, can stop an idea whose
time has come. Peace will come to Southern Africa
eventually, whatever the cost.

Selected Southern African Bibliography, Post-1980

Aluko, Olajide & Timothy M. Shaw (eds). Southern Africa in the 1980s. London: George Allen & Unwin, 1985.

Anglin, Douglas G. "SADCC after Nkomati." African Affairs 84(335), April 1985, 163-181.

----------. "Economic liberation and regional cooperation in Southern Africa: SADCC and PTA." International Organization 37(4), Autumn 1983, 681-711.

Astrow, Andre. Zimbabwe: a revolution that lost its way? London: Zed, 1983.

Barber, James. "South Africa: the regional setting." World Today 42(1), January 1986, 8-12.

Barber, James et al. The West and South Africa. London: Routledge & Kegan Paul, 1982.

Bender, Gerald J., James S. Coleman & Richard L. Sklar (eds). African Crisis Areas and US Foreign Policy. Berkeley: University of California Press, 1985, 27-157.

Benson, Mary. Nelson Mandela. London: IDAFSA, 1985.

----------. South Africa: the struggle for a birthright. Harmondsworth: Penguin, 1986.

Berridge, Geoff. Economic Power in Anglo-South African Diplomacy: Simonstown, Sharpeville and after. London: Macmillan, 1981.

Bhagavan, M.R. Angola's Political Economy 1975-1985. Uppsala: Scandinavian Institute of African Studies, 1986. Research Report Number 75.

----------. The Energy Sector in SADCC Countries: policies, priorities and options in the context of the African crisis. Uppsala: Scandinavian Institute of African Studies, 1985. Research Report Number 74.

Blumenfeld, Jesmond. "South Africa: economic responses to international pressures." World Today 41(12), December 1985, 218-221.

Bowman, Larry W. "The Strategic Importance of South Africa to the United States." African Affairs 81(323), April 1982, 159-191.

Bull, Hedley. "The West and South Africa." Dadalus 3(2), Spring 1982, 255-270.

Burdette, Marcia. "The mines, class power and foreign policy in Zambia." Journal of Southern African Studies 10(2), April 1984, 198-218.

Burdette, Marcia. "Zambia" in Timothy M. Shaw & Olajide Aluko (eds). The Political Economy of African Foreign Policy. Aldershot: Gower, and New York: St. Martins, 1984, 319-347.

Buzan, Barry & H.O. Nazareth. "South Africa versus Azania: the implications of who rules." International Affairs 62(1), Winter 1985/6, 35-40.

Callaghy, Thomas M. (ed). South Africa in Southern Africa: the intensifying vortex of violence. New York: Praeger, 1983.

Callinicos, Alex. Southern Africa after Zimbabwe. London: Pluto, 1981.

Campbell, Kurt M. Soviet Policy Towards South Africa. London: Macmillan, 1986.

Carter, Gwendolen M. Which way is South Africa going? Bloomington: Indiana University Press, 1980.

Carter, Gwendolen M. & Patrick O'Meara (eds). International Politics in Southern Africa. Bloomington: Indiana University Press, 1982.

Carter, Gwendolen M. & Patrick O'Meara (eds). Southern Africa: the continuing crisis. Bloomington: Indiana University Press, 1982. Second edition.

Caute, David. Under the Skin: the death of white Rhodesia. Harmondsworth: Penguin, 1983.

Cawthra, Gavin. Brutal Force: the apartheid war machine. London: IDAFSA, 1986.

Clarke, D.G. Foreign Companies and International Investment in Zimbabwe. Gweru: Mambo, 1981.

Clement, Peter. "Moscow and Southern Africa." Problems of Communism 34(2), March-April 1985, 29-50.

Clough, Michael. "Beyond constructive engagement." Foreign Policy 61, Winter 1985/86, 3-24.

Cohen, Robin. Endgame in South Africa? London: James Currey, 1986.

Coker, Christopher. "Collective bargaining as an internal sanction: the role of US corporations in South Africa." Journal of Modern African Studies 19(4), December 1981, 647-665.

Coker, Christopher. "The US and Southern African minerals resources: the East European dimension." South African International 13(1), July 1982, 1-14.

Crush, Jonathan & Paul Wellings. "The Southern African pleasure periphery, 1966-83." Journal of Modern African Studies 21(4), December 1983, 673-698.

Danaher, Keven. In Whose Interest? A guide to US-South Africa relations. Washington: Institute for Policy Studies, 1986.

Daniel, John & Johnson Vilane. "The crisis of political legitimacy in Swaziland." Review of African Political Economy 35, May 1986, 54-67.

Davidow, J. A Peace in Southern Africa: the Lancaster House conference on Rhodesia 1979. Boulder: Westview, 1984.

Davies, Robert, Dan O'Meara and Sipho Dlamini (eds). The Struggle for South Africa: a reference guide to movements, organizations and institutions. London: Zed, 1984. Two volumes.

Davies, Robert & Dan O'Meara. "The state of analysis of the Southern African region: issues raised by South African strategy." Review of African Political Economy 29, July 1984, 64-76.

Davies, Robert & Dan O'Meara. "Total Strategy in Southern Africa: an analysis of South Africa regional strategy since 1978." Journal of Southern African Studies 11(2), April 1985, 183-211.

Davies, Robert. South African Strategy Towards Mozambique in the Post-Nkomati Period: a critical analysis of effects and implications. Uppsala: Scandinavian Institute of African Studies, 1985. Research Report Number 73.

Davies, Robert. "Review article: the military and foreign policy in South Africa." Journal of Southern African Studies 12(2), April 1986, 308-315.

De Braganca, Aquino & Immanuel Wallerstein (eds). The African Liberation Reader: documents of the national liberation movements. London: Zed, 1985. Three volumes.

Desmond, Cosmos. "Sanctions and South Africa." Third World Quarterly 8(1), January 1986, 78-99.

Dixon, Marlene & Rod Bush (eds). Revolution in Southern Africa. San Francisco: Contemporary Marxism #7, 1983, 89-139.

Dugard, John (ed). "Special issue on South West Africa/Namibia." South Africa International 15(3), January 1985, 129-182.

Fatton, Robert. "The Reagan foreign policy toward South Africa: the ideology of the new cold war." African Studies Review 27(1), March 1984, 57-82.

310

Fig, David. "South African Penetration of Brazil" in Jerker Carlsson and Timothy M. Shaw (eds). The Political Economy of South-South Relations: case studies of Newly Industrializing Countries. London: Macmillan, 1987.

Finlayson, Jock. "Canada and Strategic Minerals." International Perspectives September/October 1982, 18-21.

Fisher, Scott. Coping with Change: US policy toward South Africa. Washington, DC: National Defense University, 1982. Monograph Series Number 82-7.

Frankel, Philip H. Pretoria's Praetorians: Civil-military relations in South Africa. Cambridge: Cambridge University Press, 1985.

Friedland, Elaine A. "SADCC and the West: Cooperation or Conflict?." Journal of Modern African Studies 23(2), June 1985, 287-314.

Gavshon, Arthur. Crisis in Africa: battleground of East and West. Harmondsworth: Penguin, 1981.

Geldenhuys, Deon. The Diplomacy of Isolation: South African foreign policy making. Johannesburg: Macmillan, 1984.

Geldenhuys, Deon and Koos van Wyk, "South Africa in Crisis: A comparison of the Vorster and Botha eras." South Africa International (16)3, January 1986, 135-145.

Good, Ken. "Zimbabwe" in Shaw & Aluko (eds). The Political Economy of African Policy Making, 348-371.

Grundy, Kenneth W. "The social costs of armed struggle in Southern Africa." Armed Forces and Society 7(3), Spring 1981, 445-466.

——————. "Black Soldiers in a White Military: political change in South Africa." Journal of Strategic Studies 4(3), September 1981, 296-305.

——————. Defending Apartheid. Bloomington: Indiana University Press, 1985.

——————. "The new role of South Africa's security establishment." Munger Africana Library Notes 75, March 1985.

Guelke, Adrian. "Southern Africa and the Superpowers." International Affairs 56(4), Autumn 1980, 648-664.

Hanlon, Joseph. Mozambique: the revolution under fire. London: Zed, 1984.

——————. Apartheid's Second Front: South Africa's war against its neighbours. Harmondsworth: Penguin, 1986.

——————. Beggar Your Neighbours: apartheid power in South Africa. London: James Currey, 1986.

Harshe, Rajan. "France, francophone African states and South Africa." Alternatives 9(1), Summer 1983, 51-72.

Haysom, Nicholas. Apartheid's Private Army: the rise of right wing vigilantes in South Africa. London: CIIR, 1986.

Hill, Christopher R. "Regional Cooperation in Southern Africa." African Affairs 82(327), April 1983, 215-239.

Holland, Martin. "The EEC Code for South Africa: a reassessment." World Today 41(1), January 1985, 12-14.

Huntington, S.P. "Reform and stability in modernizing society." International Security 6(4), Spring 1982, 3-25.

Husain, Azim. "The West, South Africa and Israel: a strategic triangle." Third World Quarterly 4(1), January 1982, 44-73.

Innes, Duncan. Anglo American and the Rise of Modern South Africa. London: Heinemann, 1984.

Isaacs, Arnold H. "South Africa and BLS: a Galtung approach to dependence relations" in Carlsson and Shaw (eds). The Political Economy of South-South Relations: case studies of Newly Industrializing Countries.

Isaacs, Henry. Struggles within the Struggle: an inside view of the PAC of South Africa. London: Zed, 1986.

Jaster, Robert S. South Africa in Namibia: the Botha Strategy. Washington, DC: UPA for CFIA, 1985.

——————. "South African Defense Strategy and the Growing Influence of the Military" in William J. Foltz & Henry R. Bienen (eds). Arms and the Africans: military influences on Africa's international relations. New Haven: Yale University Press, 1985, Council on Foreign Relations, 121-152.

Jenkins, Simon. "Regional Stability in Southern Africa." Optima 32(2), July 1984, 50-55.

Johnson, Phyllis and David Martin (eds). Destructive Engagement: South Africa at War. Harare: Zimbabwe Publishing House, 1986.

Joseph, Helen. Side by Side. London: Zed, 1984.

Klare, Michael T. "Evading the embargo: illicit US arms transfers to South Africa." Journal of International Affairs 35(1), Spring/Summer 1981, 15-28.

Konczacki, Zbigniew, Jane L. Parpart & Timothy M. Shaw (eds). Economic History of Southern Africa. London: Frank Cass, 1986 and 1987, two volumes.

Leach, Graham. South Africa Today. London: Methuen, 1986.

Leape, Jonathan et. al. (eds). Business in the Shadow of Apartheid: US firms in South Africa. Lexington: Heath, 1985.

Legassick, Martin. "South Africa in Crisis: what route to democracy?" African Affairs 84(337), October 1985, 587-603.

Lemarchand, Rene (ed). American policy in Southern Africa: the stakes and the stance. Washington, D.C.: University Press of America, 1981, second edition.

Leys, Roger & Arne Tostensen. "Regional cooperation in Southern Africa: SADCC." Review of African Political Economy 23, January–April 1982, 52–71.

Libby, Ronald T. Toward an Africanized US Policy for Southern Africa: a strategy for increasing political leverage. Berkeley: Institute for International Studies, 1980. Policy Papers in International Affairs, 11.

Lipton, Merle. Capitalism and Apartheid: South Africa: 1910–1986. Aldershot: Wildwood, 1986.

Lodge, Tom. Black Politics in South Africa since 1945. Harlow: Longman, 1983.

Low, Allan. Agricultural Development in Southern Africa. London: Heinemann, 1986.

Lotta, Raymond. "The political economy of apartheid and the strategic stakes of imperialism." Race & Class 27(2), Autumn 1985,

Maasdorp, Gavin. "Reassessing economic ties in Southern Africa." Optima 30(2), September 1981, 113–125.

"Making the New South Africa." New Internationalist 159, May 1986, 1–32.

Mandela, Nelson. The Struggle is my Life. London: IDAFSA, 1986.

Mandela, Winnie. Part of my Soul. Harmondsworth: Penguin, 1985.

Martin, David & Phyllis Johnson. The Struggle for Zimbabwe. Harare: Zimbabwe Publishing House, 1981, passim.

Mazrui, Ali A. "Zionism and apartheid: strange bedfellows or natural allies?." Alternatives 9(1), Summer 1983, 73–97.

Mission to South Africa: the Commonwealth Report. Harmondsworth: Penguin, 1986.

Morikawa, Jun. "Japan's South African Policy." Journal of Modern African Studies 22(1), March 1984, 133–141.

Myers, Desai et. al. US Business in South Africa: the economic, political and moral issues. Bloomington: Indiana University Press, 1980.

Nicol, Davidson. "United States foreign policy in Southern Africa: third-world perspectives." Journal of Modern African Studies 21(4), December 1983, 587–603.

Ncube, Don. The Influence of Apartheid and Capitalism on Black Trade Unions in South Africa. Johannesburg: Skotaville, 1985.

"Nkomati Accord – destabilization and the defence of apartheid." IDAFSA, Ottawa, November 1985.

313

O'Brien, Conor Cruise. "What can become of South Africa?" Atlantic Monthly 257(3), March 1986, 41-68.

O'Meara, Dan. "Crisis of apartheid: the Canadian response." Peace and Security 1(2), Summer 1986, 2-3.

Omer-Cooper, J.D. A History of Southern Africa. London: Heinemann, 1986.

Omond, Roger. The Apartheid Handbook. Harmondsworth: Penguin, 1985.

Picard, Louis A. The Politics of Development in Botswana: a model for success? Boulder: Lynne Rienner, forthcoming.

Price, Robert M. "Pax or Pox Pretoria?" World Policy Journal 2(3), Summer 1985, 533-554.

Redekop, Clarence G. "Commerce over conscience: the Trudeau government and South Africa, 1968-74." Journal of Canadian Studies 19(4), Winter 1984/5, 82-105.

Rossiter, Caleb. The Bureaucratic Struggle for Control of US Foreign Aid: diplomacy vs development in Southern Africa. Boulder: Westview, 1985.

Rotberg, Robert I. et. al. South Africa and its Neighbours: regional security and self-interest. Lexington: Heath, 1985.

Saul, John S. "Nkomati and after" in his collection on A Different Road: the transition to socialism in Mozambique. New York: Monthly Review, 1985, 391-418.

----------. "Socialist transition and external intervention: Mozambique and South Africa's war." Labour, Capital & Society 18(1), April 1985, 153-170.

Schatzberg, Michael (ed). The Political Economy of Zimbabwe. New York: Praeger, 1984.

Sejanamane, Mafa M. "The Crisis of Apartheid: South Africa and Destabilisation in Southern Africa", Dalhousie African Working Papers, 5, 1985.

Shaw, Timothy M. & Lee Dowdy "South Africa" in Edward A. Kolodziej & Robert Harkavy (eds). Security Policies in Developing Countries. Lexington: Heath Lexington and Aldershot: Gower, 1982, 305-327.

Sithole, Masipula. "Class and fractionalism in the Zimbabwe nationalist movement." African Studies Review 27(1), March 1984, 117-125.

Sommerville, Keith. Angola: Politics, economics and society. Boulder: Lynne Rienner, forthcoming.

"South Africa in Struggle." Monthly Review 37(11), April 1986.

South Africa in the 1980s: state of emergency. London: CIIR, 1986, third edition.

South African Review 3. Johannesburg: Ravan, 1986; 2, 1984.

314

<u>South Africa: time running out. The Report of the Study Commission on US policy toward Southern Africa</u>. Berkeley: University of California Press, 1981.

Southall, Roger. "Botswana as a host country for refugees." <u>Journal of Commonwealth & Comparative Politics</u> 22(1), March 1982, 69-86.

——————. "South Africa" in Shaw & Aluko (eds). <u>The Political Economy of African Foreign Policy</u>, 221-262.

——————. "Regional trends and South Africa's future" in Timothy M. Shaw & Olajide Aluko (eds). <u>Africa Projected: from recession to renaissance by the year 2000?</u> London: Macmillan, 1985, 81-111.

Seegers, Annette. "Review Article: The Military in South Africa: a comparison and critique." <u>South Africa International</u>, 16(4), April 1986, 192-200.

Spence, J.E. "South Africa: the nuclear option." <u>African Affairs</u> 30(321), October 1981, 441-452.

——————. "South Africa: between reform and retrenchment." <u>World Today</u> 40(11), November 1984, 471-480.

Spencer Hull, Galen. <u>Pawns on a Chessboard: the resource war in Southern Africa</u>. Washington: UPA, 1981.

Stoneman, Colin (ed). <u>Zimbabwe's Inheritence</u>. London: Macmillan, 1981.

Sylvester, Christine. "Continuity and Discontinuity in Zimbabwe's Development History." <u>African Studies Review</u> 28(1), March 1985, 19-44.

Tennyson, Brian Douglas. <u>Canadian Relations with South Africa: a diplomatic history</u>. Washington: UPA, 1982.

Thompson, Leonard. <u>The Political Mythology of Apartheid</u>. New Haven: Yale University Press, 1985.

Tostensen, Arne. <u>Dependence and Collective Self-Reliance in Southern Africa</u>. Uppsala: Scandinavian Institute of African Studies, 1982.

Unger, Sanford J. & Peter Vale. "South Africa: why constructive engagement failed." <u>Foreign Affairs</u> 64(2), Winter 1985/86, 234-258.

Vukani Makhosikuzi Collective. <u>South African Women on the Move</u>. London: Zed with CIIR, 1986.

Weitzer, Ronald. "In Search of Regime Security: Zimbabwe since Independence." <u>Journal of Modern African Studies</u> 22(4), December 1984, 529-557.

Wiley, David and Allen Isaacman (eds). <u>Southern Africa: society, economy and liberation</u>. East Lansing: Michigan State University African Studies Center, 1981.

Winter, Gordon. <u>Inside BOSS</u>. Harmondsworth: Penguin, 1981.

Wolfers, Michael & Jane Bergerol. <u>Angola in the Front Line</u>. London: Zed, 1983.

Zartman, I. William. Ripe for Resolution: conflict and intervention in Africa. New York: OUP, 1985 for CFR, 152-219.

Zimbabwe's first five years: economic prospects following independence. London: Economist Intelligence Unit, 1981. Special Report Number 111.